Martin Fletcher was educated at Edinburgh University and the University of Pennsylvania. He joined *The Times* in 1983, became its Washington correspondent in 1989, and US editor in 1993. Married with three children, he is now based in Belfast.

'A gourmet's guide to the boondocks'
Independent

'A well-observed, warm-hearted travelogue, with plenty of good humour and a cast of amazing characters'
TLS

'Fletcher is not only capable of excellent penmanship, but is also able to view the country and its people as both outsider and insider, and does so without being judgmental. I found his warm and subtly humorous style very appealing, and I highly recommend this book'
Independent on Sunday

'Blooms with deft observation'
The Times

Almost Heaven

*Travels through the
Backwoods of America*

Martin Fletcher

An *Abacus* Book

First published in Great Britain by
Little, Brown and Company 1998
This edition published by Abacus 1999
Reprinted 1999

A CIP catalogue for this book is available from the British Library.

ISBN 0 349 10935 4

Typeset by M Rules in Adobe Garamond
Printed and bound in Great Britain by
Clays Ltd, St Ives plc

Abacus
A Division of
Little, Brown and Company (UK)
Brettenham House
Lancaster Place
London WC2E 7EN

To Katy, Hannah, Barney and Imogen,
and all our friends in America

Contents

Map   viii
Acknowledgements   xi

1 Continental Divide   1
2 Sooks and Jimmies   8
3 High-Tech Hillbillies   21
4 For Heaven's Snakes   32
5 High in Kentucky   42
6 The Greatest Melungeon   49
7 Chasing Mr Moonshine   59
8 African Experience   69
9 The Preacher from Plains   88
10 Rogues and Rednecks   94
11 Winners and Losers   113
12 The Incarceration Station   132
13 Gators, Coons and Mudbugs   143
14 Matters of Life and Death   151
15 Living in Hope   171
16 Cow Patty Bingo   184
17 Richard the Lionheart   194
18 Cowboys and Indians   209
19 Husband and Wives   227
20 Lost in Space   235
21 Prophet without Honour   257
22 Their Own Private Idahos   275
23 End of the Road   298

Bibliography   305

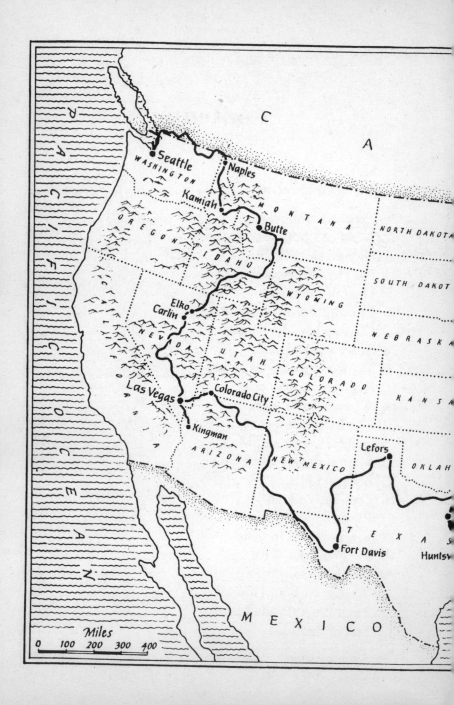

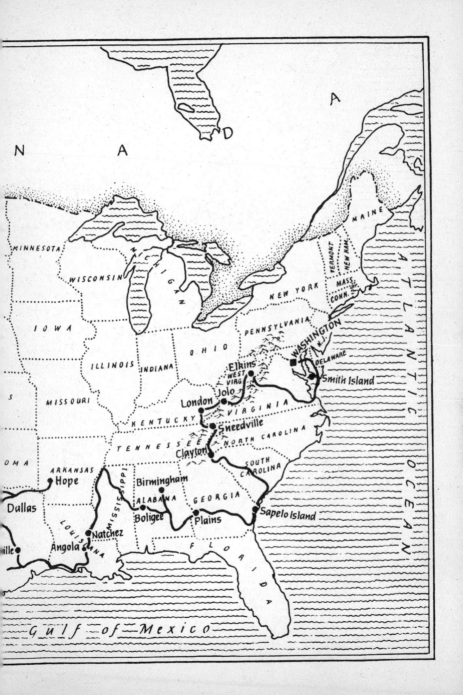

Acknowledgements

Before anyone else I must thank my wonderful wife, Katy, who gave me so much moral support and practical help and not once complained about my long absence. She will never know how deeply I missed her and the children.

I am blessed with a marvellous father-in-law, Richard Beney, who pored over the first draft of this book, corrected countless errors and offered many constructive suggestions. I was also blessed, in the Washington bureau of *The Times*, with a tireless researcher and assistant, Cathi Stallings, who did no end of work on my behalf. To both I am extremely grateful.

I would like to thank my literary agent, Derek Johns of A. P. Watt, for taking me on, finding a publisher, and giving me constant encouragement and good advice. Richard Beswick, the editorial director of Little, Brown, took a considerable risk by signing up an unknown commodity like myself. Antonia Hodgson, my editor at Little, Brown, was hugely efficient and a pleasure to work with. To both of them I extend my thanks. Peter Stothard, editor of *The Times*, made the book possible by kindly allowing me to take time off between postings. Peter Wilson, the former Washington correspondent of *The Australian*, Tom Rhodes, my valued colleague in the Washington bureau of *The Times*, and my good friend Kees Dutilh all offered counsel and ideas that I much appreciated.

I am greatly indebted to Donna Dozier Gordon, the public relations manager of Days Inn of America, who cheerfully arranged accommodation in various Days Inns across the country and helped defray the costs of my journey.

Finally I would like to thank the many, many kind and generous people – sadly too numerous to mention by name – who fed me, put me up, guided me or gave up precious time to talk to me during my months on the road. I learned that travel writing can sometimes be a lonely business, but these people made it a whole lot easier and imbued this Brit, at least, with a deep and enduring love of America and Americans.

Continental Divide

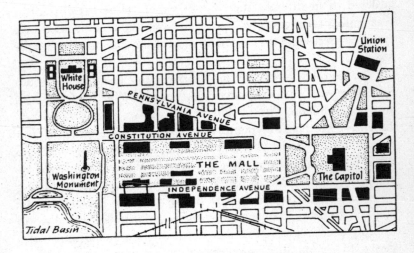

One hot summer's afternoon when the news was slow I slipped away from the Washington office of *The Times*, three blocks from the White House, to witness a daily ceremony that would be inconceivable in any other country in the world.

I took a taxi down Pennsylvania Avenue to the US Congress. There I met a silver-haired gentleman named Herbert Franklin whose title is Executive Officer of the Office of the Architect of the Capitol. Together we stood on the western steps of the famous building and watched three men emerge on to the roof at the foot of the great white dome. Using a mechanical hoist, they hauled a crateful of American flags up from the terrace in front of us, and for the next two hours ran the flags up and down three adjacent poles at a rate of about one a minute until that day's batch was finished.

Mr Franklin then took me deep down into the bowels of the Capitol and the warren of windowless rooms known as the 'Flag

Office' which he oversees. On the outer door is a framed photograph of the Stars and Stripes above the words: 'This is Our Flag. Be PROUD of it.' Inside, the walls are lined with shelves holding hundreds of boxes of flags. Half a dozen men and women were packing up the flags that had just been flying. They would be dispatched, Mr Franklin explained, to the citizens across the country who had ordered them through their congressmen, either as gifts or as mementoes for themselves, and each would be accompanied by a certificate recording the exact date on which it had flown above the Capitol.

The demand for these flags is amazing. The office sends out 135,000 a year. Since the practice first began in 1937 it has provided nearly 2.5 million. The all-time record was set on 4 July, 1976 – Independence Day in America's bicentennial year – when a crew augmented by several Capitol Hill policemen managed to run up 10,471 flags on eighteen poles in a marathon round-the-clock session. Mr Franklin said he had heard stories of Americans bursting into tears when presented with a flag that had flown over the Capitol. It's hard to imagine any other government in the world offering such a service to its citizens, or there being much of a demand for it, but then no other country has such an extraordinary reverence for its flag.

I doubt if one British household in fifty even possesses a Union Jack, but American homes are festooned with the Stars and Stripes on every major national holiday. During the seven years I reported for *The Times* from Washington my three children solemnly pledged allegiance to the flag at the start of every schoolday – albeit with their fingers crossed behind their backs. Old Glories the size of bedspreads flutter in their millions over America's offices, malls and used-car lots. In 1988 George Bush coasted into the Oval Office after making a campaign issue of Michael Dukakis's alleged disrespect for the flag, and there is nothing – absolutely nothing – that makes an upright American's blood boil hotter than the sight of some hairy protester deliberately desecrating the Stars and Stripes.

Having proudly shown me his flag-flying operation, Mr Franklin gave me a fifty-two-page government booklet entitled 'Our Flag', which tells America's citizens precisely how they should treat the Stars and Stripes.

During the national anthem 'all present except those in uniform should stand to attention facing the flag with the right hand over the heart', it begins. The flag should be flown 'only from sunrise to sunset on buildings and stationary flagstaffs in the open. However, when a patriotic effect is desired, the flag may be displayed twenty-four hours a day if properly illuminated during the hours of darkness'.

It 'should be hoisted briskly and lowered ceremoniously'. When flown at half-mast it should 'first be hoisted to the peak for an instant and then lowered to the half-staff position'. It should 'not be draped over the hood, top, sides or back of a vehicle or of a railroad train or a boat. When the flag is displayed on a motorcar the staff shall be fixed firmly to the chassis or clamped to the right fender'.

The instructions go on and on. The flag 'should not be dipped to any person or thing'. It 'should never touch anything beneath it, such as the ground, the floor, water or merchandise'. It 'should never be used as wearing apparel, bedding or drapery'.

By the time I'd finished the booklet I deemed myself lucky to be still at liberty. At the end of the 1992 Republican convention, I had joined the general plundering of the myriad flags that had decorated the Houston Astrodome. I had no time to pack my booty before flying home, so I simply wrapped it around its pole, secured it with an elastic band and thrust it at the woman behind the airline ticket counter. The flag emerged on the baggage belt at Washington's National Airport besmirched, torn and – I now realise – quite criminally despoiled.

It's easy of course for cynical Europeans like myself to mock America's reverence for its flag, but that reverence is really very understandable. Unlike the nations of Europe, which are basically tribal in origin, America is a nation of immigrants from every country in the world. They came to escape oppressive governments in their native lands, and because they were attracted by the American ideals of equality, liberty and independence. The one thing all Americans have in common – and which is drummed into them from kindergarten onwards – is a love of those ideals, and the flag alone embodies them.

Mr Franklin is a case in point. His parents were Ukrainian Jews who fled to America to escape the pogroms in their homeland. 'They didn't want any identification with the old country,' he recalled. 'They wanted to be Americans. My father felt very, very strongly that the flag should be flown outside our home on all the important national holidays as an emblem of his belief in this country and the life it enabled him to find for him and his family. That feeling gets passed from generation to generation.'

The flag unites the nation. It is a symbol behind which the whole country rallies. But what it cannot do is disguise the fact that there are really two Americas that co-exist on the same continent but hardly ever overlap.

The first, most visible America is the richest, most advanced nation on the globe, though it contains pockets of appalling urban deprivation. It's a land of big cities, national parks and man-made wonders, the country that put man on the moon and pioneered the computer and the microchip. From the roof of the Capitol where the flags are flown you get a panoramic view of this America – its obvious splendour and its less advertised squalor.

Look west and you have a magnificent view of Washington's famous Mall with its fine museums and gleaming white monuments, which an English friend once mischievously described as 'the ever more elaborate creations of a master confectioner'. Beyond, across the Potomac River, begin the prosperous Virginia suburbs – a green paradise of spacious homes and swimming clubs and far-too-tempting shopping malls where the Fletcher family lived so happily.

Look east and within the space of a few city blocks you move from the First World to the Third, from gentrified townhouses to a virtual war zone where guns and drugs are common currency and few whites go on purpose. Two thirds of the children in this ghetto are born to single mothers, one third are born into poverty, and the infant mortality rate is the highest in America. It has a violent crime rate three times the national average, and an estimated forty-two per cent of its young black males are either in prison, on parole, on probation or awaiting trial. Each year more are arrested than graduate from high school, and the highest form of technology in many of its rundown schools are the metal detectors at their entrances.

The *Washington Post* has run many stories about the dark side of America's capital, but few more harrowing than that of a forty-eight-year-old woman named Olivia Taylor whose daughter and three sons were each killed on the streets by gunfire, one by one, all in their twenties, in the space of just eight years. Ms Taylor was still paying the funeral bills for her third child when she heard of the death of the fourth.

This, then, is the America, both glorious and gruesome, which the rest of the world sees endlessly on its cinema and television screens. But the other America is almost entirely unknown to most metropolitan Americans, let alone foreigners. It also goes largely unreported by the city-based, city-centred US media. It is a vast, raw, untamed land found far from the sophisticated coastal conurbations. It is an extraordinarily insular and conservative place whose inhabitants consider New York and Washington as foreign as London or Paris. They seldom travel beyond the boundaries of their states, or even to their state capitals. They meet few outsiders and are exposed to practically no outside influences. They hardly ever see foreign films or television programmes, and a Woody Allen film with all its New York 'psychobabble' would seem utterly alien. In much of this land even *USA Today* is unobtainable and ultra right-wing radio chat-show hosts are often the major source of 'news'.

There is more than a grain of truth in those cartoon posters entitled 'A New Yorker's View of America' that show a giant Manhattan tailing off into California with only the Grand Canyon, Las Vegas and a couple of little mountains in between. In Europe most city-dwellers love the country and get out to the villages whenever possible. In America the division between urban and rural is almost absolute. This is partly due to the tremendous distances involved, but it is also a reflection of mental attitudes. Metropolitan Americans – who comprise three-quarters of the population – scoff at the 'boondocks', and at the 'rednecks' and 'hillbillies' who live there. If they do go into the country it is usually to some resort for golf or skiing. They occasionally speed through the hinterlands on interstates, but 'speed' is the operative word and the interstates have made it possible for them to cross the country without ever entering small-town America. If they must stop for a meal or a night en route they do so at intersections monopolised by motel or restaurant chains that actually boast of being identical wherever they are.

Younger people sometimes move from small towns to cities, but there is little movement the other way. In election years politicians like President Clinton and Bob Dole extol their rural birthplaces – Hope, Arkansas, and Russell, Kansas – as repositories of the finest American values, but Mr Dole certainly did not rush back to live in Russell after he lost the 1996 presidential contest and there is not the faintest chance of Mr Clinton returning to deepest Arkansas after he leaves the Oval Office in 2001. The nearest these politicians go to such places (when there are no elections looming) is several thousand feet overhead as they fly from Washington to Los Angeles.

This second America is, in short, an almost pristine, undiluted culture isolated by sheer distance and largely by-passed even by the information superhighway. Here it is easy to see how the country's short but unique history has shaped the national character. Here the religious fundamentalism, fierce independence and profound distrust of government that distinguish Americans from their distant European cousins are not only manifest but becoming – in some respects – even more pronounced.

I visited this second America periodically during long summer camping trips with my family, or on assignments for *The Times*, and was intrigued by what I saw. For example, I vividly recall making a trip to Cando, North Dakota, during the build up to the Gulf War. All 120 members of Cando's National Guard – almost every able-bodied man in town – had been called up and sent to Saudi Arabia, leaving their wives to run vast prairie farms through an arctic winter. I was the only person on the only plane from Minneapolis, and the only person in Cando's only motel. Within a couple of hours of my arrival the entire town seemed to know who I was, and here – as in other small communities – I found myself the subject of a story in the newspaper of the town I'd come to write about.

When my posting to Washington finally ended I was forty, and a little stale after writing almost exclusively about politics for the previous ten years. I resolved to take time off to explore this over-looked land more deeply, to travel far beyond the famous sights and cities in search of this little-known America. Thus it was that one overcast autumn morning I watched my children – Hannah, Barney and Imogen – climb into their yellow school bus, hugged my wife, Katy, and set off in a battered old Dodge Colt that I'd bought secondhand for $3,600 the week we'd arrived in America seven years earlier. Before that day this car had seldom done more than my daily 16-mile round trip to work and back. Its right front wing had been crumpled in an accident that had reduced its worth to less than the $190 I paid to park it outside the office every month. It lacked air-conditioning, electric windows or any other accessories. Its heating and windscreen washers didn't work, but Bruce, our local mechanic, insisted it was not worth spending money on. It was now embarked, however, on a journey of heaven knows how many thousand miles that would end, I hoped, on the north-western tip of Washington State sometime the following spring.

2

Sooks and Jimmies

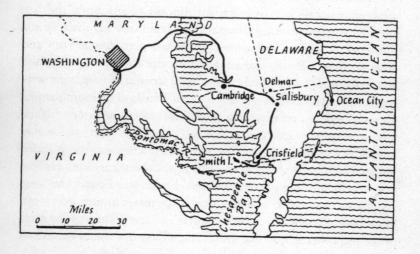

The first leg of my journey across the continent took me not west at all, but east towards the Atlantic coast.

From the Virginia suburbs I could have cut straight through Washington, but for symbolic reasons I decided to take the Beltway – the ring road that encircles the capital like a modern-day city wall. This thunderous ten-lane monstrosity has spawned a phrase beloved of Washingtonians. To be 'inside the Beltway' describes less a physical location than a certain status. It suggests you are either a part of America's governing élite or, at the very least, privy to its machinations. It implies a distinct superiority over the masses condemned to live in the hinterlands beyond the city wall, and I was now speeding round that wall towards its eastern portal.

I felt a distinct apprehension that first morning. The grey clouds hung like bruises on pale white skin and did nothing to leaven my mood, but as I crossed the Potomac River the sun broke through. I glanced northwards and spotted a rainbow over the distant white needle of the Washington Monument. At that omen my spirits began to rise, and when I passed the Andrews Air Force Base a few miles on they soared still further.

Three times in the past few years I had left Andrews for trips with the President to Europe and the Middle East. To be more accurate, the President had left in Air Force One, his giant retinue had followed in Air Force Two, and we the media brought up the rear in a chartered 747 loaded with gourmet food, the latest movies and even, on one occasion, a masseuse until the women of the White House press corps ruled her politically incorrect. Those trips were certainly fun – and vastly expensive – but I'd found no lasting attraction in defying time zones and body clocks for days on end while frantically meeting London deadlines. One visit to Jerusalem only lasted from dusk to dawn, and an even shorter one to Amman, Jordan, took from 9.00 p.m. to 4.00 a.m. Looking back, I recall we never did see much of the President, whose movements we were supposed to be reporting. He could hardly take a jumbo jet's worth of journalists and camera crews to every event. What actually happened – and here I'm giving away trade secrets – was that the White House set up huge temporary press offices wherever he stopped. Most of us had to sit in those, watch his appearances on closed circuit television, and rely on secondhand reports from a tiny, select pool of colleagues who were actually with him. Were it not for the datelines, we might just as well have been reporting from Washington.

I was suddenly seized by a sense of liberation. The months stretched ahead with no more daily deadlines, no more sub-editors mangling stories, no more broken nights, bleeping pagers or telephones that would not stop ringing. That morning, for the first time in seven years, I hadn't jumped from my bed to read the *Washington Post*, the *New York Times* and the *Wall Street Journal* before first light, and as I turned off the Beltway for Route 50 – a mere six lanes – I calmly and deliberately let twelve o'clock pass without snapping on the radio for the news.

The eastern edge of Washington is all black, and lacks the endless sprawl of malls and new developments on the opposite side of the city where the wealthy white folk live. I was soon in open country, savouring the last reds and golds of autumn, and within another half-hour I was climbing high over the northern narrows of Chesapeake Bay on a magnificent 4-mile ribbon of elegantly curving bridge. Far below, a container ship from Baltimore was steaming southwards into a vast expanse of blue-grey water flecked by occasional white sails and lit by rods of sunlight slanting through the patchwork clouds.

I stayed on Route 50 as it curved southwards down the Delmarva Peninsula, the tapering strip of rich, flat farmland that separates Chesapeake Bay from the Atlantic Ocean. I would not include Delmarva on a list of evocative American place names. It is a crass abbreviation of Delaware, Maryland and Virginia, the three states that divide the peninsula between them. There is even a town spanning the Delaware-Maryland border called – you've guessed it – Delmar.

Route 50 leads to Ocean City, and in the summer it would be packed with holidaymakers from Washington and Baltimore, but now I had it to myself. The roadside fruit and vegetable stands were closed for the season, and the fields had long since been harvested. I passed a turning to Oxford. After crossing the broad Choptank River I found myself, inevitably, in Cambridge. Next came Salisbury, whose Baptist temple stages drive-in nativity and passion plays each year. The stage is a long low hill. The audience sits in its cars and listens by tuning the radio to 95.7 FM. It applauds by honking its horns. Most nights there are three hundred cars or more in the stalls.

A few miles beyond Salisbury I branched right on to a mere two-lane road. I suddenly realised I'd been dawdling, stopping to read each historical marker on the way, and was late. I sped the last 10 miles and reached Crisfield, a small town on the edge of Chesapeake Bay, in the nick of time. The 4.30 p.m. ferry was just untying. I parked the car, sprinted down the jetty, and within another minute was churning away from the present day towards a truly unique community that has survived for three and a half centuries in the middle of America's biggest estuary.

Smith Island is not really an island at all. It is a 20-square-mile expanse of wild marshland teeming with herons, ospreys and egrets, and so far from either shore that neither can be seen. In the midst of the marshes are three patches of dry land where the Pocomoke and Assateague Indians camped each summer until a band of English and Welsh settlers dislodged them in the 1650s. Some 400 descendants of those first settlers still live there, in the tiny villages of Ewell, Rhodes Point and Tylerton. They still earn their livelihoods by harvesting seafood from the watery cornucopia that surrounds them. They still bear the same few surnames – Marshall, Marsh, Bradshaw, Jennings, Evans, Tyler, Dize – and still speak in a brogue that owes more to Elizabethan England than America.

Smith Island is less than 90 miles from Washington as the crow flies, or 180 by road and ferry, but it is another world. It has no crime, no policemen and no traffic except for boats. It has no bar, cinema, doctor, bank or supermarket. It has no mayors or town councils. The islanders obey the laws of God, nature and the Methodist church in the form of its pastor, a booming Barbadian named Dr Ashley Maxwell who is the island's only black man. They consider the state and federal governments to be interfering Johnny-come-latelies who would destroy their traditional way of life with ever more restrictions.

Besides myself there were seven substantial women and one baby huddled in the ferry's cabin. All were islanders who had 'gone off' for the day – their term for a visit to the mainland – and were returning laden with supplies. They were in raucous good spirits, but their brogue was so thick and the engine so loud that I could hardly understand them. They talked round me, looked past me and evidently considered me an awkward presence for I was a 'foreigner', or 'furr' ner', as the islanders call outsiders. I stared ahead towards Smith Island, but it was so flat and so low that all I could see until we had nearly completed the 10-mile journey was a thin black line of trees seemingly rising from the water.

To reach Smith Island by boat a little before dusk on a still autumn afternoon is to experience a rare moment of tranquillity in this turbulent world. We left the choppy waters of the Bay and approached Ewell up a wide channel bordered by banks of thick brown marsh grass. The town's waterfront bristled with rickety wooden jetties, each with a jerry-built crab hut or 'shanty' perched precariously on the end, some bearing stacks of rectangular crab pots. Behind the jetties was a jumble of pretty white clapboard houses. This mighty 'capital' of at least 200 people does actually possess a few cars, though the only road leads just 2 miles across the marshes to Rhodes Point. It also boasts a couple of restaurants. These serve the tourist boats that on summer weekends put in just long enough for the passengers to gawp at a few islanders, marvel at their accents, and demolish a 'seafood special'.

We unloaded four of the women, the baby and their bundles of shopping on to the dock, then headed southwards down another broad channel that the islanders call the 'thoroughfare', or 'thurrfer', to Tylerton, or 'Taarrlton'. Ewell was pretty but Tylerton, the smallest of the three villages with just seventy-six inhabitants, was yet more enchanting. As the ferry manoeuvred its way in between a maze of home-made jetties, a couple of boys were fishing from the dock and a waterman was closing up his shanty for the night. Narrow lanes led off between neat clapboard houses, each with a nesting-box for mosquito-eating martins. A fine white twin-towered church was illuminated by a floodlight in the gathering darkness and the whole village was framed by a backdrop of dark trees.

The air smelt of salt and marsh, the light was clear, and when the ferry cut its engine there was no sound save that of the wind and water. Tylerton has just one car, four vans for heavy loads, a fire engine, an ambulance and a golf cart that carries the elderly to church. The three ladies loaded their shopping into handcarts and trundled homewards. Nobody asked for my fare but I paid it anyway – $14 round trip. As the sky turned from deep red to black across the distant marshes, I walked half a mile along a pitted track by the water to a cottage a friend had lent me. It was 'down below', meaning at the village's southern end. It was rarely used but never locked, and there was just a wooden latch to prevent the front door flying open during gales.

For most of the 19th century Chesapeake Bay was the oyster

capital of the world. For most of the 20th it has been the blue crab capital, supplying Philadelphia, New York and cities far beyond with those savoury crustaceans, and I had come to spend a day with a master waterman named Dwight – or 'Dwoight' – Marshall. After dropping my bags I strolled back to his house, an immaculate cottage with a white picket fence right opposite the dock. He turned out to be a taciturn man of fifty-one with a handsome, weather-beaten face, bright blue eyes and silver hair. He had just returned from twelve hours on the water and was stretched out in an arm-chair in his front room. 'D'you get seasick?' he asked. 'Got oilskins?' The forecast was for high winds and heavy rain. I could return at 4.30 the next morning if I wanted, but he doubted he'd get out. Mary Ada, his formidable, no-nonsense wife, came in from the kitchen and cheerfully predicted a 'honeydoo day', as in 'honey do this' or 'honey do that'.

I wandered off to the village store to buy some food. I entered to find a dozen watermen sitting around a couple of tables talking. The room instantly fell silent. Twenty-four eyes turned on me. I felt like the bad guy who walks into a crowded saloon in the westerns, except that I lacked his boldness. I hesitated. Should I beat an ignominious retreat? That, I decided, would be cowardice. I bought some milk and a cake and perched on a stool at the far end of the counter. Slowly the old-timers resumed their conversation, but in accents so thick that again I could scarcely follow them. All wore baseball caps and thick checked shirts. All had leathery brown faces. Several smoked. Only on Smith Island, however, would you find a tough male group like that drinking cokes and eating ice creams, for all three villages are 'dry'. In 1933, when America repealed Prohibition, Smith Island voted 165 to 4 to continue it, and in 1988 the elders of the island's three Methodist churches soundly defeated an appli-cation to sell alcohol in Ewell.

The islanders practise a far stricter form of Methodism than the kind on the mainland. They 'tithe' up to ten per cent of their incomes to the church. They will not work on the Sabbath, even during peak crabbing season. Many attend morning and evening services every Sunday, and prayer meetings every Wednesday night, and each summer the island holds a week-long revivalist camp meeting in Ewell. It was during one of those camp meetings that the islanders had spotted and recruited Dr Maxwell, a visiting preacher. The islanders' fundamentalism no doubt reflects their isolation and daily battles with the elements. 'Any man who works in the open and can look at nature and say there is no God is blind,' said Dwight. 'There's got to be a creator there.'

At 4.00 the next morning I woke to a gale. The waves lapped over the path up to the village. I fought my way to Dwight's house in the darkness, and found him watching *Jason and the Argonauts* on television. He suggested we waited a couple of hours. By daybreak the winds had indeed moderated but the sky remained leaden. He then discovered his mate had flu, but decided to set off anyway. I swallowed the first of the seasick pills I'd prudently purchased before leaving Washington, followed him down the jetty, loaded six boxes of frozen fish on to the *Miss Marshall*, his 35-foot boat, and off we headed for his crab grounds ninety minutes westwards near the mouth of the Potomac.

I had omitted to tell Dwight that the last time I was on Chesapeake Bay was on a friend's yacht on a perfect summer's day, and that even then I had been violently seasick. The moment we left the shelter of Smith Island *Miss Marshall* began bouncing over the waves, lurching from side to side, spray crashing over her cabin window. Dwight opened a Coke, smoked a cigarette and munched one of the assorted biscuits littering the small cabin. 'It's rough,' he chuckled. I gripped the seat. I kept my eyes fixed firmly on the horizon – and occasionally the crucifix by his compass. I began to feel queasy, then positively bilious. I swallowed, belched, and wondered how I would ever survive a day on this heaving ocean. I decided that sitting in Washington's rush-hour traffic was infinitely preferable to this hellish commute by water, but then came a merciful distraction.

Dwight's VHF radio crackled and another waterman announced he was bringing out a mate from Ewell. Dwight slowed down. He gave his approximate position. He spotted the approaching vessel and guided it towards us. The two boats manoeuvred as close as they could in the heaving waters and a young man leaped across. He was another Marshall – Guy Marshall.

I don't know how in that vast expanse of rolling waves Dwight spotted the tiny buoys marking his crab pots but he did. He and Guy took up their positions by a second steering wheel in the back corner of the boat and set to work with production-line efficiency. Dwight snared each buoy with a boat hook and winched up the pot, a square wire cage with a rotting fish in the middle and one small entrance for the crabs. Guy grabbed it, replaced the old fish with a new one, and shook out the catch of anywhere between six to twelve substantial crabs. He then threw the jimmies – the blue-clawed males – into one wooden tub or bushel and the sooks – the smaller red-clawed females – into another. By the time he had finished Dwight had the next pot waiting, and so they steadily worked their way down watery lines all but invisible to the uninitiated.

The wind dropped, the sun came out, seagulls swooped and hovered in our wake. I finally found my sea legs and was soon happily dividing jimmies from sooks. These were not the modest little creatures you catch in an English creek. From claw-tip to claw-tip they were a foot across, and fierce to boot. Their pincers were powerful enough that even with thick gloves on you handled them with respect, and some held their fellow crustaceans in such vice-like grips that you had to break off their claws to separate them.

The hours passed. Watermen across the Bay chatted on their radios as they worked. Dwight said little, but even after a lifetime on the water he was still obviously absorbed by his work. He could sense the moods and movements of the crabs as well as anyone on the Bay. To him catching crabs was like 'finding money or treasure' and the thrill never faded. Occasionally he felt 'burned out', he admitted, but then the season would change and with it his *modus operandi*. In winter he went drift-netting for rockfish, oystering, or hunting for hibernating terrapins in the muddy shallows. In high summer he caught 'peeler' crabs which he kept in trays of shallow salt water by his shanty until they shed their shells. A dozen of those highly-prized soft-shelled crabs could fetch as much as an entire bushel – perhaps 150 – of the hard-shelled ones.

The sun moved slowly from south to west. By mid-afternoon we had filled eighteen bushels, each worth $20 to $30. On a normal day Dwight would have left home long before dawn and emptied all his 375 pots, but today he had to stop after a mere 200. We sped back to Ewell in brilliant evening light, dropped Guy and refuelled. As we headed down the 'thur'fer' towards Tylerton, Mary Ada came on the radio to invite me to supper, and fifteen minutes later we were sitting down to oyster stew followed by a great roast ham in the Marshalls' kitchen. It was then that I began to learn something of the sadness of Smith Island.

Generations of Dwight's family had been watermen, harvesting the waters in summertime and hunting for duck, fox, mink and muskrat in the marshes during winter. Dwight was one of the most contented men I've ever met. He had never lived away from the island, and never wanted to, but his whole way of life was now vanishing. Pollution and overfishing had all but destroyed the world's finest oyster beds. In the 1950s the government had declared the northern half of the island a wildlife refuge, and more recently had begun limiting what the islanders could catch in the Bay and when. Most serious of all, the island's younger generation had decided it could earn money much more easily on the mainland. The men no longer wanted to be watermen, starting 16-hour days long before dawn, and the girls didn't fancy lifetimes of rising at 2.30 each morning to pick the meat from the previous day's crab catch in time for the 7.00 a.m. ferry.

Smith Island's population peaked at 805 in 1910 but was barely half that now, while Tylerton's population had halved since 1980. There were scarcely 100 watermen left in total, and less than twenty in Tylerton. The Marshalls' three sons had all left the island, and their daughter was one of Tylerton's three remaining teenage girls. While the rest of America was struggling to recapture the islanders' values and sense of community, Smith Island itself was dying.

Mary Ada was one of those women who find strength in adversity, a life-force who would battle on till the last. She was fiercely protective of her island. She'd invited me to dinner because I was by

myself, she said, but didn't much care for writers. They always portrayed the islanders as primitive, simple or quaint. She decided I'd
asked enough questions and began quizzing me. Did I believe in
God? she asked. Did I take my children to church? Did I believe in
the Second Coming? I quickly concluded that Mary Ada was neither simple nor quaint, and that it was time to say goodnight.

I was up before dawn the next day too. I wanted to see the pickers at work. I walked through the darkness to the gleaming new
cooperative the island's women had had to build in the early 1990s
when Maryland's health inspectors suddenly decreed they could no
longer 'pick' in their homes. I could hardly believe there'd be people
working there so early, but I was wrong. Janice Marshall, a large,
jovial, middle-aged woman who turned out to be Dwight's sister-in-
law, was sitting at a stainless steel table beneath bright fluorescent
lights picking her way through a bushel of steamed crabs with a
portable television on in the background.

She was an expert picker, cracking the pink shells with the handle
of her steel knife, scooping the white meat out with the pointed end,
and flicking it into one-pound plastic tubs labelled: 'This premium
crabmeat has been carefully handpicked and packaged with pride by
the women of Smith Island, Maryland.' Janice reckoned she could
do a bushel – more than 150 crabs – in two hours and extract five
or six pounds of meat. As she worked, she talked, and from her too
I heard the same lament.

She'd wanted to be a nurse, she said, but she'd married, had children and by then it was too late. She was now encouraging her son
'to get off the water' but so far he'd been unable to find a job. Smith
Island was a wonderful place to live and rear children, but it was a
constant struggle to survive and there was more to life than crabs
and oysters. 'I'm afraid it's too late for anything in Tylerton,' she
concluded. 'We don't have a new generation coming up and so
many people have left.'

As the sun rose, I walked back to the store for breakfast and
found Mary Ada behind the counter. Besides crab picking and man-
aging the store, she was also a substitute teacher in Ewell. 'It's called
making ends meet,' she explained as I ate my first – and hopefully

last – scrapple sandwich. No one could, or would, tell me precisely what scrapple was, but it evidently had a lot to do with a pig's internal organs.

I spent the day exploring Tylerton. I found that every third or fourth house was for sale, and that even the finest would be lucky to fetch $40,000 from some city-dweller who might visit three or four times a year. I found the elementary school which had had twenty-five pupils when it opened in 1974, but had closed a few months before my visit because there were just three children left. I wandered round the abandoned playground, and peeked through the windows. There was still writing on the blackboard, pictures on the walls, and teddy bears in every seat.

Beyond the school was an overgrown baseball field with its old wooden floodlight poles all askew, the village team having folded for lack of players ten years earlier. Next to the church was a cemetery packed with graves of bygone Marshalls, Evanses and Bradshaws, and so full that people joked about whether Tylerton would run out of people or grave space first. Along the waterfront old boats had been left to sink, and a sign hanging in the one-room post office seemed an exercise in self-mockery. 'Avoid long lines,' it read. 'Best times to visit this post office and avoid waiting are from 7.30–8.30 a.m.' The one new feature, apart from the cooperative, were the road signs on every corner. These too had been imposed upon the islanders so the emergency rescue services on the mainland could respond to 911 calls.

I learned the islanders' habit of talking backwards, so that a woman might say of a handsome man: 'He's ugly.' I learned how the accents of the three communities were subtly different, and how Ewell people were known as 'bean snuckers', Rhodes Pointers as 'cheese eaters' and Tylertonians as 'herring hucksters'. I was told of the winter of 1976, when the Bay was frozen for weeks on end and the National Guard had to bring in supplies by helicopter, and of the island's superstitions. Blue paint and walnuts were bad luck, and you should always leave by the same door that you entered.

I met Lindsey Bradshaw, a tall, tousle-haired man of thirty-four who was married to Dwight's niece. He had given up being a waterman for the easier life of a carpenter, but was something of a hero in Tylerton because he had produced two children and had another on the way. He told me that of the six other children who'd been in his elementary school class he was the only one who had stayed. He wouldn't know what to do on the mainland, he said. Here, if he had time to spare, he took out his skiff and went 'progging' – rooting about – in the marshes. He showed me his shanty which was packed with the lumber, buoys, lifejackets, boat hooks and assorted debris he'd collected.

Lindsey pointed out an arthritic, grey-haired old lady pulling weeds from her garden. She was Virginia Evans, Tylerton's oldest resident at eighty-nine. When I asked if I could talk to her she beamed, told me to throw the weeds 'overboard' – meaning into the water – and led me into the old wooden house in which she had been born. In those days it had stood in Longbranch, one of a couple of other Smith Island communities that had ceased to exist in the 1930s when the inhabitants put their homes on barges and floated them down to Tylerton.

'Miss Virginia', as she is known throughout the island, showed me a faded picture of Longbranch, and dug out photographs of her elementary school in 1914 when it had forty-four pupils. 'I've dreamed of being over there like it used to be. Every house was filled with children. I crave to go back one more time,' she confided, but all that remains of Longbranch now are a few wooden posts by the marsh's edge.

She showed me entries in her diary recording the arrival of mainland electricity in 1949, the establishment of a proper telephone service in 1951, and the building of Tylerton's sewage plant in 1979. 'Before that we dumped it overboard,' she giggled. 'Nowadays,' she lamented, 'the young people go to Crisfield high school. When they graduate they want jobs and there are no jobs here. They don't want to work on the water. A lot of them move and live on the mainland and the elder people are dying. This community is a-dying, I call it.'

The next day, a Sunday, I went to church. It was a bittersweet experience. The morning sun poured through the stained-glass windows and filled the fine old chapel with light. The watermen who'd ignored me in the village store now came up and shook my hand. One by one the congregation stood and 'testified' or expressed – each in their own way – their faith in God. Dr Maxwell's baritone filled the room, and the choir gave a spirited performance, but the assembled village could no longer fill more than a third of the wooden pews.

Afterwards, in the basement, the womenfolk laid on a lavish lunch of roast beef and umpteen different crab dishes where I met another 'furr' ner', or at least a 'semi-furr' ner'. His name was Tom Horton. He was an environmental writer who had spent three years living on Smith Island with his family and had just produced a very affectionate book about the place. Talking to him, I began to feel that the island's relentless depopulation was perhaps not quite as tragic as it seemed. Until earlier this century, he said, there were several other inhabited islands in Chesapeake Bay – Watts', Jones', Holland's, Shanks's and Fox's. All had been abandoned as they were eroded by the tides. A couple still had derelict houses standing on them, but most had now disappeared beneath the water. Smith Island was one of the last two inhabited islands left but within another hundred years, Horton assured me, it too would have vanished, if not through erosion then from rising water levels caused by global warming.

3

High-Tech Hillbillies

After leaving Smith Island I meandered down the last 100 miles of the Delmarva Peninsula, by now so slender that you could drive from the shore of the Bay to the Atlantic in a matter of minutes. I crossed from Maryland back into Virginia. I passed the road to the Assateague Island nature reserve, home of wild ponies whose ancestors allegedly swam ashore from a sinking Spanish galleon in the 16th century. I stopped at a clutch of once-fine old wooden houses called Temperanceville because I liked the name.

'Why's Temperanceville called Temperanceville?' I inquired of a genial old black man who was tending his turnips in the sun.

'Ah've lived here all ma life and I jus' dunno,' he replied with a grin.

The postmistress was equally unenlightening. The girl at the petrol station suggested, improbably, that it was an Indian name. She was selling beer as well as petrol, so I guessed the noble intentions of

whoever had originally founded Temperanceville had been long forgotten. Was it possible to live in a place called Temperanceville and
not wonder where it got its name? Evidently it was. I decided against
rerunning the test in Birdsnest, Virginia, but Oyster, Virginia, was
self-explanatory. It was a charming little fishing village protected
from the open Atlantic by a string of long, low, marshy islands half
a mile offshore.

The further I went, the more rural and Southern the peninsula
became. Old black men sat outside country stores enjoying the fine
Indian summer's day. Abandoned wooden shacks were vanishing
beneath vines and creepers. I drove past cotton fields, a million
brilliant white tufts erupting from dead black pods, and acres of
peanut fields. At the peninsula's southernmost tip was a huge overgrown concrete gun emplacement, built to defend the entrance to
Chesapeake Bay during World War Two, and when the land ran out
I continued south on a low, two-lane bridge across 19 miles of
brilliant-blue, sparkling water to Norfolk, the world's largest naval
base.

Crabs, I decided, were child's play. It was time to hunt bigger
game – bears, for example. In Norfolk I turned sharp right and set
off for the mountains of West Virginia, some 200 miles to the west.
I crossed the top of the Great Dismal Swamp and came to Suffolk,
where I ate a barbecued pork sandwich in Bunny's family restaurant.
Spurning the interstate, I headed up my favourite sort of country
road – a dead straight one that followed a railway line. I went
through Windsor, Zuni, Ivor, Wakefield – 'the peanut capital of the
world' – and Waverly, then found myself in a dilapidated little place
called Disputanta. This time I had to stop.

An old-timer sitting on the porch of his tumbledown home
directed me to the post office where Roger the postmaster produced
a xeroxed sheet of paper with the history of Disputanta. 'There are
several theories on how the town got its name,' I read. 'A widely
accepted theory is that former Norfolk and Western Railroad president William Mahone took his wife down the line when it was
completed in 1851. She was a fan of Sir Walter Scott's novels and
named several towns after places in the books including Waverly,

Wakefield, Windsor, Zuni and Ivor. Disputanta, also taken from the novels, was an easy choice because two families had long been in dispute over what to name the town.'

I also read that while Disputanta's population had fallen from a peak of nearly 600 in 1920 to just 100 now 'there is hope on the horizon. In an effort to attract industry, the county is installing lines to provide sewer and water service to the area'. That optimism was not universally shared. With admirable candour the sheet went on to quote one of Disputanta's oldest residents, George Mayer, saying of the town: 'It ain't worth a damn. Everything's played out. The people ain't like they used to be. They don't associate, not even the old ones. I don't know what's going on.'

After Disputanta I relented, took the interstate, and sped across central Virginia, stopping a night *en route*. It was pretty enough country, with rolling hills and large, manicured farms, but had long ago been tamed. I regained interest when the interstate abruptly ended about 40 miles west of Charlottesville because the Appalachian Mountains blocked its way. I switched to a much smaller road, and as I snaked up higher and higher into the George Washington national forest it became clear that the Appalachians formed a barrier to much more than just the interstate. They were a barrier to progress, prosperity and the relentless homogenisation of America. There were few Holiday Inns and McDonald's where I was going, few Pizza Huts, glitzy shopping malls or hypermarkets. Big comfortable houses became rare. Battered pick-up trucks replaced leather-seated Japanese saloon cars as the vehicle of choice. Familiar radio stations began to crackle and fade. At a high mountain pass, where mist was billowing upwards and the trees were flecked with early snow, I crossed from affluent Virginia into West Virginia, the state with the lowest average household income in America. I was entering central Appalachia, a land of densely-forested mountains and deep river valleys, of stunning natural beauty and staggering human poverty, where all manner of dark and peculiar things still go on. 'Wild and Wonderful' is the slogan on West Virginia's car number plates, and highly appropriate it is too.

Most obviously this is a land where hunting is an inalienable right of the common man, not the sport of a privileged land-owning élite. Here people hunt to put meat on their tables, not just for the fun of it. If there's nothing else in season they'll go after groundhog, raccoon, possum, squirrel and even rattlesnake. By late autumn the pursuit of bear, deer, and wild turkey is practically a full-time occupation, and only the blind could fail to observe this.

I drove through the forest past clusters of parked pick-ups and smoky little encampments in roadside clearings. In the hamlet of Head Waters a group of men were skinning a deer suspended from a tree. In the tiny town of McDowell the grocery store sold hunting licences, hunting knives, camouflaged head nets, scents for attracting deer, devices for making deer-like grunts and raffle tickets with rifles as the prizes. In Durbin a large homemade sign by the road read simply 'Deer Process', and an arrow pointed up a track to where a man would chop, wrap and freeze your deer for $25 to $48 depending on its size. At a petrol station in Huttonsville I found a group admiring a dead deer stuffed into the boot of a small grey saloon car, and I saw so many men wearing camouflaged clothing I almost believed that, in my self-imposed boycott of the news, I'd missed the outbreak of a war.

West Virginia, a state of 1.8 million people, sells 300,000 hunting licences a year. Exclude children under fifteen, pensioners and various categories of ex-servicemen, who can all hunt for free, and women, who generally stay at home, and there can be very few adult West Virginian males who do not buy one. A popular christening present is a lifetime hunting licence, available for just $200 if the child is under one. Some counties even close their schools for a week at the start of the deer season.

There was a particular excitement the day I arrived, for the season for hunting bears with dogs was opening the following morning. I had telephoned West Virginia's Department of Natural Resources to ask how I could witness this event, and was put on to Joe Rieffenberger, a research biologist who had, over the past quarter-century, saved West Virginia's black bear from extinction through a series of long-overdue restrictions. Until the 1950s the state had considered the bear a nuisance and paid a bounty for each one killed. By the time Joe arrived in 1972 there were just 500 left. That number is now 5,000 and rising, even though hunters take 800 a year.

Joe not only found a group of hunters to take me out. He and his wife, Mary Moore, invited me to stay with them in the small town of Beverly. A charming couple in their seventies, they lived in a wonderful old house cluttered with books, carvings, wood stoves and what must surely be one of the last dial telephones in America. Joe, who had a big bald round head and silver beard and became red-faced with laughter whenever he told bear stories, immediately whisked me off in a jalopy even older than my own to an eve-of-season 'bear feed' organised by the group I was to join.

This was held in Bunny's breeze-block garage, Bunny being one of the hunters. You ate first, talked afterwards. There was roast bear, bear sausages and fresh venison. I'd not eaten bear before. It was a strong, dark meat and, I have to admit, pretty good. The wives ate separately. Only when they vanished with the dishes did I meet Dennis Weese, the group's leader, and the rest of his gang. Practically everyone had beards and grimy baseball caps. Most smoked and drank beer. They were loggers, bulldozer drivers and carpenters. One or two worked at a nearby prison, prisons being one of the few growth industries in rural America. They were tough working men with scarcely a high school diploma or full set of teeth between them, but they were a friendly, cheerful bunch with far more native intelligence than the hillbilly stereotype. They told jokes against themselves – 'What's the burning legal question in West Virginia? Answer: If you divorce your wife is she still your sister?' They also loathed big-city America as vehemently as metropolitan Americans abhorred the boondocks, and not for the last time on this trip I found myself an object of pity for having to live in Washington.

It was dark and beginning to snow by the time Joe and I went home. For the rest of the evening he gave me a crash course in bears, right down to the sow's extraordinary ability to delay fertilisation after copulation so she always gave birth in January. What made bears so interesting was that their behaviour was learned, not innate, he said. Each was an individual. 'Every rabbit is average – a rabbit is just a bunch of genes – but there's no such thing as an average bear,' he explained. The thrill of bear hunting was the quarry's complete unpredictability.

My alarm woke me at 4.30 a.m. Mary Moore had left out a hefty breakfast and an even more substantial packed lunch. I stepped out into the pitch darkness to find several inches of snow on the ground and Dennis waiting in his pick-up. We drove for half an hour to the mouth of a forested valley called Becky's Creek that runs up the side of the 4,500-foot Cheat Mountain, and stopped at the trailer home of some 'holler hooters' – dirt-poor people who live in the hills and hollows of Appalachia.

This was the meeting place. A dozen pick-ups came in behind us, their powerful headlights slicing through the darkness, each with rifles on their seats and a doghouse on the back. The men strapped collars with radio transmitters on to their hounds and gave the frequencies to Roger, a colossal man who was the group's communications wizard. These collars would not only enable Roger to track the movements of each and every dog with his portable antennae, they also contained mercury switches that would emit different signals when the dogs looked upwards. That way Roger could tell when they had driven a bear up a tree so the hunters could move in for the kill. These people may have been hillbillies, but they were hi-tech hillbillies.

In normal conditions the hunters put their best sniffer dogs on top of their pick-ups and set off up forest tracks until the hounds smelled where a bear had crossed. The snow made that unnecessary. Anyone could see where a bear had crossed. The trouble was, the snow also made it far less likely that the bears would be out. As dawn broke half-a-dozen of the younger men set off on foot for an area where they had recently spotted a large male bear – a boar – while the rest fanned out in their pick-ups.

Dennis and I bumped several miles up the valley, seeing nothing, till the trail ended in a clearing. There we waited, drinking coffee and listening to the Johnboy and Billy Show on the radio while a tremendous snowstorm swirled outside. We could have been sitting inside one of those toy snow bubbles children get at Christmas.

Dennis, a gaunt man in his mid-forties, was a natural leader and noticeably more pensive than the others, perhaps because he'd travelled a bit. At thirteen he had left the mountains and moved with his stepfather to Iowa, one of America's flattest states. At eighteen he had joined the Navy for four years. He then became a dry-stone waller in Iowa but had divorced, got homesick like so many mountain men, and returned to West Virginia. He now did a bit of everything – built walls, operated diggers, worked at a ski resort – but the bear hunting season was what he lived for. 'This is my time,' he said. It was not the killing. He'd rather see the bear let loose, though others in the group had 'blood in their eyes'. It was the dogs and the chase he loved. He and his second wife spent probably a quarter of their modest income on raising and training their eight hounds. 'You're taking a dog that doesn't know shit, like it's in kindergarten, and you're graduating it,' he explained. Later in the day, when he showed me the spot where a bear had killed his 'Fred dog', tears welled in his eyes.

After a couple of hours Dennis' walkie-talkie crackled. The foot party had found nothing. We drove to a rendezvous in another clearing. 'We're beating a dead horse,' said Roger. Dennis agreed. The bears were just not walking. The same footsoldiers, their beards caked with ice and looking like the cast of *Doctor Zhivago*, insisted on trying one more place so off they tramped while Dennis and I returned to the trailer home for yet more coffee.

An hour later, having admired the holler hooter's impressive collection of muzzle-loading rifles, we were driving disconsolately out of the valley to see if other hunters had had more luck when Dennis' walkie-talkie crackled again. 'Denny. Get the shit up here,' ordered Roger's urgent voice. The footsoldiers had 'jumped' a bear.

Dennis stamped on the brakes, slithered round 180 degrees in the snow, and careered back up the track, slipping and sliding, bucking and bouncing, suddenly animated. 'This is why we like bear hunting,' he shouted. 'It lets us act like teenagers again.' We found Roger pointing up a fork in the trail. We took it, engine screaming, tyres spinning up an icy hill.

*

A bunch of yelping hounds burst out of the trees and crossed the track in front of us, hot on the trail of a bear that must have passed just moments earlier. The dogs were closely followed by the foot-soldiers. The pawprints were big, they said. It looked like a good-sized bear. They and Dennis held a hasty discussion. These people knew the mountain like city-dwellers know streets. They reckoned the bear was heading up towards a narrow plateau of old strip-mines further up the mountainside. We piled back into the pick-ups and for the next forty-five minutes drove furiously out of the valley, up a mountain road and along an old mining track till we reached the plateau. There Roger whipped out his antennae. The signals were strong and fast. The dogs were somewhere close below and appeared to have 'treed' the bear. A dozen of us set off down the mountainside, rifles over shoulders, heading towards the signals until we could actually hear the dogs barking. We crept forward till we saw the bear, 30-foot up in the crook of a tree, its front paws round the trunk, peering contemptuously at the dogs below.

It was a male and it was big. Each hunter is allowed just one bear per season, but the men quickly decided this one was worth shooting. The honour was offered to Gil, who had led the trackers, but he declined. Killing a bear was an expensive proposition. The taxidermist would charge $500 and the butcher another $50. Gil offered the job to Jed, a sixteen-year-old who had yet to kill his first bear. The men caught their dogs and ringed the tree. Jed raised his rifle, aimed and fired. He hit the bear in its neck. It toppled, broke its fall on a branch, but hit the ground with a thump. It made one brief effort to get up then keeled over. The men let their dogs tear at its fur by way of reward, then slit open its stomach and gutted it, carefully saving the heart, liver and, above all, the gall bladder which is coveted by Asians and would fetch $80. They tied a rope around the bear's neck and hauled it triumphantly back up through the snow to the pick-ups.

Well, that is what should have happened but, as Joe said, bears are unpredictable creatures. What actually occurred was this. We got to the plateau, it was well below freezing, and the snow was falling harder than ever. The signals were indeed strong so seven of us set off down a path that led towards them. We trudged for more than an hour through thick snow but seemed to get no closer at all. Finally we reached a place where the path turned sharply back up the mountain in the wrong direction. We could not go on. It was getting dark. The signals were thoroughly confusing. They suggested some dogs were heading back down the mountain while others were strung out behind us. 'Ten thousand dollars worth of tracking equipment and we can't find them,' exclaimed Dennis in exasperation.

We had no choice but to return to the pick-ups. By the time we reached them night had fallen, we were wet through and frozen, and we had thirteen dogs missing. As best as we could tell, the bear had indeed headed up the mountain but somewhere near the ridge he had crossed into another valley and headed back down again, leaving a trail of exhausted dogs scattered through the forest. He had probably covered nine or ten miles and was, it seemed, still going strong.

I began to think longingly of the Rieffenbergers' cosy chestnut-panelled sitting room and of the chicken-and-squirrel stew Mary Moore had prepared for dinner, but we couldn't leave without the dogs. Most of the pick-ups headed back down the mountain to patrol the two valleys. We stayed on the plateau and grew steadily more despondent. We were out of food. Our sodden feet were numb with cold. An icy wind buffeted our lonely vehicle, and periodically we had to step out into the bitter night and scan the blackness below with our antennae. Bear hunting, I decided, was not my kind of sport. I would almost have preferred to be bouncing across a churning Chesapeake Bay.

Over the next four hours nine of the hounds were recovered, but we were getting only faint signals from Mark and Eagle and none at all from Squirt and Maggie. Even Dennis, the ultimate bear hunter, had to concede that this particular beast was 'making us pretty miserable', but claimed the day had at least shown how the odds were stacked in favour of the bears. 'This is their neighbourhood,' he said. 'They know where they're going and what they're doing. We're the ones left guessing. Mostly it's pure brute strength. They're just plain out tough. They just outlast the dogs and the hunters.'

At 10.00 p.m. we abandoned the plateau and drove down the mountain but not, alas, to our homes. Dennis wanted to try a third valley. There were now pick-ups scattered across 20 square miles or more of pitch-black mountainside. None were receiving more than the faintest signals out of the impenetrable darkness, but it was past midnight before Dennis admitted the search was hopeless and called it off. Twenty hours after setting out, we drove cold and exhausted back to Beverly having spent twice as long hunting dogs as hunting bear. I found Mary Moore asleep in her armchair, having evidently waited up for me, but by then it was far too late for stew.

There was a postscript to all this. I had just finished a very late breakfast the next morning when the telephone rang. It was a message from Dennis. His dogs had just 'treed' a bear. I jumped into my car and hurried in bright sunshine to the foot of the mountain. There Buck, one of his group, met me and drove me back up to the plateau in his pick-up. En route we passed a second group of hunters with much bigger, fancier pick-ups drinking whiskey.

We had barely arrived when we heard a single shot from the forest below. We got word that the second group would soon be bringing out a bear. We went to watch. After about twenty minutes four men came up from below, dragging a dead bear through the snow with a rope tied around its neck. Their arrival was greeted with whoops and shouts and great celebration. They dumped the bear in the middle of the pick-ups, its thick black fur encrusted with ice. An old-timer who had once hunted bears for bounty rolled the animal on to its back and drew loud cheers by cutting off its penis with a knife. He kept them as souvenirs, he explained. A nine-year-old boy sat on the carcass, raised its head, and stuck a whiskey bottle between its yellow teeth while someone took pictures. The bear was tied to a pole and hoisted into the air for weighing – 175 pounds. When the men finally tired of playing with the carcass and returned to their drinking, the once-fine beast was dragged off to a pick-up, leaving a trail of bloodied snow behind it. Exactly who had shot the bear was never quite clear. Whoever it was evidently wanted to bag another one later in the season.

I returned, rather sickened, to our group. Dennis was back at his pick-up, but so furious he could not or would not speak. I telephoned him that night instead. Still seething, he explained how he had set off early that morning to search for his dogs and had eventually found them. In the process he had come across a bear's tracks. He had loosed two fresh dogs and they had quickly 'treed' the bear, which was when he called me. Before he could reach the tree, however, hunters from the other group had heard the dogs barking, found the bear and killed it.

'They knew it was our bear but shot it anyway,' Dennis protested bitterly. 'Why would anyone want to kill a bear so bad they would shoot someone else's? I don't even want to be called a bear hunter when you have guys like that around.'

4

For Heaven's Snakes

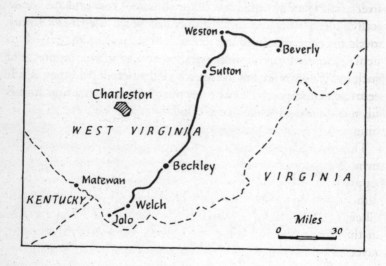

I drove south-west from Beverly and the snow vanished as fast as it had come. So did the last vestiges of civilisation, save for the satellite television dishes in every yard. That's another West Virginia joke. The satellite dish is called the state flower.

I was entering a benighted land and soon realised that I'd had a very gentle introduction to the delights that lay before me. The valleys became narrower and darker, the towns poorer and meaner, and the human deprivation began to eclipse the natural splendour of the hills and forests. This bore no relation to the idyllic West Virginia John Denver sang about in 'Country Roads', and the 'War on Poverty' that President Johnson launched in Appalachia in the 1960s had patently been lost.

Earlier this century, when coal was king in southern West Virginia, the people lived in miserable conditions and were grotesquely exploited, but at least had jobs and strong communities. Today, the coal mines are either highly mechanised or – more often – closed, their hulking 'tipples' or pitheads abandoned and their railway lines vanishing beneath the undergrowth. The people mostly live in dilapidated wooden or tarpaper shacks, some still with outside toilets, or in trailer homes plonked wherever there is a sliver of flat land in the bottom of the sunless river valleys. You practically never see 'for sale' signs for there simply is no market. Empty hovels are left standing till they collapse or someone puts a match to them. There are boarded-up motels and derelict petrol stations. Old trucks and jalopies are left to rust where they expired – especially, it seems, if that happens to be in people's front gardens. The land is still mostly owned by the coal companies, and regarded as something to be ravaged and despoiled.

The historical markers record mining tragedies. Outside the towns the roadsigns have all been used for target-practice and are peppered with bullet-holes. In a small mountainside cemetery I found rough, homemade concrete gravestones. I passed sheds with 'Chew Mail Pouch Tobacco – Treat Yourself To The Best' painted on their sides. I ate in dingy cafés where everyone still smoked, stayed in a dreary little motel whose soap was of such poor quality that even a kleptomaniac like myself left the second bar behind, and found it was easier to buy a gun or old railway sleepers than good fresh fruit or vegetables.

There were numerous Christian bookshops, but none of the conventional variety. There were lots of tanning parlours, perhaps because so little sunlight reached the valley bottoms. There was also an inordinate number of hairdressers operating from their homes, places like 'Becky's Magic Shears' or 'Cindy's Cut and Curl – The Best Little Hair House in Town'. There were, it is true, long lines outside the banks, but only because it was the third of the month – the day welfare cheques go out.

It is hard to be white and poor in America, but people around here offered spectacular proof that it was possible. Nor could they be described as anything but troglodyte in their social views. Normally a Democratic stronghold, West Virginia had just elected a seventy-four-year-old Republican as governor because the Democrats' candidate was a woman

The first town I came to after Beverly was Webster Springs, host of the annual 'world wood-cutting championships' (another town nearby holds an annual tobacco-spitting tournament). Bright yellow ribbons were tied to mailboxes, trees and lamp-posts. Sadly these were not for decoration. A clerk in the courthouse told me that a month earlier an eighteen-year-old local girl had been run off the road while driving home. Her body was later found in a flooded coal pit with cinder blocks tied around it, and her family and friends had put up the ribbons as reminders that her killer was still at large.

After crossing the spectacular New River Gorge I came to Sophia, where I was stopped for doing 38 mph in a 25 mph zone and fined $110. I had been warned about towns like this. They routinely stop cars with out-of-state licence plates to supplement their meagre tax base.

Outside the town of Iager I spotted a place selling trailer homes. A pleasant woman called Valerie showed me round. Practically no one built proper brick homes any more, she told me. Trailer homes were far cheaper, though flat land was 'scarcer than hens' teeth'. They began at $10,000, including furniture, delivery and installation, and ranged up to $60,000. That year they had sold about 200. Tucked away in the back of the lot was an old secondhand one that Valerie euphemistically called a 'fixer-upper' and offered to me for a mere $800. It was filthy, it stank, it was in a state of terminal disrepair and must have been lived in by a hermit for the past half-century. I politely declined. Someone on welfare would probably take it, Valerie sighed. Round these parts people were either miners, loggers, truckers or on welfare. 'When kids leave high school they don't give them diplomas, they give them maps to North Carolina,' she remarked. As I drove away I saw a company sign I'd missed when entering. It read: 'Lester Mobile Homes – Where Dreams Come True'.

I drove on through yet more scenes of decay and dereliction. The smartest buildings were the schools and post offices. The commonest were churches – churches of every conceivable denomination and sub-denomination. There were Free Will Baptist Churches, Primitive Baptist Churches, Missionary Baptist Churches, Seventh Day Adventist Churches, Wesleyan Churches, Churches of the Living God, Fundamentalist Christian Churches, Pentecostal Churches, Churches of the Nazarene, a Bible Missionary Church, a Church of Christ, a Jesus Church, a Church Triumphant Assembly of God and a plain, simple Church of God. Most were no more than utilitarian wooden huts, though many had big signs outside offering strictures like: 'If You Don't Want the Fruits of Sin Stay Out of the Devil's Orchard'.

This proliferation is what happens when one church does not enjoy a state monopoly as tends to be the case in European countries. In America anyone can set himself up as a preacher and you end up with hundreds of little 'privatised' churches, each vying for members by offering some new doctrinal twist in the same way that toothpaste manufacturers offer some magic new ingredient to make your teeth still whiter.

Religion is strong in Appalachia. Its wretched inhabitants need something to look forward to. There were statues of Jesus on porches, signs proclaiming 'Holiness or Hell' in windows, and 'Jesus Saves' stickers on car bumpers. It was, in fact, to a church in the tiny town of Jolo that I was heading, but this was a church like very few others in the world. It was one whose parishioners are willing quite literally to die for their faith – and on occasion do.

The Church of the Lord Jesus was easy to find. There isn't much else in Jolo. You pass the inauspiciously named Hemlock Restaurant, where I stopped for a sausage sandwich and found an official notice in the toilet warning that the water had failed a recent nitrates test. You turn left at Shirley's Snack Hut, and follow the road about a mile into the hills until you see on your left a small white wooden building perched on the edge of a gulley.

On this particular Saturday night the verges were lined with cars from out of state for it was the church's 'homecoming' weekend – an annual event that attracts like-minded worshippers from Appalachia's most distant corners. There were perhaps a hundred people packed inside – adults, children and babies – though this was hardly to be a conventional family service. Some were hugging. Others were sitting expectantly on rows of wooden pews and plastic chairs. Most were clutching dog-eared Bibles. In front of the pews was an expanse of shiny wooden floor. Beyond that was a low stage with a lectern and a jumble of musical instruments. On the wall at the back of the stage were three large notices.

The first, handwritten, declared: 'Women not allowed to wear short-sleeves, jewelry or make-up. No gossiping. No talebearing. No lying. No backbiting. No bad language or by-words.'

The second, also handwritten, read: 'No tobacco users. Men not allowed to have long hair, mustache, or beard. Men not allowed to wear short-sleeves. Women not allowed to cut hair, wear dresses above knee.'

The third was framed and the key to this whole church. It is the text of Mark, chapter 16, verses 17 and 18:

And these signs shall follow them that believe: in my name shall they cast out devils; they shall speak with new tongues; They shall take up serpents; and if they drink any deadly thing, it shall not hurt them; they shall lay hands on the sick and they shall recover.

These folk around me were extreme fundamentalists who believed that every word in the Bible should be taken literally – including the verses from Mark. Hence there were, that evening, six glass-topped wooden boxes spread out along the stage, each containing a writhing knot of rattlesnakes and copperheads culled from the surrounding mountains. There was also, behind the lectern, a large jar ringed with a bright red tape and filled with strychnine, a clear liquid used hereabouts as rat poison.

A short but strongly-built old man with thick spectacles and huge hands steps on to the stage. This is the pastor, Bob Elkins, who spent forty-four years down mineshafts. He invites the congregation to 'do what God would have you do', and with that the church erupts. A makeshift band lets loose with electric guitars, drums, and keyboards, filling the room with a deafening 'rockabilly' version of 'Reach Out and Touch the Lord'. Others pitch in with cymbals and tambourines. The congregation is on its feet and clapping. Men and women rush on to the floor and launch into a freestyle, foot-stomping dance with such energy and abandon that the building trembles. What the musicians lack in quality they more than make up for in volume and exuberance. Someone is bawling into the microphone. The dancers whirl around, arms aloft, eyes closed and praising Jesus. After a few minutes a young man breaks off and approaches a snake box inscribed with the words 'A Believer is a Doer'. He undoes its brass clasp, opens the lid and lifts out two great five-foot rattlers.

Soon others follow suit. Men and women are pirouetting and gyrating with serpents in their hands. They are gently caressing them, passing them from hand to hand, wrapping them round their necks. Men are handling three, four, five at once, draping them over their arms like ropes. A man plays his guitar with one hand while holding a copperhead in the other. Another holds a copperhead's mouth just inches from his face. There is no fear. The handlers believe God protects them. The snakes coil, squirm, stretch rigid, their tongues flicking in and out, but incredibly no one is bitten.

The music goes on and on. The noise and heat grow overpowering. Women are quivering and weeping. People are talking in tongues, babbling incomprehensibly. Some of the dancers seem in trances, their shirts soaked with sweat and clinging to their bodies. A middle-aged man staggers, collapses and crawls across the floor to the boxes. He grabs a serpent, stands up and lurches alarmingly across the room. A woman approaches the lectern, seizes the strychnine jar and takes a swig. She hands it on to others. They drink and barely grimace.

A younger man dressed in white with purple boots falls at the feet of a deathly pale silver-haired lady who wears largely black and has been watching the proceedings impassively from the stage. She is Barbara Elkins, the pastor's eighty-one-year-old wife and the church's matriarch. The man grabs her hand and begins to prophesy. He tells her that her time on earth is nearly over but she would soon be seeing God. 'Holy! Holy! Holy! I see you holier than you've ever been,' he cries, then reels wildly around the floor, bends double and screams.

Mr Elkins and other worshippers gather round an elderly man sitting in the front pew with his leg in bandages and propped up on a stool. This is Ray McCallister. He had a major heart by-pass operation just days ago. They rub oil on to his head. They lay their hands on him. They urge him to 'walk in Jesus' name', but to no avail. Someone hands him a snake instead.

Finally, after nearly an hour, the band falls silent. 'Thank you, Lord,' the dancers murmur. 'Praise Jesus.' They return to their seats and Mr Elkins asks for preachers. Over the next ninety minutes four or five men come forward. They have nothing prepared. They simply launch into scarcely-intelligible streams of consciousness punctuated by constant 'Hallelujahs' and 'Praise Gods'. They speak at the speed of auctioneers, each personally testifying to God's glory with all the force that he can muster.

One, Carl Porter, is an unemployed lorry driver and the pastor of a church in Georgia – the only other state besides West Virginia where religious snake-handling is still lawful. In 1975 he was being ejected from a church that objected to him handling serpents when a copperhead he was holding brushed against a woman. He served three months in prison for aggravated assault with a deadly weapon.

Another is Spencer, twenty-three years old, who nearly died from a snake bite while preaching at a revivalist meeting three months earlier. He was rushed unconscious to hospital where he spent nine days recovering. He had no health insurance, ran up $60,000 in medical fees, and lost his job in a carpet mill. Undaunted, Spencer delivers a thirty-minute fire-and-brimstone monologue, constantly dabbing the sweat from his face with a handkerchief. He denounces the ungodly, backsliders, churches that ignore the letter of the Bible. 'He that believeth not shall be damned,' he cries. 'This is not a game of hopscotch. This is a real battle. It's between you and the devil.'

Spencer eventually talks himself out, but still the service is not over. Mr Elkins himself preaches. 'I'm feeling good. I don't know how you feel but I'm feeling good,' he declares and launches himself like an ageing rock star into a foot-stomping dance that sets the band off once again.

I step outside to savour the cold night air and silence. There are other men out there. They show me wounds acquired from years of worship – scars, cratered flesh and atrophied fingers. One, Dewey Chafin, Barbara Elkins' sixty-three-year-old son, is a disabled miner who has been bitten 122 times in forty-four years and is something of a living legend. He has had bites that 'hurt me not at all and hurt me bad', but each has told him that 'God can take care of me when he wants to.'

The handlers offer various explanations for why God allows them to be bitten – they were being tested, they were being punished for transgressions, they picked up the snakes before the spirit moved them, or God was showing unbelievers that the snakes have not been doctored. They refuse medical help when bitten (Spencer was in no fit state to argue) and rely instead on prayer. They insist that deaths strengthen rather than shake their faith, and there is strong evidence to support that claim.

Jolo has lost two members from snake bites. The first, in 1962, was Dewey's twenty-two-year-old sister, Columbia, whose daughter, Lydia, is now the church's organist. Mr Chafin says Columbia's death told him simply 'that God was wanting her, that it was her time to die'. The second was that of Ray Johnson, a man of fifty-two with a chronic heart condition who used to make a 300-mile round trip to Jolo from Virginia each weekend until a rattler bit him twice in the left wrist in 1991. His family also continues to attend the church. Mr Elkins told me he once 'died' himself after being bitten. He was laid out dead in his bathroom, but his congregation gathered round and prayed for him and he returned to life.

There is one other point on which the handlers are unanimous. No feeling on earth compares to handling snakes. 'It's the best feeling you've ever had in your life. It's like being high on cocaine, pot, whiskey or whatever multiplied ten thousand times,' says Carl Porter.

It was nearly 11.00 p.m. before the service ended. It had lasted three hours, was the second in successive nights, and another was starting at noon the next day, to be followed by a hearty 'home-coming' lunch. I set off for the nearest motel – 40 miles across the mountains in a town called Welch – amazed at how lively a Saturday night could be in Jolo and struggling to comprehend what I had seen.

These people were hardly sophisticated, and the religious Russian roulette they engaged in was by any rational standard weird, but I had also seen a passion, a joy, a sense of communion and cleansing in that room that surpassed anything I had encountered in conventional churches. For a few exhilarating hours each week these people had found a way to transcend their grim environment. Perhaps, unconsciously, they were also sending a defiant message to the world – materially they might be poor and backward, but spiritually they were blessed and on their way to true salvation.

The church had another observer like myself that weekend. His name was David Kimbrough, an academic from Indiana who had written a well-received book on Appalachian snake-handling. The practice dates back to the early 1900s and the unlikely figure of George Went Hensley, an illiterate womaniser. Hensley agonised over the verses in Mark 16 and concluded he had to risk his life and follow them if he was to receive eternal salvation. In 1910 he climbed a mountain in Tennessee, found a large rattlesnake, and after praying to God for protection grabbed it. Hensley became an itinerant evangelist, preaching and demonstrating serpent-handling at revivalist meetings the length and breadth of Appalachia. It was he who handed Barbara Elkins her first serpent in 1947, but in 1955, aged seventy-five, a snakebite killed him.

The snake-handling movement peaked before the Second World War when it had as many as ten thousand followers. Dr Kimbrough reckons that even today there are at least thirty snake-handling churches left in Appalachia, including several in states where the practice has been outlawed, and up to three thousand handlers. He personally has traced at least seventy-six deaths from snake-handling and five from drinking strychnine.

Following my visit to Jolo I told my brother-in-law, a Church of England vicar, about serpent-handling. His response stunned me.

Plucking various biblical commentaries from his bookshelves, he demonstrated a broad consensus amongst scholars that the original St Mark's Gospel ended at verse 16. Verses 17 and 18 were almost certainly spurious later additions and – except in Appalachia – widely disregarded.

5

High in Kentucky

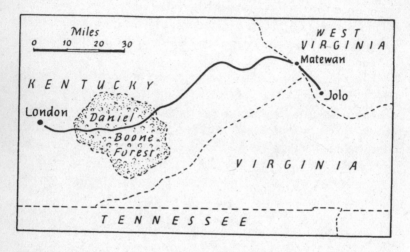

There was another traditional Appalachian practice that intrigued me, one imported by the Scotch-Irish, and that was moonshining — the distilling of illicit whiskey.

Back in Welch the next day I made some discreet inquiries, and that evening a rather feckless young man from a long and distinguished line of moonshiners made a furtive visit to my motel room. His great uncle had had his eye shot out by the 'revenuers' — the excise men who used to search the forests for illegal stills. His grandfather had worked in the mines all day and 'run liquor' at night. His father had once been shot in the leg while trying to escape from the revenuers down a forest path.

Yes, the practice still went on, the young man told me. Old-timers still drank 'shine' because it was better and cheaper than the legal stuff. You still found the occasional abandoned still in the hills, but no, he didn't make shine himself, nor did anyone in his family, and he didn't know anyone who did. Nowadays, he went on, he and his friends grew marijuana in hidden forest clearings and sold it for $100 an ounce. He had made $11,000 from that autumn's crop alone. 'I know it's illegal but a man's got to make money and there's no other jobs around here,' he explained. He had tried leaving the mountains to find work but couldn't handle cities. He had only once been to Washington, and that was to accompany his grandmother to a march demanding help for miners with black lung disease. 'I guess once you're a hillbilly you're always a hillbilly,' he concluded.

I had read about the marijuana growers of Appalachia. I called the US Forest Service and was told the Daniel Boone National Forest in Kentucky was the marijuana capital of America. Very soon I was on my way to London, Kentucky, some 200 miles to the west, to meet Mike Gay, the area's chief Forest Service law enforcement officer.

I made just one stop *en route*. I wanted to see Matewan, a gritty little coal town of about eight hundred people that spans the Tug River and the West Virginia-Kentucky border. I wanted to see the place where two prominent local Scotch-Irish clans, the Hatfields of West Virginia and the McCoys of Kentucky, had pursued the deadliest, most celebrated family feud in American history during the 1880s and 1890s. The vendetta was allegedly sparked by a dispute over the ownership of a hog, and by the time it had finished as many as one hundred Hatfields and McCoys were dead and the two states had very nearly gone to war in support of their respective families.

From my past experiences in America I expected to find a town full of restaurants selling McCoyburgers and vendors hawking Hatfield T-shirts. I expected a big visitors centre, a museum, actors in period costume. I expected to visit the exact place where, in August of 1882, three drunken McCoy brothers had stabbed Ellison Hatfield twenty-six times in the feud's first killing, and perhaps a reconstruction of the old schoolhouse where Devil Anse Hatfield, Ellison's brother and the clan chieftain, held those three McCoys before executing them.

All I actually found was an historical marker and an audio

presentation commemorating the Matewan Massacre of 1920. The massacre had nothing whatever to do with the feud. It was a shoot-out between coalminers striking for the right to join a union and henchmen brought in to evict them from their company homes. Ten died, and the massacre sparked a rebellion by miners through-out the state.

I was flabbergasted. Didn't the impoverished people of Matewan want to cash in on their past? The feud had violence, passion and sex – a McCoy girl got pregnant by one of Devil Anse's sons but the old man refused to let them marry. It was perfect tourist fodder. It was just as colourful as the 'Shootout at OK Corral' which draws visitors by the thousand to Tombstone, Arizona. But no one would trek deep into the mountains – 100 miles from the nearest inter-state – to learn about a union victory. Such things were un-American. They were excised from school textbooks. They were an offence to the nation's capitalist creed. I wandered forlornly down the deserted main street until, at the very end, I spotted an insurance agency run by one Robert McCoy.

Robert turned out to be a great big round man in his fifties with black hair and remarkably deep set eyes. Sadly, there was nothing remotely murderous about him. He didn't seem the feuding type at all. He looked like the sort of fellow your children might engage in a gentle pillow fight, but he turned out to be the great-grandson of Randolph McCoy, Devil Anse's opposite number, and a former mayor of Matewan, so he was the nearest I'd come to 'the real McCoy'. He sat me down and explained, in the nicest possible way, that he was heartily sick of journalists asking about a 19th-century feud. 'It was very embarrassing for West Virginia,' he protested. It reinforced the state's image as 'a backward and violent place'. The media harked back to the feud every time something brutal hap-pened in the state, and that was plain ridiculous. The massacre, by contrast, was a milestone in America's industrial history, an event of genuine social and historical importance.

Duly chastened, I slunk away from Matewan – but not com-pletely empty-handed. In the back of the car, hidden beneath a blanket, was a half-gallon jar of clear-as-dew moonshine to be borne in triumph back to Washington. Alas, I may not reveal how I got it. I can say only that it came from one of the scores of McCoys who still live around Matewan, and that he or she was given it by one of the many Hatfields still resident in the area. Happily the two families have long since been reconciled and in 1976, during the dedication of a McCoy family monument, the two families officially if belatedly declared peace in the Tug River valley.

Early the next morning I presented myself at the front desk of the headquarters of Kentucky's Daniel Boone National Forest and picked up a glossy little tourist brochure. It contained lovely photographs of a clear stream tumbling through sylvan glades, sunbathers by a deep blue lake, and a pioneer's restored log cabin. It waxed lyrical about the trails, the wildlife and the eighty natural arches to be found in the forest's 670,000 acres. What it utterly failed to mention was that the forest was also a frontline in America's war on drugs, the site of a battle against marijuana growers commonly believed to be occurring thousands of miles away in Mexico and Colombia. To be high in the mountains of eastern Kentucky had, I realised, two very distinct meanings.

For me this other, less-advertised side of the Daniel Boone National Forest was vividly underscored a few minutes later when I walked into the law enforcement office and found Mike Gay standing with five burly colleagues around a deer and a box of curious contraptions. The deer turned out to be dead, though its head revolved thanks to a battery-powered mechanism concealed in its neck. It was a decoy used to trap poachers. The contraptions turned out to be horrendous booby traps with which marijuana growers had sought to protect their clearings.

Mike, a plumpish, red-headed fellow in his forties who makes diphthongs or even triphthongs of every syllable, proceeded to show me the booby traps one by one, caressing and lingering over each one for dramatic effect. There were planks of woods with long rusty nails protruding from one side. These had been placed on the ground near clearings and covered with leaves. There was a line of barbed steel fishhooks that had been suspended between trees at eye height and concealed with creepers. There were heavy iron leg traps, grenades, and an assortment of explosive devices designed to be triggered by tripwires. I had to admit that none of these would have looked very enticing in the brochure.

When Mike had exhausted this box of goodies he put on a grainy video showing shreds of coloured cloth inexplicably hanging from the trees around a clearing. Having aroused your curiosity, the cameraman then honed in on three largely naked and horribly mutilated bodies lying on the ground. They were growers who had accidentally blown themselves up while setting traps.

Mike had one other charming titbit to impart. In one clearing, he told me, officers had found poisonous snakes tied to the marijuana plants.

These traps were evidently designed more to protect the plants from theft by rival growers than discovery by Mike's officers. If such measures sound extreme, consider this. Each plant in this prolific forest produces up to a pound of top-grade marijuana worth roughly $3,600 on the streets of New York or Washington, and that is not far short of the price of gold.

Until the early 1980s the Daniel Boone forest had been exactly what the brochure suggested – a vast expanse of unspoilt hills and forest where people could fish, hunt, walk, or simply commune with nature. About that time, however, baby boomers and Vietnam veterans began achieving a certain affluence, boosting the demand for pot. The Reagan administration cracked down on imported marijuana, suppressing supply. South American drug barons found dealing in cocaine much easier. Street prices for marijuana soared, and domestic production did likewise.

South-eastern Kentucky is not like the state's bluegrass country to the north and west. Its inhabitants do not trot off to the Kentucky Derby every year. They are mostly dirt-poor hillfolk, and for many the temptation was simply too great. Why live off welfare, grow tobacco for just $5,000 an acre, or work for $5 an hour in a hamburger joint when they had the climate and soil to grow the ultimate cash crop on their very doorsteps? Growing it actually on their doorsteps – or even in their gardens or on their farms – was perhaps a little dangerous, as the authorities could then legally seize their property, but they could easily eliminate that risk by using the surrounding forest.

Today Kentucky and neighbouring Tennessee are the top two marijuana-growing states in the country. The Daniel Boone forest produces roughly a third of Kentucky's output and some of the world's best marijuana. That year alone Mike and his team had found no less than 3,553 clearings and 133,125 plants. How many more they failed to find is anyone's guess.

The Forest Service has only one real weapon in its battle against the growers, and that is aerial surveillance. Mike's men spend hundreds of hours in helicopters and light aircraft each summer, scouring the vast forest for those pinprick clearings, but finding them is only half the battle. They must then secure convictions. Most people in the small communities of south-eastern Kentucky have a pretty good idea who the growers are. They are the 'holler hooters', ostensibly living off welfare, who pay cash for brand new pick-up trucks each autumn. They are the ones pumping money into wretched local economies. They may be friends, even neighbours. In some of the poorest counties, said Mike, it was well nigh impossible to persuade a jury to convict.

By way of a grand finale, Mike and two colleagues strapped on their gun belts, put me into a patrol car, and drove me thirty minutes into the forest. We turned on to a dirt track, parked, and climbed up through the trees to the top of a low hill, the dead leaves crackling beneath our feet. On the far side was an unusually large marijuana clearing, perhaps 60 feet long and 20 feet wide, that Mike's officers had spotted from the air last May. They had installed two hidden surveillance cameras, one at the clearing and one by the track. The cameras recorded regular visits by a fifty-year-old unemployed man who lived in a trailer home three or four miles away. In July the man had crashed his vehicle and a second, younger man began delivering him to the site in his jeep. This second man was also unemployed but lived in a remote area and was building a brand new house right next to his old one. In August Mike's officers obtained search warrants, found $25,000 in cash in the younger man's home, and surmised that the older man was one of several he employed to do his dirty work.

It was a lovely sunny day, and for a few minutes we lingered in the forest admiring the growers' handiwork. They had picked a south-west facing slope in an area of poplars and pines because neither produce nuts. No nuts meant no squirrels and consequently no hunters. They had sawn halfway through trees around the clearing so they toppled but did not die, rendering the clearing completely invisible from the ground during the summer. They had chopped the tops off other trees to let in sunlight without – they hoped – making the clearing too obvious from the air.

The growers had been caught because they had become too greedy. They had created a clearing big enough for 240 plants – compared with an average plot of 30 to 40 – and it had been spotted. Had they got away with it the growers and their distributors would have cleared $800,000 – a veritable fortune in a region where $25,000 was a handsome annual wage. As it was, they faced several years in prison.

Little now remained of their efforts. There were a few empty beer cans on the ground, a scrap of fertiliser bag, a sheet of corrugated iron for trapping rain water and, protruding from the earth, the occasional stalk of a chopped-down marijuana plant. At one end of the clearing was the blackened remains of the bonfire on which all that green gold had gone up in smoke.

6

The Greatest Melungeon

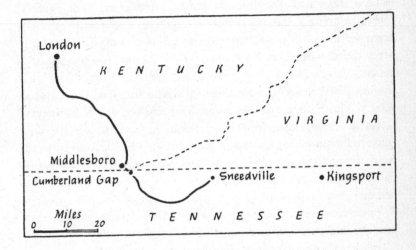

You hear countless examples of the American Dream coming true, but seldom of the opposite.

In 1886 an ambitious young Scotsman named Alexander Arthur rode through the Cumberland Gap, a break in the mountains at the point where Kentucky, Virginia and Tennessee meet, and just a few miles to the north found a bowl-shaped valley surrounded by apparently rich deposits of coal and iron ore. 'This is where I will build my city,' he declared in much the same way that Brigham Young and his fellow Mormons hailed the site of what is now Salt Lake City.

Arthur persuaded a group of English and Scottish financiers to back him. In no time a marvellous new city was rising in the valley. Arthur called it Middlesboro after the industrial town in England, and its broad streets were all named for British nobility – Cumberland, Gloucester, Exeter, Doncaster and so on. He built a golf course (using baking powder cans for holes) and an opera house, and began constructing another town called Harrogate – named after its more genteel English namesake – in the nearby hills. This was to be full of English-style mansions for the factory bosses, but its first buildings were a splendid home for himself and a magnificent 700-room hotel called the Four Seasons which cost $1 million and was, at the time, the largest in America.

Unfortunately Arthur's empire collapsed before it had even been completed. The iron ore deposits proved mediocre. In London, in 1890, Baring Brothers bank ran into trouble (as it would again a century later) and several of Arthur's British backers lost their money. Three years later America suffered a financial crash and all four of Middlesboro's banks failed. The city, on which Arthur had lavished $30 million, went from boom to bust. It was left with huge mills but little ore, with a giant brewery but few to drink the beer, a wonderful tannery but no hides, splendid churches but no congregations. All it had left was coal, and that is what Middlesboro became – a coalmining town subject, like so many others in Appalachia, to the boom-and-doom cycles of that steadily contracting industry. Arthur died in 1912, a broken man.

I didn't know any of this when I left the Daniel Boone forest and headed south towards Tennessee. I stopped in Middlesboro only because I vaguely remembered hearing that it had America's oldest golf course. What I found was one of the sorriest places – given its grand ambitions – that I've ever visited.

The highway just east of Middlesboro had sucked the remaining vitality from the town. Fast-food joints and motel chains lined Route 25, a major link between eastern Kentucky and eastern Tennessee, but behind that thin ribbon of apparent prosperity lay the empty shell of Arthur's grand design. The main street, Cumberland Avenue, was still lined by imposing red-brick buildings but most were now either abandoned or occupied by pawn and tacky discount shops. The adjacent streets were still broad, and still bore the names of British peers, but were largely deserted and bordered by tracts of derelict land. Arthur envisioned a city of 150,000, but the present population barely exceeded 12,000.

I drove down Worcester Avenue, transmuted over the years into 'Worchester' Avenue, to the golf course which is now part of the Middlesboro Country Club. A sign in old English lettering proclaimed that it was indeed the oldest continuously used golf course in America (a club opened in Yonkers, New York, in 1889, a few months before Middlesboro's, but subsequently changed sites). There was nobody in the clubhouse except for the golf pro, a genial young man named Jerry Shoffner whom I found watching basketball on television in the basement bar. He seemed delighted to have some company. 'Stay a while,' he urged. 'Have a drink.' Unfortunately the choice did not extend beyond coke or iced tea. This was a dry county, Jerry explained. Members could bring their own bottles and keep them in 'liquor lockers' in the changing room, but that was all.

We studied the course through the window. Arthur and his cronies had certainly chosen a beautiful location, with mountains all around, and more than a century later the club was still using the same nine holes. It began to drizzle, but that didn't matter. There was no one out on the course. In fact, said Terry, nobody had played all day. To be perfectly honest the club was down to 188 members and struggling to keep going. To generate a little extra income it had just decided, for the first time in its history, to let non-members play.

I left Jerry watching basketball and went to find Arthur's grave in an old cemetery on a hill overlooking the town. No fine monument commemorated Middlesboro's founder. In fact I couldn't even find his gravestone. Having spent a fruitless hour searching in driving rain, I went into a Kentucky Farm Bureau insurance office just outside the gates. I reckoned someone in there would know where the great man lay. Three men and three ladies scratched their heads. They telephoned friends and local officials. No one knew. I gave up, went to buy something to eat in a Piggly-Wiggly supermarket and locked myself out of the car. As I waited disconsolately for a garage to come and rescue me I read the *Middlesboro Daily News*. Arthur had certainly not imported British tabloid journalism to Middlesboro. One headline proclaimed: 'No Fish Killed In Waste

Spill'. I read on, breathlessly. 'No fish appear to have been killed in Kentucky as a result of a massive coal-waste spill in Virginia last week . . .'

It took two mechanics all of thirty seconds to unlock the car. Poorer by $15, I fled that depressing town, hoping that rather more of Arthur's dream survived a few miles up the road in Harrogate. Alas, there was nothing whatsoever. The $1 million hotel was sold to a wrecking company for $28,000 and demolished within a couple of years of its completion. Arthur's home, The Conservatory, had become the music school of a pleasant little college called the Lincoln Memorial University, but was torn down in the 1950s. My visit to Harrogate was not entirely profitless, however. While wandering around the college I picked up a leaflet advertising its 'magnificent Abraham Lincoln Museum'. The museum was certainly remarkable, though 'magnificent' was perhaps not quite the adjective I would have chosen.

It possessed a lock of Abe's hair, which was pretty impressive. So was the silver-topped cane he had with him when he was shot in his box at Ford's Theatre by John Wilkes Booth. The shred of black cloth taken from the dying president's coat was, I suppose, moderately significant, but that was more than I could say for the exhibits that followed.

One exhibit was an inch-long piece of tassel taken from the flag that had hung in the presidential box. There was a small piece of stone from the front step of the house across the street from the theatre into which the mortally-wounded president had been carried. The climax of this riveting sequence was a tiny piece of wood and a scrap of wallpaper taken from the room in that house where he died. In the midst of all these wondrous artefacts was a big black carriage. Lincoln's? Not quite. The marker said it probably belonged to Lincoln's Secretary of State, and was evidently judged worthy of inclusion because the man had once said of Lincoln: 'The President is the best of us'. As a resident of the city in which Lincoln was shot I momentarily considered offering the museum one of my used hankies or a speck of dandruff.

*

It was dark by the time I left and I still had a way to go before I reached my destination. I was heading for Sneedville, a town of just 1,600 people in the remote mountains of north-eastern Tennessee that had a far more compelling tale to tell than the Abraham Lincoln Museum.

For centuries a fierce and reclusive people called the Melungeons have lived in the hollows and on the ridges surrounding Sneedville. They are of striking appearance with dark skin but distinctly European features and, in some cases, blond hair and blue eyes. No one knows where they came from, but they were there when the first English and French explorers reached the area in the mid-to-late 1600s. It has been improbably suggested that they are one of the lost tribes of Israel, or survivors of Sir Walter Raleigh's 'lost colony' from Roanoke Island, off the North Carolina coast, but they themselves have always claimed to be 'Portyghee', or Portuguese. If that is true – and there is a growing body of evidence to support their claim – then all those history books that say the English were the first Europeans to colonise the New World permanently need to be rewritten.

Sneedville was on the way to nowhere. It lay 21 miles up a dark and windy road in the heart of Tennessee's poorest county. I passed few cars – fewer still with both headlights working – and only the occasional dimly-lit home. I arrived to find a town enveloped in fog and eerily devoid of living creatures. Its only motel, named simply 'Town Motel', consisted of eight rooms on the top floor of a breeze-block building and was locked. It was with some relief that I found an open grocery store where a check-out girl called Amanda, or 'Ammeender', kindly telephoned the motel owner.

'Wot yer doin' in Snaydveeal?' she asked. Strangers were evidently rare, especially ones with English accents.

'Hunting Melungeons,' I replied.

'Well, ah'm wurrn,' piped up a second check-out girl, and she did indeed look remarkably Mediterranean. Before we could fully explore the implications of being a Melungeon, the motel owner arrived, admitted me to his cold and distinctly uninviting premises, and gave me his telephone number. 'If yer wan' anythin', jus' holler,' he said cheerily and vanished. In Sneedville's spartan 'Drive-In Restaurant' I ate a late and lonely supper beneath a framed text reading: 'For the wages of sin is death, but the gift of God is eternal life through Jesus Christ our Lord.' I walked back through the drizzle to my comfortless room, locked myself in and went to bed.

Things looked better the next morning. A heavy mist cleared to reveal a town surrounded by small tobacco farms and steep wooded hills. Playing 'Spot the Melungeon', I walked over to the courthouse to meet Scott Collins, Hancock County's clerk and master and a founder member of the Melungeon Research Committee. On his office wall was a faded photograph of Maried Hatfield, the first and last man hanged in Sneedville and a member of West Virginia's infamous feuding family. Scott was patently a Melungeon – tall and dark-skinned with handsome, aquiline features – and over coffee at Aunt – 'Aint' – Bea's café he expounded on the possible provenance of the mysterious Melungeons.

The latest and most plausible theory runs something like this. In 1567 – forty years before the English established their first successful colony at Jamestown – the Spanish established the Santa Elena colony on the coast of what is now South Carolina. They sent Spanish and Portuguese soldiers – some of them Moors – inland to build forts. When the British overran the colony in 1587 the Spanish fled, abandoning the soldiers. About the same time, Sir Francis Drake is believed to have dumped two or three hundred Turkish and Moorish slaves on the coast of what is now North Carolina. Drake had captured the slaves from Spanish and Portuguese ships that were transporting them to the Caribbean and South America.

These two abandoned groups joined, retreated into the Appalachian foothills and intermarried with local Indians. In 1673 an English explorer named James Needham ventured into the Tennessee River valley and wrote of 'a white people which have long beards and whiskers and weares clothing . . . ye white people have a bell which is six foot over which they ring morning and evening and att that time a great number of people congregate together'. French explorers brought back similar reports. When the first waves of English and Scotch-Irish settlers reached the area in the mid-1700s they also found these strange people speaking broken English, bearing English surnames, practising Christianity and claiming to be Portuguese.

Scott and other researchers believe that they had Anglicised their names so that, for example, Colina became Collins and Molina became Mullins, and that they described themselves as Melungeons because that was, apparently, an early Portuguese term for a white person. 'What they were trying to say when the English walked in was "we are white like you. Why kick us around?",' Scott argued.

If that was the goal, it didn't work. The Melungeons had the best land. The newcomers, having travelled thousands of miles, wanted it. Their solution was simple. They used the first censuses in the 1790s to label the Melungeons 'free persons of colour'. They deprived them of their land and most basic rights, including the vote, legal redress and public education. They essentially treated them as blacks. The Melungeons were driven high into the barren mountains, to places like Newman's Ridge which overlooks Sneedville, and completely ostracised. A Melungeon, remarked one 19th-century Tennessee senator, was merely a 'Portuguese nigger'.

The Melungeons grew bitter and aggressive in their exile. They counterfeited silver coins and sold moonshine to survive. They spawned infamous characters like 'Brandy Jack' Mullins and 'Counterfeitin' Sol' Mullins. They would come down to town, drink and cause mayhem, but local sheriffs feared to tangle with them. White mothers would warn their children to 'be good or the Melungeons will get you'. To be a Melungeon was to be the lowest of the low and considered shameful. Over time the Melungeons naturally began to conceal their identity and play down their heritage, and that attitude still persists.

Scott, now in his late forties, said he didn't realise he was a Melungeon until well into his adulthood because 'people didn't like to talk about it. It was poor taste. I asked my father why he never talked about it and he said it was not something you needed to talk about. You couldn't change anything. That's what Melungeons tried to do – forget.'

Aunt Bea told me she had thought of the Melungeons as 'blond-haired, blue-eyed niggers' until she discovered she was one herself. 'They hide it,' said a white car mechanic that I met in Sneedville. 'They think it's along down with the negroes.' As we spoke, he pointed to a carful of Melungeons driving by in a rusty jalopy even older than my own.

Brent Kennedy, the leading authority on the Melungeons, only discovered that he was a Melungeon in 1988 after contracting sarcoidosis, a rare disease that primarily afflicts Mediterranean and Middle Eastern people. He began to ask himself why so many of his family had a decidedly Mediterranean appearance, why his family had lost its land without a penny of compensation and now lived on the most mountainous ridges, why it was treated so harshly by neighbours and why his great-grandfather had been barred from voting well into the 20th century. 'All these questions had previously been written off by family elders as simple bad luck, or "politics", or for this reason or for that,' Kennedy says in his book *The Melungeons: The Resurrection of a Proud People.*

'Their answers nearly always were accompanied by a faraway look in their eyes, if there was any eye contact at all . . . As I now know, the truth had been hidden, generation after generation: photos and family records burned time and again as each generation tried to eliminate evidence of the one that preceded it . . . As I clawed my way into the closets of our family history I uncovered layer after layer of purposeful deceit, a veritable diary of self-imposed exile from the land of the living. We had always been on the run, dreading each door that would close in our face until we avoided all doors, even those that might have opened.'

Scott, Kennedy, and others are now struggling to change the stereotype of the Melungeons as a 'bunch of poor trashy people'. They have set up their research committee, produced a book on the Melungeons, and are planning a Melungeon museum in Sneedville. They claim Abraham Lincoln and Elvis Presley may have had Melungeon blood. They believe the Melungeons should be proud of their history and of their survival in the face of so much adversity. After all, said Scott with a grin, 'We were here before the British and that's going to piss a lot of you off.'

Besides Melungeons, there is not much to see in Sneedville beyond a couple of banks, three cafés and a single working payphone. I decided to drive up to Newman's Ridge, where many Melungeons still live, and pay homage to a woman who was in one sense indisputably the greatest of them all. As I climbed the steep mountain road the homes became poorer and poorer till they were mere hovels surrounded by rusting junk. One was ringed by an electric fence. Outside another a gaunt, bearded man stood and stared from his porch until I'd passed. Some had dogs and 'Keep Out' signs. An ancient Chevrolet truck lay abandoned in a field, its windscreen riddled with bullet holes, and I began to sense that the Melungeons fully deserved their reputation for ferocity.

At the top was a Melungeon cemetery and the Goins Chapel Baptist church, a white wooden hut with a breathtaking view across line after line of bluish-grey hills to North Carolina's distant Smoky Mountains. I later learned that this was another snake-handling church, and that Melungeons also believed in planting and harvesting according to the state of the moon, or 'by the signs'.

Beyond the church the road deteriorated into a gravel track, and a mile after that a rusty iron post on the left marked where a muddy trail led off into the forest. I walked down that trail for fifteen minutes until, in what had once been a clearing, I found a derelict log cabin with the skeletal remains of a shed and animal pen behind it. The late afternoon sun slanted through the bare trees, and as I approached a large deer bounded away through the undergrowth. There was a sagging verandah, a fine stone chimney, and three rooms with rotting floorboards. Scraps of yellow newspaper, used for lining, were still plastered on the inner walls, but most striking of all were the cabin's highly unusual arched window frames, which did indeed suggest some ancient Iberian influence

This was once the home of Mahalia Mullins, a celebrated moonshiner, and I called her the greatest of all the Melungeons because she weighed about 35 stone. A Sneedville sheriff once tried to arrest her but had to abandon the attempt because of her size. She was 'ketchable but not fetchable', he explained to the judge. When Mahalia died her family had to knock down part of a wall to get her body out of the cabin. They managed to carry her a few hundred feet into the forest where, a few years ago, Scott discovered her long-lost grave. It is still there, a slab of rough sandstone with this misspelt inscription chiselled on it: 'Mahalia Mullins – Dide May 15 1882'.

I poked around for a few more minutes, reciting Walter de la Mare to myself:

> *'Is there anybody there?' said the Traveller*
> *Knocking on the moonlit door*
> *And his horse in the silence champed the grasses*
> *Of the forest's ferny floor.*

No one answered me, either, so I left.

7

Chasing Mr Moonshine

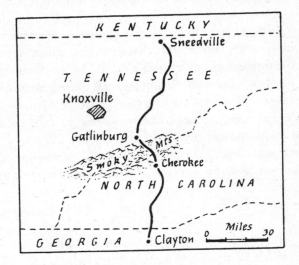

I can't reveal exactly where I went after Sneedville, but it was south across the Clinch Mountain in the general direction of Knoxville, Tennessee. Someone I'd met in West Virginia had arranged for me to go to an illegal cockfight, but in return I'd promised to disclose neither the place nor the identity of those that took me. It was all delightfully cloak-and-dagger.

I was told to go to a certain motel just off an interstate and I would be collected the next day. It was a very nice motel. On my pillow I found a printed greeting card. 'Because this motel is a human institution to serve people, and not solely a money-making organisation, we hope that God will grant you peace and rest while under our roof,' it said. 'May this room and motel be your "second home". May those that you love be near you in thoughts and dreams. Even though we may not get to know you, we hope that you will be as comfortable and happy as if you were in your own house.'

At 9.00 the next morning – Saturday – a red pick-up truck arrived on schedule. I climbed in somewhat apprehensively, but found a genial man in an old jacket and baseball cap sitting at the wheel. He was a former construction worker in his early sixties whom I'll call Doug. His first words were hardly what I expected from a cockfighter. 'You'd better buckle up. Round here it's illegal not to.'

Doug drove me back to his rural bungalow to meet his wife and then, with the same sort of pride that a gardener might show off his prize chrysanthemums, gave me a tour of the 'chickens' he raised behind his home. There were a hundred and twenty birds in six long rows of cages. They included fifty magnificent fighting cocks – multicoloured, broad-breasted, lustily-crowing creatures each tightly tethered to the upright plastic drums in which they lived so they could not attack each other. Doug knew the precise genealogy of each. He bred them for strength, aggression and above all 'gameness' – a willingness to keep fighting however badly wounded. Some breeders used steroids, he said, but personally he didn't think they helped.

Doug took me into his shed and showed me the darkened 'rest boxes' in which he kept his roosters before a fight so they conserved energy. He also denied them food on 'derby' days to give them an extra edge. He showed me the steel weaponry he attached to the natural spurs on the roosters' legs. There were gaffs – curved, two-inch needles designed to puncture – and two sorts of blades for slashing: the Mexican short knife and the Filipino long knife. On a wooden work bench were three electric grindstones to keep these ugly little devices razor sharp. He had several shelves of gold and silver trophies and back in the house he dug out, for my benefit, a yellowing booklet on the rules and etiquette of cockfighting rather like those the Victorians produced for croquet or lawn tennis.

It was time to go. It was a lovely sunny morning, and we followed a broad river towards the Smoky Mountains whose lower reaches were still shrouded in mist. My avuncular guide continued to surprise me. He pointed to an old burned-out motel. 'That used to be a whorehouse,' he said. Half a mile further on he pointed to a grey trailer home perched between the road and river. 'That's the whorehouse now.' He gave me some last-minute instructions. No cameras. No notebooks. The pit operators might think I was a federal agent or one of those 'do-gooders' – his derisive term for animal rights activists. Nobody was worried about the local sheriffs, however. They turned a blind eye, said Doug. If they heard of an impending raid by federal agents they'd tip you off. Some even attended the cockfights.

Just when it seemed we'd run into the mountains Doug turned left on to a side road, and soon branched on to an even smaller road. We rounded a corner and there, invisible until you were right in front of it, was a narrow hollow in the hills filled with cars and pick-up trucks. A big beefy man stood at the entrance collecting $10 from each person. At the top of the hollow was a jumble of old caravans and wooden huts clustered round a new, low breeze-block building. This was the pit. On one side of the anteroom was a counter selling food and soft drinks. On the other was a stand selling baseball caps and sweatshirts with the pit's name on them, an array of cockfighting equipment and little coloured bottles. I asked Doug what was in them. 'Dope,' he replied. Drugs to stimulate the cocks.

Beyond the anteroom was the actual pit – a small raised circle of dirt perhaps ten foot across, enclosed by a high wire fence and ringed by sharply rising tiers of rough wooden benches. This was my first cockfight, but even I could tell this was a lacklustre, early-season affair. There were scarcely a hundred people there, the cocks were feeble, and most of the fights developed into long, dull wars of attrition. After a couple of hours Doug had had enough. 'That's the saddest damn bunch of chickens I've ever seen,' he complained as we drove home for a stupendously large lunch that his wife had spent the morning cooking. The only trouble with Doug's cocks, she confided, was that their crowing woke her up at 4.30 every morning.

That night Doug directed me to a different pit, one of three in eastern Tennessee, and this one was hillbilly heaven. It was two minutes off the Interstate. Its car park was packed, pick-ups lined the verges, and it was inconceivable the local authorities did not know of the place. Inside, the circular tiers of benches were jammed with two or three hundred big-bellied, atavistic men, their equally overweight wives, and even a few children. It was hot. The cigarette smoke was so thick you could scarcely see across the room. The pit itself was lit up in the darkness like a snooker table, and before each fight the place erupted. Men with thick wads of money stood and bellowed 'I bet twenty-five on the red' or 'I lay forty', looking for someone to take them on. The two cock owners bet fifty or a hundred dollars, held their birds close enough for them to take a few sharp pecks at each other, carefully removed the small leather covers from their steel spurs, then turned them loose.

This time the fights are short and brutal. The cocks fly at each other. There are flurries of wings and feathers, flashes of steel, darting beaks, sudden splashes of blood in the dirt. The crowd cheers and groans and curses. The owners circle the pit, shouting at their birds. Some fights are over in a minute, with one cock lying dead from a skewered heart or paralysed by a broken spinal cord. In others one bird is quickly disabled by a broken leg, a punctured lung or blinded eye, but the fight continues until it cannot or simply will not fight on. When the two birds become entangled, their owners quickly retrieve them, pinch their beaks, blow into their feathers to revive them, and with bloodied hands set them down behind two parallel white lines until the referee restarts the fight. If there is no speedy resolution the fight is moved to a smaller pit behind the benches and fresh birds are introduced.

During occasional breaks in this carnage the crowd stands, spits, scratches and buys yet more hot dogs, Cokes and greasy cheeseburgers in a sideroom that also includes a full-time sharpener for the roosters' steel spurs. I wander round, trying to be as unobtrusive as possible and marvelling at the incongruities of the place. The whole outfit is illegal, but it has strict rules of its own. There are large signs banning alcohol and drugs. Another warns of severe reprisals against anyone caught 'throwing' fights for money – favoured means of doing that include feeding your bird aspirin or injecting water into its wing sockets so they quickly dislocate. On the door of the sole toilet is a notice that reads 'Women Only. Men Outside or Lift the

Seat', and on the wall behind the food-and-drink counter is a plaque honouring the pit's generous contributions to a local childrens' hospital. The pit also makes large donations to local politicians, of course, which is one reason it is left alone.

It is nearly midnight before the fighting ends, and by this time the pit is carpeted with blood and feathers. Outside in the darkness is a dustbin full of dead and not-quite-dead roosters. Not all these discarded birds were losers. Some had won, but were so maimed that their owners had wrung their necks in any case. Indeed few birds ever survive more than three or four fights. The man with the most winning cocks leaves with the few thousand dollars of gate money, minus the pit operators' standard fifteen per cent, and as the pick-ups stream from the car park I half expect to see a policeman directing the traffic or to read about that evening's 'derby' in the next day's local paper.

I drove away thinking about Doug. He was not a cruel man. He had been most hospitable to me, a complete stranger, and had proudly shown me pictures of his daughters and grandchild, yet he engaged in what seemed to me a pretty hideous sport. He had insisted that the cocks were born aggressive, that they were natural fighters from the moment they were hatched, and that 'all we do is condition them'. It is also, of course, a part of man's darker nature to be drawn to blood and gore, and these country folk see less reason to suppress that instinct. Doug cheerfully admitted as much. 'We're just a bunch of hillbillies,' he said.

The next day I returned briefly to 'sivilisation', as Huckleberry Finn would say, and it was not pleasant. The Great Smoky Mountains National Park stood squarely between me and my next destination and I had no choice but drive across it. Don't get me wrong. The park itself was gorgeous. Being out of season, only about a dozen of its nine million annual visitors were there and the weather was sublime. When the road peaked at a little over 5,000 feet, mountains rolled away in every direction, fading from dark blue to grey with white mist filling the valleys in between. I parked and hiked two miles along the Appalachian trail, which runs 2,000 miles from

Georgia to Maine. It was so lovely I considered doing the whole lot, but decided to save the last 1,998 for another day.

No, the problem was the two truly vile towns – Gatlinburg and Cherokee – that you must pass through to enter and leave the park. The first was a hideous neon-lit sprawl of tacky motels, fast-food restaurants, mini-golf, go-Kart tracks, fun fairs, false windmills, 'candy shoppes', 'kampgrounds' and Chapels of Love. If not satiated by so much kitsch, you could take an aerial tramway up to Ober-Gatlinburg.

Cherokee was even worse. I passed in rapid succession Chief Saunookee's Trading Post, the Cherokee Fun Park, the Little Princess Restaurant, Tepee Village, the Ocanaluftee authentic living Indian village, the Totem Pole Craft Shop, the Wigwam Craft Shop, the Cherokee mini-mart, Minnetonka Moccasins, Medicine Man Crafts and the Redskin Motel – and that was just the outskirts. Stuffed bears and live Indians in headdresses stood outside these businesses to attract tourists, and it was hard to say which looked more miserable. It was the sort of place that my children, having yawned their way through the national park, would go nuts about, but I found it hard to believe that adults drawn to the park by its natural beauty could be anything but repulsed by such crass commercialism. I could only assume the park was bordered by these two monstrosities for much the same reason that pretty girls allegedly consort with plain ones – to make them seem still prettier.

It was time to leave Appalachia, but I still had one piece of unfinished business. I had yet to find a moonshiner, and there was only one place left to try. I headed for Rabun County, in the extreme north-eastern corner of Georgia, which consists of the town of Clayton (population 3,000) and great tracts of the Chattahoochee National Forest. This is the last real stronghold of moonshining in America. It is also the home of Dillard Barron, the country's last great hunter of illegal whiskey makers. With his help the US Forest Service had found and destroyed well over a hundred stills in the 900,000-acre forest over the previous ten years – stills that had kept low-life bars in cities like Atlanta amply supplied with cheap, strong liquor.

At sixty-two Dillard is the Forest Service's oldest law enforcement officer, but he is tall, strong and still in peak physical condition. He has leathery skin, a square jaw and sparkling pale blue eyes, and bubbles with boyish enthusiasm. What makes him so good at his job is his intimate inside knowledge of the trade, for his father and grandfather were both moonshiners. 'There weren't no other jobs back then,' he explained. 'Had it not been for moonshining we would have starved. That's what bought shoes for our feet. Seventy-five per cent of the people in these remote areas were involved in whiskey.'

While still a boy Dillard began helping those moonshiners, and later he drove a bootlegger's lorry. In those days federal anti-moonshine regulations stopped anyone from buying more than sixty pounds of sugar or twelve half-gallon fruit jars, so Dillard would drive the lorry down to the coast, pick up large illicit consignments of those vital commodities, and bring them back to the mountains.

In 1955 he was actually convicted for moonshining and put on probation for two years. That conviction threatened to cause problems when he decided to join the law enforcement business in the early 1970s, but a friendly federal judge secured him a presidential pardon in return for half a gallon of moonshine and a country ham.

'I ain't saying you've got to have been involved in illegal activities to be a good law enforcement officer,' Dillard told me, 'but there are things you can't learn in school. You know them from your previous doings.'

There was nothing very funny about marijuana growing in the forests of Kentucky, but there was something distinctly comic about moonshining in Rabun County, Georgia. Everyone knew which families made moonshine – the Englishes, the Welches, the Mosses. They knew where they got their supplies and which welding shop made their stills. The moonshiners were mean, but they were characters. Dillard had grown up with them, counted some of them as friends, but still did his level best to catch them. It was like a game of cat-and-mouse or checkers, he said, with each side constantly watching and trying to outwit the other. When caught in the act, moonshiners considered themselves honour-bound to try to scarper through the woods even though most were now old men and often inebriated by their own product. The wiliest moonshiner of them all was probably Dewey Thomas, now in his late sixties, and as luck would have it Dillard was hot on Dewey's trail when I arrived.

Dewey had been a moonshiner all his life and knew every trick there was. His car even had adjustable shock absorbers so it could carry a bootful of moonshine without looking loaded down. He had a particular talent for persuading others to do the risky manual work on his behalf, and that way he had generally managed to avoid arrest, but in December 1995 he had been caught red-handed. Dewey was now awaiting trial, but Dillard strongly suspected that he was continuing to make moonshine. Dewey owned seventy acres in a remote little valley west of Clayton that was surrounded by national forest and accessible only from one end. In recent weeks Dillard had twice spotted two young men up there who could only be 'still hands'. As Dewey's wife had remarked to Dillard following her husband's 1994 arrest: 'He's hard to stop from his old ways.'

Dillard kindly let me join his search for Dewey's latest still. At 6.00 a.m. the next day he and three colleagues picked me up from my motel and we drove out to Dewey's property in a large black van with tinted windows. It was still pitch black and freezing cold when we arrived. One man took up position on a hill overlooking the dirt road into the valley so he could alert us by radio if Dewey came out from Clayton. A second man drove the van back out of the valley. The remaining three of us – all dressed in camouflaged clothing – set off into the darkness to search the entire forested perimeter of Dewey's property.

Dillard was in his element, grinning like a boy scout. He scrutinised every tyre mark and footprint with his torch. He steered us away from muddy patches lest Dewey spotted our tracks. He skirted gates lest Dewey had left a twig or leaf to show if they'd been opened. He concentrated his search around the many streams flowing down the hillsides because stills need cold running water. He frequently sniffed the air for the tell-tale smell of fermenting 'beer', and hunted for the paths moonshiners made as they carried supplies and equipment into the forest from their vehicles.

Those supplies and equipment are considerable. You need 800

pounds of sugar plus corn, yeast, malt and water to make 1,000 gallons of 'mash'. You need several large wooden or plastic barrels in which to ferment the 'mash' and turn it into 'beer'. You need the still itself – a copper or steel tank big enough to hold all the 'beer'. You need bricks or breeze blocks to line a furnace beneath the still, 100-pound propane cylinders to boil the alcohol from the 'beer', car radiators in which to condense the steam and containers for the ensuing 100 gallons or so of moonshine.

It is not enough to search for paths leading directly off the road, however, since some moonshiners park their pick-ups near a rock and put a plank across the gap so they can unload while leaving the verge unmarked.

As dawn broke we moved off the road and into the forest. We spent the next five hours scrambling through the trees and undergrowth. We walked about seven miles and passed copious evidence of Dewey's past activities. Dillard showed me the still Dewey was caught operating in 1994. It had been destroyed, but the debris still littered the surrounding area. There was a rough shelter about the size of a double garage made of branches and tarpaulins. Beneath this was a deep pit, the mangled steel of the actual still, scattered breeze blocks, lengths of thick black rubber hosepipe and dozens of plastic, gallon milk jugs for the moonshine.

On the far side of the valley we inspected the remains of a second still that Dillard and his colleagues had found earlier that same year. This was also one of Dewey's, but they had only been able to convict the 'still hands' who ran it for him. Because it was not near the road the moonshiners had had to drive their vehicles across a field to reach it, but Dewey had made cattle trample across the field to obscure the tracks.

Further on was a third still that Dewey had apparently abandoned shortly before Dillard found it in 1990. We found the remains of two stills Dewey's father must have operated during World War Two – they were made of tin because copper was unavailable during the war. We twice stumbled across two clusters of fermenting barrels. We found, in short, everything save the still we were looking for.

'It's not up here, but I'm going to find it,' said Dillard as we prepared to leave. 'He wants me to believe it's up here, but it's not.'

At that moment the lookout man came on the radio. Dewey was driving into the valley. We dropped to the ground and watched him pass below us in his grey Ford saloon. Over the next hour the lookout man kept us informed of his movements. He fed his cattle, went briefly into a cabin on his property, and left. It was then that our driver blundered. He gave Dewey insufficient time to leave the area before coming to fetch us. The two vehicles passed on the dirt road into the valley. Dewey stopped, turned round and followed the van to see what it was doing. Our driver, seeing Dewey behind him, turned and left, but Dewey stayed put, his suspicions aroused. He sat there for what seemed an eternity while we shivered in the cold, unable to move. Finally, mercifully, he left, and after a decent interval we drove back to Clayton frozen, empty-handed and having probably alerted our quarry to the fact that he was being chased.

It had been Dewey's day, but there was a side of me that was not so sorry. I felt I'd been hunting an endangered species. Moonshiners were making moonshine long before the practice was deemed illegal (in 1794 farmers in western Pennsylvania rioted when Congress first enacted an excise tax on whiskey). They were craftsmen keeping a tradition alive. They were meeting a demand. They sold their whiskey for about $20 a gallon and it was generally about ninety-five per cent proof, making it considerably cheaper and stronger than the legal stuff. There was something almost romantic about these old rogues, and America would be a less colourful place without them.

I sensed that Dillard felt the same. When I suggested it would be a shame if moonshiners became extinct he chuckled. 'It would,' he replied. He was like Dennis Weese, the bearhunter back in West Virginia. The fun lay almost entirely in the chase.

8

African Experience

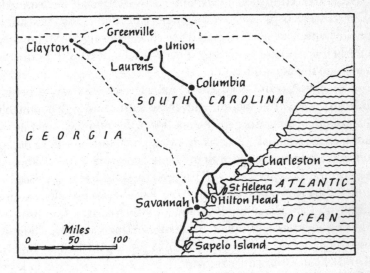

Talk to metropolitan Americans about backwoods America and a surprisingly large number will ask if you've seen a movie called *Deliverance* in which four men from suburban Atlanta are terrorised by rednecks during a weekend canoeing trip in the wilderness. The film captured and reinforced that secret horror of their country's dark interior which many city-dwellers harbour. I mention this only because *Deliverance* was shot on the Chattooga River which I crossed soon after driving away from Clayton. As I did so I left Appalachia behind and entered the schizophrenic state of South Carolina, where the 'Old South' and much-vaunted 'New South' live side by side, where areas of dramatic economic progress and social enlightenment sit cheek by jowl with pockets of poverty, racism and reactionary conservatism.

As I descended from the mountains the earth grew redder, the temperature warmer, and the roads flatter, straighter and wider till at length I found myself rolling along an interstate into Greenville, a city that neatly encapsulates those two South Carolinas. The enormous amounts of foreign investment it has attracted over the past decade are reflected in the gleaming new plants of multinationals like BMW, Fuji, Michelin, Bic, Hitachi and Bosch. Greenville is also home, however, to Bob Jones University which had its charitable status removed by the US Supreme Court in 1983 because it banned inter-racial dating and marriage amongst its students. Indeed it barred blacks entirely until 1971 and even today only has a few token black students.

The university insists its ban on miscegenation is based on a biblical injunction, not racism, and chose to surrender that valuable tax-exempt status rather than back down. It considers itself a bulwark against godless, depraved modernity and boasts of being 'unmovable in its allegiance to the Holy Scriptures'. It refused to let me spend a day on its prim, 1950s-style campus, but I had visited it briefly during South Carolina's 1996 Republican presidential primary and immediately understood why the original Bob Jones, a fire-and-brimstone preacher from rural Alabama whose son and grandson have since succeeded him as president, dubbed it 'The World's Most Unusual University'.

The male students all wear jackets, ties and short-back-and-sides haircuts, the girls long hair and dresses below the knee. There is mandatory daily chapel, student 'prayer captains' lead nightly prayer meetings in the dormitories, and creationism is taught as fact, evolution merely as a theory. Dating is permitted only in a huge 'Dating Parlour' where couples can sit and talk on sofas but matronly chaperones make sure they do not touch. Students may not leave the campus alone. To avoid moral contamination the university's sports teams do not compete against other universities. Drinking and smoking are banned, as are television, films, newspapers and all 'questionable music' including jazz, rock and rap. The university has an impressive collection of religious art, but any nudity is concealed. Some of its library books even contain disclaimers that read: 'It is sometimes necessary to include in this library books whose contents the university cannot wholly endorse.'

Initially, I was a bit put out when I was barred from visiting, but I consoled myself with the knowledge that the university had once awarded Ian Paisley an honorary degree so its judgement had to be a little suspect.

I had encountered little racial tension in Appalachia, doubtless because there were so few black people. West Virginia is ninety-six per cent white and was actually created during the Civil War because its mountain folk, who had no use for slaves or aristocratic slaveowners, refused to join the rest of Virginia in seceding from the Union. Likewise, mountainous north-eastern Tennessee remained largely loyal to the Union, though the state as a whole seceded, and remains ninety-seven per cent white. By contrast South Carolina, whose cotton plantations depended entirely on slave labour, was the first state to secede back in 1860, remains one-third black, and despite its best efforts to present itself as a modern, progressive place is still frequently embarrassed by unreconstructed whites. It has a lot of 'poor white trash' – the sort of people who feel most threatened by black advancement. It has lots of people who have yet to get over the South's Civil War defeat and still delight in defying edicts – especially racial ones – handed down by Washington.

My arrival in South Carolina came shortly after a white couple had been convicted for tying a black boy to a tree and terrorising him. It coincided with the sentencing of two former Ku Klux Klansmen for burning down a black church. It also coincided with a furious controversy over a proposal by the state's Republican governor, David Beasley, that the Confederate battle flag should be removed from the top of the statehouse dome because right-wing racists had turned it into a symbol of white supremacy. Angry white conservatives were accusing him of betraying his heritage and kowtowing to the state's one million blacks. A couple of months later the proposal was defeated.

Forty miles south of Greenville I came to the old mill town of Laurens – population 9,500 and forty-three per cent black – where the same sort of battle was being fought in microcosm. The town's civic leaders had erected signs by the highway declaring 'Laurens is a Great Town' and 'We are Proud of Laurens'. They would probably have liked to rework the war memorial in the pretty town square which lists separately the white and 'colored' soldiers who gave their lives. What they unquestionably wanted to get rid of was the monstrosity that had recently opened in the old Echo cinema in the square's far corner, a stone's throw from the courthouse. Across the canopy, where the cinema would once have advertised its films, big black letters now proclaimed: 'The World's Only Ku Klux Klan Museum' and 'The Redneck Shop Now Open'.

I found the proprietor, a veteran Klansman named John Howard, sitting at a counter in the old foyer from where he commanded a clear view of the square. He was one of the more loathsome creatures I met on my trip – a big, blubbery man in his early fifties with a dirty baseball cap, bright blue eyes above a stubbly chin or two or three, and a definite attitude problem. An interview? That would cost me a couple of thousand dollars, he said. Him racist? Hell no! Sure, he'd burned crosses and worn white robes, but he'd been attracted to the Klan only by its rituals and traditions. He'd even had blacks in his shop. The media had lied about him, he whined. His goal was simply to promote understanding and, with the Klan now splintered and largely impotent, to preserve a bit of history. He was really a concrete contractor, and the museum and Redneck shop were just a sideline – 'pure fun'.

The shop filled the old foyer, and I doubt 'fun' was the adjective that had sprung to the minds of those blacks who had allegedly ventured into it. There was a table full of sweatshirts with slogans like 'Ain't Racist – Just Never Met A Nigger I Liked', 'The KKK Is Getting Bigger – Ain't You Glad You Ain't A Nigger?' and 'If You Ain't Redneck You Ain't Sheet'. There were stickers declaring 'Racial Purity is America's Security' and, alongside a KKK insignia, 'It's a White Thing – You Wouldn't Understand'. There were KKK belt buckles, KKK ceremonial swords, and grotesque little models of black men that Mr Howard called 'little nigglets' and sold for $1.57 each. The museum, which occupied the actual cinema and consisted primarily of white KKK robes and hoods, was closed. Mr Howard told me it opened only on Fridays and Saturdays when his son was available to stand guard, and he was not about to make an exception for me.

The shop did not seem to be doing much business. Just two customers came in during the hour I was there, both wanting the biggest Confederate flags it sold. But Mr Howard had certainly succeeded in inflaming passions. The town council had tried but failed to deny him a trading licence. There had been demonstrations. Bricks had twice been thrown through the shop's windows, and one man had driven a vehicle through its front. Signs warned that the premises were protected by electronic security devices, and that South Carolina's minimum sentence for armed robbery was seven years. Stuck prominently on Mr Howard's telephone were numbers for the local police and fire station but the shop, he insisted, was here to stay.

Months later I read of a delicious twist to the saga of the 'Redneck Shop'. It turned out that long before it opened, Mr Howard had sold the old cinema building to a fellow Klansman named Michael Burden – an 'Exalted Cyclops' no less – with the legal proviso that Mr Howard could continue using the premises for the rest of his life.

Unfortunately for Mr Howard, Mr Burden got married and his bride persuaded him to renounce his racist past. Mr Howard was so angry he ejected Mr Burden, his new wife and her two children from an apartment he'd lent them. In desperation Mr Burden threw himself on the mercy of David Kennedy, an outspoken black pastor who had spearheaded the opposition to the Redneck Shop. Mr Burden even claimed to have planned, at Mr Howard's prompting, to assassinate Mr Kennedy and bomb his church.

Mr Kennedy took pity on the destitute family. He fed them, and his all-black congregation found them a trailer home in their previously segregated neighbourhood. In return, Mr Burden sold Mr Kennedy the cinema for a mere $10. Mr Kennedy may be legally barred from evicting the Klansman and his pernicious shop, but can at least now enjoy the satisfaction of imagining Mr Howard's fury at having a black landlord.

The Redneck Shop was an intense embarrassment to Laurens, and not just because it had attracted so much national publicity. It had also resurrected an ignominious past that the town had evidently been striving to conceal and forget. Shortly before my visit Mr Kennedy told the *New York Times* how in 1913 a white mob had lynched his great-uncle, Richard Puckett, for allegedly attempting to rape a white woman, and how the rope had been left dangling for decades from the railway bridge as a grim warning to the town's black folk.

The story intrigued me, so I went along to Laurens' fine new library to find out more. I scoured the local reference section. I read histories of the town. I found not a single mention of the lynching. It was as if it had never happened. It reminded me of the way the word 'nigger' was beeped out of old black-and-white movies shown on television back in Washington. I approached one of the librarians who eventually managed to dig up a solitary ancient cutting from the local newspaper.

The report bore remarkable testimony to the attitudes of the time. It described how a 'negro' had hidden behind a bush and pounced on 'a lady of a prominent Laurens county family' as she approached the town to visit a sick relative. Her screams frightened him away. Search parties were sent out. Puckett was arrested when several white men 'stopped at a negro house to get a drink of water' and he 'seemed to act in a suspicious manner'. The lady could not positively identify him, the newspaper reported, but 'the evidence pointed so positively in his direction that no doubt can be entertained but that he is the right man'. That evening an angry crowd gathered outside the jail. It would not be appeased by promises of an immediate trial, or by a conference with the lady's family to see if it favoured a lynching. Puckett was seized, strung up from the railway bridge and riddled with bullets. 'The lynching crowd was a very quiet and orderly one,' the report concluded with evident approval. 'It was a sullen, silent and determined body of men, bent upon putting a quick end to the life of the would-be rapist.'

Such an event could never happen today, of course, but traces of that mentality survive. Look what happened in Union, another textile town of about 11,000 people 30 miles from Laurens. In 1994 a young white mother named Susan Smith claimed a black man had stopped her, taken her car and driven away with her two children aged three and fourteen months. Initially, because this highly improbable story played to racial stereotypes, no one questioned it and an immediate manhunt was launched. It subsequently transpired that Smith had drowned her children by driving them to a nearby lake and rolling her car down a steep concrete boat ramp. This time it was the falsely accused black community that was outraged.

I drove over to Union out of morbid curiosity and discovered the story had an appalling sequel. Two years after Smith drowned her children a party of four adults and six children had driven out from Union one evening to see the infamous spot. They parked their van so its headlights lit up two memorials to the Smith children that had been erected near the top of the ramp. Three of the adults and two children got out. The van then suddenly and inexplicably rolled down the steep bank into the water. The five people inside drowned, like the Smith children before them, and so did two others who tried to save them.

I made a point of parking well away from the water. The Smith case had made national headlines, and the site had attracted thousands of sightseers from across the country, but this was a grey winter's day and I had the place to myself. It was curiously affecting. The lake was black and still and ringed by fir trees. The two memorials were shaped like tombstones. One was made of black marble and inscribed: 'Dedicated to the memory of Michael and Alex Smith, whose precious lives touched the hearts of all of us.' Above this inscription was an etching of the two children in a rocking chair, and below an etching of toy bricks, a toy car and a teddy bear. The second was made of grey granite and topped by a small, solar-powered angel that glows at night. There was a picture of the two boys, and some dreadful doggerel:

> *Two little angels with beautiful smiles*
> *Graced this earth for a little while*
> *They touched the hearts of all around*
> *More precious children could not be found.*

Behind these two stones was the stump of a tree that had been planted in the children's memory. The van had snapped the tree off as it ran down the bank into the water.

As I was leaving this sad spot I noticed a large board with the lake's rules and regulations. There were thirteen in all – no alcohol, no littering, no fishing without a licence. At the bottom some moron had scribbled a fourteenth. 'No killing your kids.'

I returned to Union in need of something cheerful and found it in a modest roadside diner with formica tables called Gene's. I ordered fried chicken at the counter and offered my money to a smiley old fellow with thick glasses and two patently false front teeth who was standing at the till. He stuck out his hand.

'Where yer from?' he asked.

'England,' I replied.

'Sure preshate yer droppin' bah,' he said, beaming.

This was Gene, and after I'd eaten, just as I was climbing into my car, he came rushing out. 'Just wanted to say I preshate yer comin' in,' he said.

We chatted a while. It turned out he was a self-made millionaire. He had begun life pushing a refreshment trolley round a local cotton mill. At thirty-two he had borrowed the money to open the diner. Thirty years later he owns a big old house in Union, a beach house, a cabin in the mountains, a trailer park and four vintage cars. He serves 300 people a day, seven days a week and at sixty-four could easily retire but 'I just love people'. Not long afterwards I read a review of a book called *The Millionaire Next Door* that showed two-thirds of America's millionaires were not sportsmen or filmstars or chief executives, but humble folk like Gene whose watchwords are hard work and frugality.

Enough of these white folk. They were not the reason I had come to South Carolina. They just happened to be on my route. I hopped on to an interstate and rattled 200 miles down to the coast, where the air is heavy with the sweet smell of pulp mills, to search for the last traces of Africa brought over in 17th- and 18th-century slave ships.

I say the coast, but that is misleading. Down in the Low Country the land doesn't abruptly end in glistening white beaches at the Atlantic's edge. Rather it dissolves into marshes laced with creeks and rivers, and between the marshes and the open sea is a long line of lush, semi-tropical islands that extends more than 200 miles from north of Charleston right down to Georgia's border with Florida. It was to those islands and their rice, cotton and indigo plantations that tens of thousands of African slaves were diverted after the ships that brought them docked in Charleston and Savannah. Their descendants were amongst the first slaves freed during the Civil War, their white masters having fled inland, and many were allowed to keep the land they worked. They lived on undisturbed for the best part of another century, and because the islands were so cut off they remained African long after their fellow blacks on the mainland had become fully-fledged Americans.

They were called the Gullah or Geechee people. They had their own creole language, also called Gullah, which was a mixture of African languages and pidgin English developed so slaves from different parts of Africa could communicate with each other and with their masters. They had their own cuisine, heavily dependent on rice and fish. They had their own unique skills – boat-building, basket-weaving, making fishing nets – and extracted medicines from roots and herbs. They had their own forms of religious worship including 'seeking', or looking for messages in dreams, and 'shouting', a shuffling, stamping, rhythmic dance. They believed in spirits and witchcraft. They would place cherished objects on graves, pass babies over coffins to appease the spirits of the newly-dead, and build their cemeteries by the water so those spirits could more easily return to Africa. They developed their own negro spirituals, including 'Michael, Row the Boat Ashore', and were great storytellers who gave the world the tales of Brer Rabbit.

This Gullah culture remained vibrant in its island strongholds until shortly after World War Two, but then developers began building bridges to the islands and turning them into playgrounds for the rich. The most dramatic example of this was the island of Hilton Head, President Clinton's New Year haunt, which is where I headed first with my twelve-year-old daughter Hannah, who was joining me for the last few days of her Christmas holidays.

We went to see Emory Campbell, King of the Gullahs, a tall, loose-limbed man in his mid-fifties with sparkling eyes, greying hair and great charm. He wasn't really the king, but he was the Gullahs' most eloquent spokesman. He was a native of Hilton Head who had trained as a microbiologist, worked at Harvard, then returned to help his people. For the last fifteen years or so he had been executive director of the Penn Centre on neighbouring St Helena Island, an institution which began life in 1861 as America's first school for freed slaves and now laboured to preserve the Gullah culture.

Emory did not exactly live in one of Hilton Head's many million-dollar homes. Like most of his fellow Gullahs, he had a modest bungalow in one of the least desirable corners of the island where holidaymakers never ventured. In fact he still drew his water from a well beside his house. He greeted us in bare feet, sat us down on a sofa beneath a slowly-revolving ceiling fan, and gave us a potted history of the island.

Following the Civil War northern industrialists bought about two-thirds of Hilton Head – some 20,000 acres – for winter hunting and its freed slaves bought the rest. The industrialists rarely visited. As late as the 1940s, when Emory was a young boy, there were just three resident white families and the 3,000 Gullahs had the freedom of the island. They caught fish from its pristine beaches and harvested crabs, shrimps and oysters from its bountiful marshes. They hunted for deer, squirrel and raccoon in forests of majestic pine and ancient 'live' oaks dripping with Spanish moss. They grew watermelons, corn, beans, okra and other vegetables. They were self-sufficient, virtually autonomous, and would visit the mainland only to sell surplus produce.

Then, in 1956, the state built a bridge to Hilton Head and two white businessmen, Fred Hacks and John Fraser, began developing it as a resort. Today the 12-mile-long island is covered no longer with forests but with hotels, condominiums, golf courses, tennis courts, swimming pools, boutiques and manicured, palm-lined boulevards. Those Gullahs who have not sold out or been forced from the island by soaring property taxes are vastly outnumbered by Hilton Head's 25,000 white residents, and have returned to a sort of economic servitude, working for paltry wages in the most menial jobs on the island – gardening, cleaning, waiting, maintenance.

'We call it a more comfortable form of slavery,' said Emory. 'Our people are working in great discomfort to make sure the rich are comfortable. It's no different to what it was when there was slavery, only now we get something called wages that really don't meet the requirements of the cost of living.'

The developers have, to Emory's disgust, named the island's various resort communities 'plantations'. 'It connotes slavery,' he said. 'It's a marketing device for the developers because they know most northerners longed for the southern way of life – big houses, yard hands and house maids,' he said. Moreover they have walled off those 'plantations', meaning that three-quarters of the island is now off-limits and Emory needs a special pass to visit a family cemetery sandwiched between a yacht basin and the 18th hole of the Harbourtown Heritage Links.

Having almost completely destroyed the Gullahs' way of life, the island's new white masters suddenly decided a few years back that these black folk were actually rather quaint and could be turned into a tourist attraction. The island's visitors centre and 'museum' now trumpets the fact that they were the first slaves freed after the Civil War, but fails to relate any of their subsequent history. It sells framed Gullah poems, books with cute titles like 'We Lived in a Little Cabin in the Yard', and Gullah recipes for 'sqayrill stoo' (squirrel stew), 'roas' skonk' (roast skunk) and 'swimp en' grabby' (shrimp in gravy). Having been taught for most of their lives that their language was primitive, backward and something to be ashamed of, the Gullahs are now accosted by tourists begging them to speak it. To Emory's amusement the mayor of Hilton Head had recently asked him, without any apparent irony, to stage a celebration of Gullah culture, but the truth is that here at least there is precious little left to celebrate.

*

We had not intended to visit St Helena island, but after meeting Emory we changed our minds. He let slip that the island still had a practising witchdoctor, a certain Dr Buzzard who attracted customers from far afield. Hannah's eyes lit up. To return to school saying she'd met a witchdoctor would be cool beyond belief. Emory was adamant he would not talk to us, but we decided at least to try.

St Helena is about 10 miles north by water, but 50 by road because of the estuaries and marshes. To reach it you pass through Beaufort, a town of exquisite mansions built before the Civil War as retreats for white plantation owners who found steamy, marshy, tropical St Helena too unhealthy. St Helena is still overwhelmingly black and has not been developed like Hilton Head, primarily because the freed slaves acquired much more of the land, but in a sense it is almost worse. It has become a living museum written up in the travel pages, a place where tourists come to gawk at the Gullahs like they gawk at the Dutch Amish of Pennsylvania. Gullah-N-Geechie Mahn Tours will take you round the Penn Centre, the Gullahs' tiny old clapboard 'praise houses' or churches, and the remains of the plantations. There is a Gullah House Restaurant, a Gullah Boutique, a Candied Yam Bakery and the 'Tuc in De Wood' campground. The Red Piano art gallery sells T-shirts proclaiming 'Gullah Spoken Here' and Gullah translations of St Luke's gospel entitled 'De Good Nyews Bout Jedus Christ Wa Luke Write'. There is even a children's television show made on St Helena called 'Gullah Gullah Island'.

The gallery's owner had indeed heard of 'Dr Buz'. She believed he lived somewhere down by the old Oaks Plantation, though she too insisted he would turn us away. We set off, and halfway down the Oaks Plantation Road we stopped to ask directions from a black woman walking along the grassy verge. We were in luck. She not only knew Dr Buzzard. She was his cousin. Evidently believing we were customers, she hopped in the car and guided us to the old plantation gates where we turned left down a sandy track. A few hundred yards further on she pointed to his home.

I have to admit that it was not quite what I'd expected of a witch-doctor. It was a modern brick bungalow surrounded by a lawn and shaded by a great oak tree. There were Christmas lights around the windows, a flowering camelia bush by the front door, and a large satellite television dish in the back yard. We drove our guide to her home and returned to look for Dr Buz.

We knocked on the front door. Nobody answered so we went round the side and there he was, a gaunt man in his fifties or sixties wearing an old white cap and red jacket. He was bending over a car with a much younger man, his son perhaps. He had not heard us approaching so I called 'Hello'. He turned and calmly sized us up as we approached.

'Hi!' I said cheerily as we shook hands. 'I'm from England. I was wondering if I could talk to Dr Buzzard?'

A faint smile crossed his face. 'Ain't nobody called that here,' he said.

'But aren't you Dr Buzzard?' I asked.

'No sir. Dr Buzzard's just a name. It doesn't mean anything. What would you want with Dr Buzzard anyway?'

I explained that I was writing a book about America and would like to ask him about his craft. 'If you paid me five hundred and fifty thousand dollars I'd write the book for you,' he replied with a sly grin.

We verbally sparred for a few more minutes. He would admit to nothing, but seemed to enjoy our little tussle. I finally had to admit defeat. We shook hands again and left, but Hannah and I were not downcast. We'd met our witchdoctor. We knew it was him because of one particular physical characteristic we'd been told about. When he smiled, he displayed a row of three lower teeth all capped with gold.

I doubt Dr Buz had anything to do with it, but the next day Hannah and I found our first little piece of authentic Africa.

Back in 1932 a linguist named Lorenzo Turner had travelled through the Low Country making recordings of the Gullah people. One of the islands he visited was Harris Neck, Georgia, roughly 100 miles south of Hilton Head, where there was a healthy community of perhaps sixty Gullah families. There he recorded a woman named

Amelia Dawley singing a curious lilting song with words that sounded decidedly African. In 1989 Joseph Opala, an American anthropologist working in Sierra Leone, found that scratchy old recording in Turner's archives. He and a colleague, Cynthia Schmidt, an ethnomusicologist, travelled from village to village playing the song until eventually, in the small village of Senehun Ngola in Bagbo Chiefdom, a woman recognised it and began singing along.

What Amelia Dawley had sung for Lorenzo Turner was a Mende funeral song that had been passed down from one generation to another for the two centuries since her ancestors had been shipped in chains to North America.

It was a remarkable discovery. No other African text carried to America in a slave ship had survived so long or so completely. Unfortunately the federal government had ejected the Gullahs from Harris Neck in 1942 in order to build an air base on the island. The families had scattered far and wide, and it was generally assumed that the song had died with Amelia Dawley in 1955.

It took a considerable coincidence to dispel that assumption. That same year, 1989, the government of Sierra Leone invited thirteen prominent Gullahs to a 'homecoming' in Africa. One of the thirteen was Lauretta Sams, who worked for the county that includes Harris Neck. When she said she knew the place Dr Opala begged her to search for any descendants of Amelia Dawley. She asked around and discovered that not all the families had left the area. A few had settled just across the marsh that divides Harris Neck from the mainland, vainly hoping that one day the island would be returned to them. Amongst those families Ms Sams found Mrs Dawley's only surviving child, an elderly woman named Mary Moran. Dr Opala and Dr Schmidt played her the recording. Mrs Moran not only recognised the song her mother had taught her as a child. Despite a lapse of more than half a century she was able to sing along. The song had, miraculously, survived another generation.

Hannah and I went to visit Mrs Moran. She lived in one of several ramshackle homes scattered around a pine wood near the end of the quiet country road that leads to Harris Neck. It was the exact same place where she and her husband Roosevelt, a crab fisherman, had thrown up their first rough shelter in 1942 after being ousted from Harris Neck. She was then nineteen and seven months pregnant with her fourth child. She was now seventy-five with ten children, 'thirty-some' grandchildren and, she told us, twenty-two great-grandchildren 'last time I counted'.

A small, dignified woman with frizzy grey hair tied back in two small buns, she invited us in, sat us down in her simple living room and talked about what her family had dubbed 'the little ugly song'. Her mother had taught it to her on her knee, she said. As a child she had danced to it, not realising it was a funeral song. She had tried to teach it to her own children but they'd not been interested. Then, cradling a three-month-old great-granddaughter, she began softly to sing.

'A wahkah, mu mohne; kambei ya le; li leei tohmbe . . .' she intoned, her slippered foot tapping to the rhythm. 'Everyone come, let us struggle; the grave is not yet finished; the deceased is not yet at peace . . .' It was one of those tingly moments that linger in the memory – and another cool story for Hannah to take back to school.

Mrs Moran has now taught the song to a thirteen-year-old granddaughter, ensuring its survival for at least one more generation, and in Sierra Leone she has become a celebrity. A few weeks after our visit she was flown out there, was taken by helicopter to Senehun Ngola, met distant relatives she never knew existed and was received by the President. It was the first time she'd ever left America.

The one sadness in her life is that her people never got their island back. The air base had barely been completed before the ground was found to be too soggy to support heavy aircraft, but there was no way the white authorities were going to return Harris Neck to the Gullahs and it eventually became a national wildlife refuge. On a still, warm January afternoon Mrs Moran's son Bill took us over there. The overgrown runways were still visible, slicing through the forest. All other signs of human habitation had long since been destroyed save for a single Gullah cemetery where a small stone marks Amelia Dawley's grave.

*

On Hannah's final day we struck gold. We found an entire African village just off the coast of the United States. It is called Hog Hammock on Sapelo Island, just a few miles south of Harris Neck.

About seventy Gullahs live in Hog Hammock, which is the last surviving community on an island where 800 slaves once toiled on the plantation of a Scotsman named Thomas Spalding. The rest of the island's 11,000 acres are now a nature reserve and marine research facility owned by the state of Georgia. You can only reach Sapelo by ferry, and you can only board the ferry if part of an official tour or invited by a resident. We had telephoned Cornelia Bailey, Hog Hammock's unofficial historian, and she had somewhat reluctantly agreed to show us round. So shortly before noon on a warm but misty day we walked down a small jetty near nowhere in particular, boarded the *Annemarie*, and set off along a channel through the marshes. The thirty-minute ride to Sapelo cost $1, making it surely the cheapest form of public transportation in America, and we were the only whites on board.

From the water Sapelo seemed merely a dense dark-green forest surrounded by acres of waist-high reeds. As we approached we saw a narrow track had been built across the marshland to a small dock where several battered old cars were awaiting the ferry's arrival. Cornelia was there with her ten-year-old granddaughter, sitting in an ancient burgundy-and-cream van with a chronically cracked windscreen (there were no police or traffic regulations on Sapelo). She was a large lady in her mid-fifties dressed in a purple sweatshirt, green tracksuit bottoms and a bright red headcloth. She did not get out. She shook hands through the window and told us to jump in the back. Cornelia, we quickly learned, was an intelligent and assertive woman who made no concessions at all to white folk.

Sapelo was a magical island, replete with pelicans, snakes and alligators. Cornelia drove us along green tunnels through the lush forest. She showed us Nannygoat beach and Behaviour cemetery, where graves date back to the 1700s. She took us past old dairy buildings and Spalding's palatial mansion, later acquired by the tobacco magnate R. J. Reynolds, with its empty turquoise swimming pool and classical statues shaded by palms and giant oaks. The island's white masters have long since gone, however, and the plantations have reverted to nature, leaving the Gullahs to themselves.

Cornelia stopped by the sign at the entrance to the 434 acres of private land that comprise Hog Hammock. 'Notice it doesn't say "welcome",' she told us. 'We make you feel welcome, but we don't want you to stay.'

Hog Hammock was amazing. It was a Disneyesque version of an African village. Shacks and trailer homes were randomly scattered around the pine woods. There were sandy tracks for roads. The air was scented with woodsmoke, and rang with the cawing of rooks and the buzzing of cicadas. It was immeasurably peaceful. Had you arrived there blindfolded after a very long journey you would never have believed it was America, that it was on the same continent as New York City. America, said Cornelia, was what you saw on television.

She showed us the tiny store which sold only non-perishable goods, the two white wooden churches, the old schoolhouse, a state-funded senior citizens centre that nobody used and Lulu's Kitchen, a tiny eating place that catered for the official tours. Twice she pointed to new homes in amongst the trees. 'Infiltrators', she snapped. 'We don't like newcomers. They dilute the culture. They are basically domineering. They want us to conform to their ways but we like our ways.'

We ended up at her husband's bar, a blue plywood hut with a circle of rough wooden benches beneath a tree outside. Had Cornelia been able to put us on the 2.30 p.m. return ferry without giving offence I think she'd have done so, but we'd missed it and would now have to wait for the 4.30 departure. We sat and drank Cokes. She was not unfriendly. She just disliked whites in general. It was as if she had never forgiven them for tearing her ancestors away from Africa.

'Once a buckra, always a buckra,' she insisted, 'buckra' being the Gullah word for a white person. 'If I could put a fence around myself and cut off whites altogether I would do so. We could meet in the middle of the road. A lot of people would prefer it to be that way. Not every black community is dying to integrate into white communities and go to their schools. All we ever wanted was to be treated equally.'

Cornelia didn't actually need to put a fence around herself. She was ringed by water which was – she conceded – almost as good. 'This is a little bit of Africa. This is a little bit of home . . . Here we can live as we want to. We don't like other people coming and telling us you can't cook like this or speak like that. We don't want that bull from other people. We want them to leave us alone. We want to be just us. We want to cast our nets, row our rowboats and sing our songs in church on Sundays our way.'

Many of the old Gullah customs had died, she admitted. There was only one basket-weaver left, an old man of eighty-nine named Allen Green. Her ninety-four-year-old father had been the last boat-builder, and the islanders were now 'stuck with modern medicine'. But they still had their own superstitions, customs and distinctive lifestyle. They still spoke Gullah amongst themselves. Were I to sit in on a family meal, she said, I would understand about two words in every six.

Cornelia was the only American I could remember meeting who was not proud of her country. She didn't even consider it her country. She called herself and Sapelo's other inhabitants Africans. 'I would rather be African than American if I'd not had the misfortune to be born here,' she said. 'If I had the funds I would abandon this country and go back there.' She had returned once. She was another of the thirteen Gullahs who had been invited to Sierra Leone in 1989. 'I felt a wholeness again,' she recalled. 'I had a sense that that was where I belonged. There were people who looked just like you, who behaved just like you, and ate food that was very similar. It was the best feeling in the world.'

The sun had finally penetrated the mist and it was almost hot. We still had time to kill so Hannah and I went in search of Glasco Bailey, Cornelia's eighty-three-year-old uncle and the last man on Sapelo to make circular cast nets for fishing. Despite our conversation with Cornelia we were hardly prepared for what we found. The old man was chopping sticks on an upturned tree trunk in his yard. He was surrounded by cats and chickens pecking around in the dirt. His home was a tiny old wooden shack with a corrugated iron roof shaded by centuries-old oaks bearded with Spanish moss.

We followed him on to his verandah and sat for a while on a threadbare sofa while roosters crowed outside. He was a friendly soul, but almost impossible to understand as he was almost toothless and spoke only pidgin English. He had never lived off the island and had never wanted to. He went inside and came back with a faded black-and-white photograph of R. J. Reynolds' yacht on which he had once worked. He produced an ancient bible whose leather binding had long since fallen apart and took out a certificate recording the births of himself and his five brothers and sisters. He was the only one still living. His wife had also died many years ago and he had no children.

When we asked about his fishing nets he took us inside. We were dumbfounded. The tiny rooms were cluttered with junk and lit by single naked lightbulbs. He cooked on a primitive woodstove. There was just a rumpled worn blanket on his bed. The only vaguely modern appliance was not one but two aged televisions. The string nets, however, were works of art. He took us out the back to show us the moulds in which he made the lead weights. Outside was an old water pump with a broken generator, tumbledown sheds, homemade cages in which he kept turkeys and a sun-dappled vegetable patch in which he grew castor beans as a laxative. On the edge of the clearing was a beaten-up truck. He said the battery was flat but it didn't look as if it had moved for years. Cornelia was right. This was definitely Africa, not America.

Cornelia drove us back to the dock. We thanked her, and were just climbing out of the van when she asked for petrol money. Still no concessions to white folk. The boat set off back towards mainland America and within a few minutes Sapelo had vanished in the mist like some imaginary land.

9

The Preacher from Plains

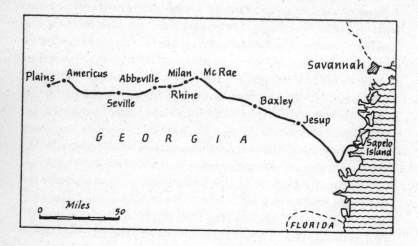

That evening I put Hannah on a plane back to Washington and momentarily succumbed to a feeling of great loneliness. This was compounded by my choice of a motel so profoundly dismal that it would have graced a Hitchcock movie, though to be fair it only cost $20. Such moods rarely outlast the night, however. I woke to brilliant sunshine and balmy weather, and this was the moment when I left the Atlantic coast for the final time and headed directly westwards once again.

I had a wonderful day. I meandered 200 miles through the heart of rural Georgia along country roads that were so straight and flat and empty that I could balance my coffee on the dashboard without fear of spillage. At first I travelled through endless pine forests broken only by the occasional swamp or by rivers with exotic Indian names like Canoochee, Ohoopee or Ocmulgee. At Vidalia, 'home of the sweet onion', I joined a road that followed the main railway line from Savannah, and almost exactly every 10 miles after that there was a quiet little town built, originally, to provide water for the old steam engines. I went through McRae, Milan, Rhine, Abbeville, Rochelle, Pitts, Seville and Bland Villa. They all had neat town squares, and the civic-minded had erected signs like 'Don't Be A Litter Critter'. The further I went the more agricultural the land became. There were ploughed-up cotton fields speckled with tiny tufts of white, regimented orchards of tall grey pecan trees, and roadside stalls selling great sacks of peanuts boiled, shelled or roasted. At about 3.30 p.m. I arrived in Plains, home of Jimmy Carter, the former President.

Back in 1977, during Mr Carter's first year in the White House, as many as 15,000 tourists a day would flock to this town of just 700 people, and the cars would be bumper to bumper the entire length of the one road through it. Such crowds are long gone. In fact I had the place virtually to myself. I checked into Grace Jackson's bed-and-breakfast, the only accommodation there is in Plains, and spent a delightfully tranquil two hours wandering around in the late afternoon sun.

The town is all of about eight blocks long, stretched out either side of the main road and a railway line. At one end is Mr Carter's old peanut warehouse, now owned by the Golden Peanut Company. Next to that a short row of old brick stores includes the 'antiques' shop where Hugh Carter, Jimmy's first cousin, still sells faded political memorabilia from the Carter era. Another block along is the little white weatherboarded railway station from which the former Georgia governor ran his quixotic but ultimately victorious campaign for the White House in 1976, and from which the 'Peanut Express' left for his inauguration with virtually the entire town on board.

Across the road is his late brother Billy's petrol station, preserved just as it was in the days when he was America's national joke, and behind that is the old colonnaded, red-brick high school where Jimmy's teacher, 'Miss Julia' Coleman, allegedly inspired the future president with dreams of greatness. The echoing classrooms with their polished wood floorboards now house a museum and visitors centre where I sat all by myself and watched a film of Mr Carter and his wife, Rosalynn, giving a guided tour of their house. Mr Carter had, it seemed, built all the furniture – even their bed – himself.

The Carters still live at the far end of the main road. I wandered down there past pretty white shingled houses with well-trimmed lawns. One man was having a bonfire. Another was washing his car. I met a couple of people out strolling and each wished me a polite good evening. The Carter residence is a long low house set well back from the road and surrounded by trees and a high iron fence, but someone had obligingly built a short brick path across the grass to give visitors a better view. A Stars and Stripes hung limply from a single flagpole. The water hydrant was painted red, white and blue. There was a guard house at the entrance to the compound but it was empty, and across the road were a couple of tumbledown shacks occupied by poor black families – Mr Carter's closest neighbours.

Besides the Billy Carter softball field, the Lillian G. Carter nursing home where Jimmy was born, and his childhood home a couple of miles outside town, that's about everything of interest there is in Plains. As I wandered back to my bed-and-breakfast I began to marvel that a man from such a tiny place could reach the White House, but then I caught myself. Bill Clinton came from Hope, Arkansas; Ronald Reagan from Tampico, Illinois; Richard Nixon from Yorba Linda, California; Harry Truman from Independence, Missouri and Dwight Eisenhower from Abilene, Kansas. Lincoln, of course, was raised in his legendary log cabin. Americans love to see the American Dream come true, and love to boast of how the most humble man can become the world's most powerful.

They are also fervent populists, and it is no accident that America's Constitution begins 'We, the people . . .' or that its leader is addressed as 'Mr President'. They profoundly distrust Washington's political élite and would much rather their leaders were drawn from the ranks of common men. Mr Carter particularly benefited from this sentiment in the wake of the Watergate scandal, of course, and on reflection I decided it was probably harder to win the White House if you were not raised in a small town than if you were.

What made Mr Carter exceptional was that he returned to his small town after his political career was over. When not circling the globe resolving conflicts, monitoring elections in banana republics or building low-cost housing for Atlanta's poor, he is often seen jogging or riding his bike through Plains. He mows the grass at his church. He also teaches an adult Sunday school class there, and that was what I'd really come to witness.

The Maranatha Baptist Church is a newish, low brick building surrounded by fields and pecan trees on the edge of town. I arrived there about 9.45 the next morning to find the pastor, Dan Ariail, briefing a congregation swollen by perhaps fifty other visitors like myself. Take pictures only when Mr Carter arrives, not while he's speaking, Mr Ariail insists. The President will hang around afterwards to meet you all, but please don't ask for autographs. Any questions? Someone asks what it is like to be pastor of a President's church. A great opportunity, Mr Ariail replies cheerily. Every Sunday, after Mr Carter has done his bit, he gets to preach to dozens of people who would not normally go near a church. A few of us wriggle uncomfortably in our seats.

As Mr Ariail finishes his introduction, the 39th President of the United States appears unannounced beside him. Rosalynn and a grandson take their place in the front row. There are audible whispers and giggles from the pews. Mr Carter is dressed in an open shirt, dark checked jacket and grey trousers. He is seventy-two and silver-haired, but tall, unbowed and obviously fit.

'Are there any visitors here today?' he asks disingenuously. A few dozen hands shoot up.

'Where y'all from?' he asks. People shout out umpteen different states. There are people from England, Australia, Brazil and India. One man says he is from the Dominican Republic.

'You have a new president there,' Mr Carter says. 'D'you like him all right? We helped conduct the election there the 30th of June. I think he's doing a fine job.'

Mr Carter jokes about how only about one in six visitors to the church are Baptists and the rest are 'all kind of strange denominations'. He starts to recount how he and twenty-two members of his family (people forget he had three sons before Amy came along) spent New Year's Eve on Harry Truman's old estate in the Florida Keys.

'Tell them about the gate,' Rosalynn interjects.

'Okay,' he replies obediently. It seems the main gate to that estate is traditionally only opened for presidents, and New Year's Eve was the first time it had been opened since Kennedy went there in 1960 while preparing for the invasion of Cuba at the Bay of Pigs.

The preamble is finally over and Mr Carter switches on a video of Jay Leno, a late-night television comic, interviewing New Yorkers on the street about the Bible. 'How many animals in Noah's Ark?' Leno asks one woman.

'Five?' comes the querulous reply.

'Name the four gospels,' he asks another.

She can't.

'Okay, name the four Beatles?'

'John, Paul, George and Ringo,' the woman shoots back.

Leno challenges a man to cite one of the Ten Commandments.

'Freedom of speech,' he replies after a very long pause.

The congregation is roaring with laughter. Mr Carter has made his point. He takes a verse from Timothy as his text: 'All scripture is given by inspiration of God, and is profitable for doctrine, for reproof, for correction and righteousness.' For the next forty minutes he paces from side to side, explaining how we should read the Bible to learn how to live just as we use a manual to learn how to use a computer or new motorbike. Life should be about much more than becoming rich or important. We should strive to 'stretch our hearts'. We should aim for 'transcendence'. By reading the Bible we could learn how to follow the examples of Jesus, including particularly his love for his enemies. That was the way to 'a peace that passeth all understanding'. He ends by urging us all to resolve to read at least a few verses from the Bible every night.

It is a persuasive discourse, perfectly pitched for the irreligious in the congregation, but then you do not become President of the United States unless you can communicate. Nor, for that matter, can you become President of this God-fearing country without at least professing to be an active Christian, though in Mr Carter's case his faith is unquestionably sincere.

There is a brief break before the service proper begins. Mr Carter joins Rosalynn and one of their grandsons in the congregation. A few of the visitors slip away, but there is still a sizeable congregation, including several secret service agents who stand out a mile because they neither sing nor pray. An hour later we all pour out into the sunshine where the Carters happily pose for photographs with anyone who wants. They are in no hurry. It is all amazingly informal. You almost expect to be invited home for Sunday lunch. That does not happen, alas, and after twenty minutes the man often described as 'the best former President America has ever had' climbs into a grey Chrysler saloon with his wife and a secret service agent drives them home.

10

Rogues and Rednecks

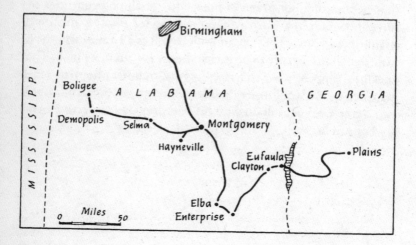

West of Plains the pine forests returned, and the earth became so red it stained car tyres and the edges of the roads. The land grew steadily hillier till the empty highway resembled a rollercoaster. I rode up and down until eventually I reached a huge reservoir marking Georgia's border with Alabama.

Georgians call this the Walter F. George Lake after some local dignitary. Alabamans call it the Eufaula Lake after the little-known gem of a town that sits on a bluff on its western shore. In the 19th century every plantation within 100 miles would send its cotton to Eufaula, from where it was shipped down the Chattahoochee River by steamboat to the Gulf of Mexico. The planters and merchants built themselves magnificent mansions which still stand, in pristine condition, on either side of elegant tree-lined boulevards. Alabama has always been synonymous in my mind with lynchings, cross-burnings, bloody civil rights clashes and sinister happenings in the swampy backwoods, so Eufaula's laid-back charm caught me by surprise.

I drove on through undulating forest, looking in vain for aboriginal wannabees as Alabama had recently become the first state to legalise the hunting of deer with spears.

I went through the town of Clayton, whose greatest claim to fame is a grave in its cemetery shaped like a whiskey bottle. It was erected by the mother of a young man named W. T. Mullen who drank himself to death in 1863 at the age of twenty-nine. The tombstone was apparently her way of saying 'I told you so'.

Thirty miles beyond Clayton is a town called Enterprise which boasts the only monument in the world erected in honour of a pest. It is thirteen feet high and consists of a lady holding aloft a boll weevil, the beetle that destroyed the region's cotton crops in the early 1900s. In desperation the local farmers switched to peanuts which proved so successful that they all grew rich. 'In profound appreciation of the Boll Weevil and what it has done as the herald of prosperity,' the inscription reads.

It's amazing what turns up in these backwaters of the old Deep South. Who would have thought, for example, that in the little town of Elba, which straddles the Pea River west of Enterprise, you'd find the widow of a Confederate soldier still alive more than 130 years after the last shots of the Civil War were fired? Alberta Martin claims to be the only Confederate widow left, and almost certainly is, but you never know. Until she came to light that title had been accorded to South Carolina's Daisy Wilson Cave, who died in 1990 aged somewhere between ninety-seven and one hundred and five.

Ferrin Cox, publisher of the *Elba Clipper* newspaper, told me how to find Mrs Martin. Watch out for her son, William, he warned. He could be aggressive, but take no notice. She's the one who pays the bills. I drove to the very edge of town, beyond the levee built to protect Elba from flooding, and followed a narrow lane past a lumber yard and a couple of trailer homes till it petered out. There, on the left, was Mrs Martin's tiny white house.

She turned out to be a surprisingly sprightly, large-framed lady of ninety with a wizened face, silver hair drawn back in a bun and a reputation for playing a mean game of dominoes. I explained who I was. She invited me into her cramped front room with its linoleum floor, sat herself down in a rocking chair beneath a large Confederate battle flag, and began telling me her story. It wasn't the easiest interview I'd ever conducted. Her mind was still sharp and she was disarmingly candid about her convoluted life, but her hearing aid was, as she put it, 'torn up bad', making it hard for her to understand me. She had a deep Alabama accent and toothless gums, making it equally hard for me to understand her. She also insisted on writing the first of her three husbands out of the script, so it was not always clear which one she was talking about. William was on his best behaviour, however, and with him acting as interpreter we got by.

Mrs Martin was a sharecropper's daughter who left school when she was about thirteen and went to work in a cotton mill. Aged eighteen or nineteen she married her first husband but he drank, killed himself in a car crash, and left her penniless with an infant son to support. She returned to her family in the nearby town of Opp, and that was where she met William Martin who had been drafted into the Confederate army more than sixty years earlier. He was at least eighty-one and possibly older. He had already been married twice, had twelve children and several grandchildren.

There was no courtship. 'We jus' met at random, first one thing then another. We jus' talked over the fence and he asked me to marry him,' Mrs Martin recalled. She consented, but love had nothing to do with it. They hadn't even kissed. She hated living at home with eight overbearing brothers and 'I needed somebody to help me raise my son. He drawed a good pension. He drawed $50 a month which was a lot of money back then. It was during the Hoover times. You could get a sack of flour for 25 cents, yer know, and a gallon of cooking oil for 25 or 30 cents.'

They married on 10 December, 1927, when she was twenty-one. A year later they had William Junior. She kept house for the old man, cooked for him, cut his hair, shaved him. 'I liked him all right. He was good to me,' she said, but he was 'jealous as he could be' and prone to rages if he thought other men were eyeing his pretty young wife. 'Everyone said I was nice-looking,' she recalled.

They had been married five years when her husband collapsed at a Confederate reunion in Montgomery, the state capital, and a few days later he died. Within six months she had married his seventeen-year-old grandson, Charlie Martin, and although he was a chronic drunkard the marriage lasted fifty years until Charlie died in 1983. Her own weakness was for snuff.

Local people knew Mrs Martin was a Confederate widow, and the *Elba Clipper* reported as much when Daisy Cave died in 1990, but the national media paid little attention to claims by a tiny newspaper from deepest Alabama. That changed only in 1996 when Ken Chancey, a local dentist and Civil War buff who was distressed by her poverty, did some research, discovered she was eligible for a Confederate widow's pension, and persuaded the astonished state of Alabama to give her a generous monthly stipend. Confident there were no more widows left alive, Alabama had dismantled its arrangements for supporting Confederate pensions back in the early eighties.

Mrs Martin was suddenly able to buy herself new false teeth, a new hearing aid, and air-conditioning, though none were in evidence when I visited. More than that, she became an instant celebrity and an icon for the legions of white southerners who still wallow in nostalgia for the Confederacy and the 'Lost Cause'. Mrs Martin was fêted at the Sons of Confederate Veterans centennial convention in Richmond, Virginia. She led a parade in Georgia, opened a Confederate museum in Tennessee and met George Wallace, the former governor of Alabama and arch-segregationist, who declared he would not have missed the meeting for $10,000.

On her living-room wall are framed proclamations from Alabama's governor, the state senate, the Military Order of Stars and Bars and Elba's mayor. On her table is a silver trophy presented to her by the Georgia branch of the Sons of Confederate Veterans, and on the television flowers delivered by an unknown well-wisher the previous day. She receives mail from admirers across the country. She is, after all, the last living link to the bloodiest and most momentous conflict in American history, but she is also, to be honest, an extraordinarily fragile link.

Mrs Martin was only married to her second husband for five years, and that was well over sixty years ago. Press her about his role in the Civil War and she can recall practically nothing except some fragment about how 'when it was sleet or rainin' they would build a lil' ol' bridge across a creek and put their blankets and things on it to keep from sleepin' in the mud and water'. She dimly recalls that he fought in Georgia and Virginia but 'no, sir,' she told me, 'he never did talk to me about none of his doings in the war'.

Mrs Martin has no letters, no possessions, no mementoes whatsoever of her second husband save for a single oval-shaped photograph that hangs amid the proclamations on her wall, just beneath a portrait of the Confederate general Robert E. Lee. 'It's bin in the family all these years,' she said. 'After he passed away someone brought it back to me. Dunno who.' The photograph's edges are torn. It is faded and yellowed with age but there he is – a trim, handsome, unsmiling white-haired man with a thick moustache who, by enlisting in a rebel army in 1864, enables his widow to receive roughly $2,500 a month in the final years of the 1990s.

I stayed in Elba at Aunt B's bed-and-breakfast, a lovely old southern home with polished wood floors, high ceilings and white wicker rocking chairs on the verandah. Aunt B was a warm, bubbly woman whose real name was Barbara Hudson. The day after I visited Mrs Martin, she happened to be hosting the Elba study group – seven or eight genteel ladies who met monthly to have an elegant afternoon tea and hold discussions. Would I mind talking to them, Barbara asked? Of course not, I said.

I told them what I'd seen and where I was going, the discussion broadened, and before long we were arguing about creationism. To my amazement I was the only one there who subscribed to the theory of evolution. Without a single exception the ladies believed the world was created in six days exactly as described in the Book of Genesis. They utterly rejected the idea that man had evolved from apes, though one volunteered that she knew a black man who looked very like a monkey. 'This,' I was forcibly reminded, 'is the Bible belt.'

The topic had arisen because Alabama had recently become the first state in the nation to insert a disclaimer in its schools' biology textbooks casting doubt on the theory of evolution. It reads: 'This textbook discusses evolution, a controversial theory some scientists present as a scientific explanation for the origin of living things, such as plants, animals and humans. No one was present when life first appeared on earth. Therefore, any statement about life's origins should be considered as theory, not fact.' In addition, Alabama's Republican governor, Fob James, had sent every science teacher in Alabama a book called *Darwin on Trial* that highlights supposed weaknesses in the theory of evolution.

Alabama was not alone in questioning Darwinism. A few months before my visit the Tennessee legislature only narrowly rejected a bill to ban the teaching of 'godless' evolution as a fact. In states like Texas, Ohio, Florida, Georgia and New Mexico, and in numerous counties and school districts around the country, creationists were pressing hard, and with some success, for restrictions on how evolution could be taught. Polls showed more than half of all Americans inclined more to the biblical than the scientific version of creation. The issue had become so controversial that some teachers were now avoiding it altogether, while the superintendent of one Kentucky county simply had the relevant pages of his schools' textbook glued together. More than seventy years after the celebrated 'Monkey Trial' that ended with John Scopes being fined $100 for teaching evolution in his Tennessee classroom, America's creationists were on the offensive again, only this time the ground rules were somewhat different.

For decades following the Scopes trial America's textbook publishers had almost entirely omitted the theory of evolution, but by the early 1980s they had grown sufficiently bold that Louisiana was provoked into passing an 'equal time' law insisting creationism and evolution be taught side by side as alternative theories. In 1987 the US Supreme Court overturned that law, declaring that creationism was a religious belief and its teaching violated the constitutionally

mandated separation of church and state. No longer able to promote creationism in the classroom, its supporters were forced to
change tactics and were now trying to discredit evolution.

I was curious. Who were these people? Did they really believe
that Genesis should be taken literally, that the earth was created in
six days, and that all mankind was descended from Adam and Eve?
I telephoned Eunie Smith, president of the Alabama branch of the
Eagle Forum, an ultra-conservative Christian organisation that had
led the fight for the disclaimer. We arranged to meet in what turned
out to be a very comfortable suburban house in the hills above the
once-great steel city of Birmingham. It also turned out that I was
meeting not just Eunie but Joan Kendall, another Eagle Forum
God-and-country type whose house this was, Norris Anderson, an
academic who had prepared the Eagle Forum's case against the
offending textbooks, and Norris' wife, Judy, who was no shrinking
violet either.

What followed can only be described as a rout. I had just driven
120 miles up from Elba in lashing rain. I was playing away. My
familiarity with the finer points of the theory of evolution left much
to be desired, and it was one against four. For two hours I was verbally pummelled, assaulted with facts and figures, assailed with
arguments. I would inwardly groan as Norris produced from his
briefcase yet another file or fat book with yellow markers protruding from relevant pages. The women bustled in and out, making
photocopies of quotes, votes and documents I simply had to have.
With the sweetest of smiles they battered me with science, or anti-
science, or pseudo-science, until they had comprehensively crushed
my last pathetic displays of resistance. In the following weeks, lest
my heretical ideas might be trying to reassert themselves, they sent
books, videos and pamphlets to my home in Washington.

They were not religious zealots, they insisted. The zealots were
the textbook writers who presented their 'religion of evolution' as
absolute fact, who were indoctrinating American kids with the belief
that they were created not by God for some higher purpose, but –
like the worm or the fish – by a complete fluke. Listen to this,
they'd say, and rattle off quotes from textbooks – 'Evolution is

random and undirected . . . You are an animal, and share a common heritage with earthworms . . . There is no doubt among scientists that humans evolved from common ancestors they shared with other living primates.'

Such teachings had dire social consequences, Joan argued. 'When students are taught day after day for twelve, fourteen, sixteen years that they are animals that share a common heritage with earthworms we should not be surprised when we see children acting out their common heritage – shooting up drugs, killing one another, being totally amoral. They are just acting out what they are taught.'

The Darwinian theory of evolution was full of holes, Norris continued. He produced a simple mousetrap and pointed out the constituent parts. What were the chances of such a device being created by accident, he asked? Infinitesimal! Someone had to have designed and assembled it, yet evolutionists refuse to accept that some outside intelligence created vastly more complex life forms. What's more, he said, evolutionists cited natural selection, or survival of the fittest, as the means by which life evolved into higher forms, but suppose you had a row of mousetraps, each missing just one part. They would all be equally useless, so how could natural selection ever have produced a working mousetrap? And another question. Where did the constituent parts themselves come from?

That was not all. There were, Norris contended, glaring gaps in the fossil chains. The major groups of animals all appeared quite suddenly. No new major groups of living things had appeared in 500 million years. There was no physical evidence of one species turning into another. In the heat of the moment I struggled to produce any answers to those assertions.

My tormentors insisted their goal was merely 'intellectual honesty' and 'academic excellence'. They denied trying to foist their religious beliefs on anyone. They refused even to admit they were creationists or to discuss their religious convictions. Their beliefs were not relevant, they insisted. I did manage to extract an admission from Eunie that she was a Baptist and definitely did not believe she shared common ancestors with monkeys. Joan's religious orientation was obvious from the shelf full of Bibles and biblical studies behind Norris' right shoulder. Norris remained thoroughly opaque. When I asked if he went to church on Sundays he replied: 'What do you mean by church?' It was like talking to Dr Buzzard.

The next morning I went to Montgomery to see Fob James, the governor, in his great, dark wood-panelled office in Alabama's white domed Capitol. He'd entertained the Board of Education meeting that had ordered the disclaimer with a theatrical performance designed to ridicule the idea that man evolved from apes. According to the *Montgomery Advertiser* he 'lumbered across the front of the auditorium bent at the waist and dragging his arms to mimic a monkey, gradually standing upright as he moved about the room'.

Getting to see the governor was not particularly difficult. Montgomery is only a little place. The streets around the Capitol are practically deserted. The demand for parking spaces is so low that the city has what must surely be the world's cheapest meters – five cents an hour – and the fine for a parking ticket is a mere $4 (I know because I got one).

It was hard to believe that this somnolent town on the Alabama River had witnessed so many tumultuous events. It was the birth-place of the Confederacy, and a little bronze star on the steps of the Capitol marked the spot where Jefferson Davis was sworn in as the Confederacy's first President in 1861. A few blocks away is the Dexter Avenue Baptist Church from which, after Rosa Parks refused to surrender her bus seat to a white man in 1955, a young pastor named Martin Luther King masterminded the year-long bus boy-cott that launched America's Civil Rights Movement. From the governor's office George Wallace had led the battle against racial desegregation in the 1960s, famously proclaiming 'segregation now, segregation tomorrow, segregation for ever'. In that same office Fob James announced to a British journalist named Martin Fletcher that Alabama's remaining evolutionists – all six or seven of them – were to be summarily executed.

I exaggerate, of course, but Mr James is nothing if not blunt – delightfully so after my experience the previous evening. He didn't want evolution taught as a fact. He didn't like it as a theory, even. 'I would reject the idea that I came from a monkey,' he declared, 'though I would protect your right one hundred per cent to believe that you came from a monkey.'

'So where did man come from?' I asked.

'I think God created man.'

'Do you believe the world was made in six days?'

'I take the Bible literally. I haven't seen any book yet that I thought contradicts it accurately.'

Was he concerned that Alabama might be seen as a hotbed of crazy religious-right creationists? 'No,' he replied, and that was that.

Mr James was in his shirt-sleeves and had a window wide open despite the cold outside. He was a bluff, gruff, likeable character of sixty-two. His first name was really Forrest, and his middle name Hood, the surnames of two famous Confederate generals. He had been a star football player at college who went on to play professionally for the Montreal Alouettes, and his Alabama accent was so thick a Canadian petrol pump attendant once told him: 'I'm sorry, sir. We only speak English and French here.' He made his fortune by developing plastic-covered concrete barbells, became governor in 1978, left to run a Gulf Coast marina and won the governorship a second time in 1994. His second term had been most memorable up to that point for his reintroduction of chain gangs, and his promise to have the National Guard protect a state judge who was refusing to remove the Ten Commandments from his courtroom wall.

'Let me ask you a question,' Mr James abruptly demanded when I'd finished asking mine. He started rummaging through papers on his vast expanse of desk. 'Where's that report?' he demanded, and sent an aide off to search for it.

While we were waiting he waxed lyrical about the 'old girl', Margaret Thatcher, and said he'd read every book Churchill ever wrote. It was Sir Winston who had really inspired him to enter public service. The governor was warming up. 'Let me tell you another reason Churchill inspires me,' he continued, flourishing a box of cigars. 'I think we ought to shoot anybody who smokes cigarettes, but to take your cigars away from you is a form of oppression. Only communists would do that, so you see Churchill was also a great inspiration to those of us who smoke cigars.' The cigars were Cuban, I noticed. I politely refrained from asking the governor where he'd got them, because importing them into America is illegal.

The aide returned with the missing report. The governor came round from behind his desk and sat down on a leather chair beside me. He explained how he had recently been pilloried in the liberal media for suggesting a bit of 'buttwhipping' did a child good, and had begun to doubt his own civility. The report was a wire service story on how the Archbishop of Canterbury had come out in favour of corporal punishment. Mr James began reading it out in tones of mock horror.

'Lord Tebbit, former chairman of the Conservative party, described the advice as eminently sensible – "I was caned at school and I suspect I would have been more unruly had I not been." Can you imagine it? Can you imagine my British friends caning somebody?' the rumpled governor exclaimed. 'You're a bunch of damned rednecks!'

'Look here!' he continued. 'Sir Ivan Lawrence, Conservative MP for Burton, said the Archbishop's comments were in total accordance with common sense and the experience of most parents. "I got a good hiding . . ." Hiding! Hiding!

'There's another word here that shocked me. It borders on child abuse and came from Mr David Plunkett (sic), Labour's Education spokesman. "There are very few children who have never been smacked . . . I think it's a perfectly reasonable way to bring home the severity of what a child has done." Smacking! You're smacking your children in Great Britain? I always thought my friends in Great Britain were genteel and refined!

'Here's what I conclude. I plead guilty to being a redneck, but evidently the Archbishop and many Members of Parliament are also rednecks. That means the world's redneck population is increasing, and if it continues to increase I think we can be very optimistic about the next century. I think it will be one of civility, decency and courtesy and one of people acting like ladies and gentlemen.'

With that ringing declaration the governor concluded our

interview. 'Thank you so very much,' he said, shaking my hand. 'Take care.'

It was quite a performance – all the more so if you consider that a convicted murderer was due to be executed in Alabama that night and the governor alone had the power to commute his sentence. I don't mean to suggest that Mr James was ignoring the matter. Indeed he assured me he took his duties exceptionally seriously where capital punishment was concerned. It was just that the impending execution did not seem to be preying on his mind or in any way oppressing him, and it duly went ahead.

The day became increasingly surreal. I went off to lunch at the columned-and-porticoed Montgomery Country Club with Alfred Sawyer, the governor's communications director. He was as much of a character as his boss – a former journalist who had found God, become an Episcopalian priest, and spent three years in a parish in Finchley, north London, before going to Jerusalem to run the Middle East's oldest Protestant church.

We ate in a palatial dining room overlooking the golf course with a young state congressman named Perry Oliver Hooper II whose father, Perry Oliver Hooper I, was the chief justice of Alabama's Supreme Court. One quick telephone call and Judge Hooper, the embodiment of Southern charm, spent the rest of the afternoon giving me a personal guided tour of the court as if he had nothing else in the world to do.

The next day, which was sunny but still bitterly cold, I took Route 80 west from Montgomery through a string of counties known as the Black Belt. The name came from the colour of the rich alluvial soil, but could equally well refer to the colour of the overwhelming majority of the inhabitants. After a while, I began to understand how exposed and lonely a black person must feel in somewhere like Idaho or New England.

Fifteen miles beyond Montgomery I made a brief detour to Hayneville, the seat of Lowndes County, to see if it had erected a sign saying 'Welcome to the Tort Capital of America'. It hadn't, but it should have, for over the previous few years the impoverished people of Lowndes County had developed a brilliant wheeze for redressing America's widening income gap.

It works like this. Some impoverished citizen finds a pretext to file a lawsuit against a giant manufacturer or insurance company, preferably from the Yankee north. The plaintiff's lawyer uses his twelve vetoes to obtain a jury of similarly downtrodden citizens – not hard in a county of 12,000 people where seventy-five per cent are black, forty per cent live in poverty and the average per capita income is barely $7,000. He plays on their deep-seated sense of grievance, of having been exploited for far too long, and invites them to teach the offending company a lesson. The jurors happily comply, awarding the plaintiff not just compensation but some astronomical sum in punitive damages. The judge in such cases will sometimes reduce these damages, but that requires courage as the lawyer is likely to be a big contributor to his re-election campaign. Some giant out-of-state company is screwed, the plaintiff's lawyer pockets a third of the proceeds and everyone – at least in Alabama – goes home laughing.

Between 1989 and June 1996 juries in Lowndes County had in this way enriched their peers by a staggering $155 million, according to a Yale Law School study. Nor was Lowndes County alone. Half the counties in Alabama had cottoned on to this ploy, though few so brazenly. During that same six-year period Alabama juries had smashed all records by awarding their fellow Alabamans no less than $767 million in punitive damages, all but $129 million of which was against out-of-state defendants. People were now rushing to sue for the most piddling offences and matters had reached such a pass that insurance and other companies were pulling out of Alabama.

The Lowndes County courthouse was a white stucco building on one side of Hayneville's pleasant, grassy town square. I had time to spare, so I found the circuit judge's office and asked the clerk for a rundown of recent punitive damage awards, hoping to extract some particularly juicy examples. She smiled knowingly and led me into a sideroom. She pulled a fat blue file off a shelf, then another and then another. I began to comprehend the scale of the task I was taking on. No more, I cried, and fled out into the sunshine.

I walked around for a while, being excessively polite to everyone I passed in case they sued me for causing emotional distress. I then drove away, reflecting with wry detachment on what I'd seen.

Few places in America had suppressed black people as ruthlessly as Lowndes County. Not until 1965 had a black person been allowed to register to vote there. In March that same year three Klansmen had shot dead Viola Liuzzo, a thirty-nine-year-old white woman from Michigan who had been giving some black civil rights activists a lift. Five months later a state employee shot and killed a twenty-six-year-old white theological student, Jonathan Daniels, following his release from the county jail for participating in a civil rights demonstration. In both cases all-white juries sitting in the Hayneville courthouse acquitted the defendants despite overwhelming evidence against them.

Now the blacks had gained control and – like whites before them – were twisting the system to their advantage. In a sense it was payback time, and who could blame them?

I rejoined Route 80 and drove on to Selma. This is one of the most famous stretches of highway in America, though the surrounding land was flat, agricultural and pretty dull to look at. On 7 March 1965 600 civil rights activists tried to march 65 miles from Selma to Montgomery to petition George Wallace, the governor, for the right to vote. Egged on by Wallace, state troopers confronted them on the Edmund Pettus Bridge which crosses the Alabama River outside Selma and brutally turned them back with billy clubs and tear gas. 'Get those god-damned niggers,' shouted Jim Clark, Selma's infamous Sheriff, as he unloosed his men. Two days later Martin Luther King tried to lead another march to Montgomery and that too was blocked. A federal court intervened, Wallace was forced to back down, and King finally arrived at the Capitol in Montgomery with a following of 25,000. The media coverage of these events shocked millions of Americans and helped secure the passage of the historic Voting Rights Act.

A couple of hours further on I came to Greene County, 631 square miles of old cotton plantation land near the Mississippi border where Nathan Forrest recruited the first members of the original Ku Klux Klan in the late 1800s. Greene County was one of the first to take advantage of the Voting Rights Act and in 1969 became only the second county in the South where a black majority seized political power from a segregationist white establishment. Unfortunately that was probably the county's finest hour, and if the late Dr King could visit the place now he would find his famous 'dream' quite spectacularly unfulfilled.

After nearly three decades of black rule, Greene County is still the poorest in Alabama. Its population has dropped to a mere 10,000, of whom more than eighty per cent are black and forty-five per cent are living below the poverty line. It is $3 million in debt and recently became the first county in the state ever to file for bankruptcy. Alabama's attorney general was investigating the disappearance or misuse of nearly $800,000 from the county's coffers. The county's chief of staff, who treated himself to regular trips to Paris, owed thousands of dollars in travel advances, and the FBI was investigating allegations of voter fraud following elections in 1994 in which absentee ballots accounted for an incredible third of all votes cast.

Moreover, Greene County was, in practical terms, as segregated now as it was in the 1950s. Blacks and whites lived side by side but seldom mixed. Black kids went to the public schools, and white kids to the private Warrior Academy in the county town of Eutaw. There was a black swimming pool and a white swimming pool, a black bank and a white one, black cemeteries and white ones. The two races worshipped at different churches. One newspaper, the *Democrat*, catered for black readers and another, the *Independent*, for whites. I was told some doctors had separate waiting rooms for blacks and whites, though I did not see them. And while blacks had a virtual monopoly on political power, those whites that had not fled retained the economic power. They still owned most of the businesses and land.

I had first visited Greene County early in 1996 after three black churches tucked away in forests surrounding the tiny town of Boligee had been mysteriously burned to the ground in the middle of the night. Dozens of Southern black churches had been destroyed in a similar manner during the previous three years. Along with scores of other reporters from Washington and New York I flew in for a day to write what seemed a straightforward story about how white racists, emulating the 'night riders' of the KKK during the civil rights era, were destroying the traditional centres of rural black life.

Local black leaders certainly encouraged us in that belief, and Buddy Lavender, a sixty-eight-year-old white catfish-and-crawfish farmer with shaggy grey beard and dungarees who served as Boligee's mayor, fire chief and police chief, played into their hands. He made what seemed at the time preposterous hints that blacks might have torched the churches themselves to divert attention from their own misdeeds. As a result of all the publicity, donations and white volunteers poured into Boligee from across the country to help rebuild the churches. That all happened, however, before the charges of corruption and mismanagement by the county's black officials came to light, and I began to wonder whether the media had not been hoodwinked.

I wanted to revisit Boligee in any case because it was such a wonderful throwback. It was unbleached, utterly unhomogenised. It could have been the set for one of those nostalgic films about the Old South like *Fried Green Tomatoes*. The town is so small it appears on maps only because there is nowhere bigger in this remote corner of western Alabama. Its 270 inhabitants live in shacks or antebellum homes that are equally decayed. It straddles a railway line, and is cut in half for fifteen minutes at a time while 100-car freight trains trundle through on their way south to New Orleans. It has a dilapidated café with one end for whites and the other for blacks, a single blinking traffic light, one payphone, a post office and a dark, cavernous store with tin cans on wooden shelves around the walls that can't have changed in fifty years. 'There used to be eleven stores, but there ain't but me left,' said the man behind the counter. There were also two abandoned cotton gins, one with a faded, peeling advertisement for Leonora Flour painted on its brickwork, and a boarded-up building that was once, according to the chiselled lettering above the doorway, the Boligee Banking Company.

This time, however, I arrived to find that the 20th century was just reaching Boligee – and a good job too as it is so nearly over. The town was finally having a proper sewage system installed and it was crawling with workmen. Previously, said Buddy Lavender, three quarters of its homes had either no septic tank at all or tanks that didn't work. Buddy's life had also changed. He was no longer mayor, his wife had left him, and he had suffered a heart attack.

He blamed the furore surrounding the church burnings for all three, particularly his electoral defeat. About $40,000 of the donations that had flowed in from around the country had been sent directly to him as mayor, but he had refused to hand that money over to a rival fund organised by Greene County's black leaders because he didn't trust them. In light of later revelations that may have been prudent, but the county's black political machine had extracted its revenge by orchestrating his defeat in that summer's election. Buddy, who had won five previous elections with bi-racial support and was one of the last two white mayors left in Greene County, lost by sixty votes to thirty with all but three black votes going to his opponent.

I spent an enjoyable few hours with him on this second visit. His various reverses had not extinguished his *joie de vivre*. We toured his catfish pond and he explained the difference between Louisiana swamp and Australian red claw crawfish. He showed me a beaver dam, his orchard, his vegetable patch and his menagerie of chickens, dogs and cats. We ate what he called 'good ol' country cookin'' – stew, mashed potatoes, beans, gravy and cornbread – at the white end of the Boligee café. We bumped into a deputy sheriff who wanted to serve him with divorce papers from his wife, but Buddy refused to take them. 'You ain't seen me,' he grinned, and roared off in his pick-up.

He also showed me his amazing arsenal. He had ten rifles in a cupboard in his living room, one by the backdoor, three behind his bedroom door and four more in his bedroom cupboard. He kept three revolvers in a box in his bedroom and a fourth beneath his mattress. Each had a purpose, he insisted. There was a squirrel gun, a turkey gun, a snake gun and so on. He was still Boligee's police and fire chiefs, jobs for which he got little more than his expenses. His police patrol car was rusting away beside his home so he had simply transferred his handcuffs and blue flashing light to his pick-up. There were more guns in there – two revolvers, a rifle and a semi-automatic which he jokingly called his 'people gun', though he admitted there were few riots to suppress in Boligee.

Buddy loaded the semi-automatic and we ended the afternoon by using a plastic Coke bottle for target-practice in the field behind the abandoned school next to his home. Afterwards we went inside to escape the cold. 'That big mama'll get you warm,' he said, pointing to a large gas fire.

Buddy is easy to portray as a racist redneck. He certainly looks the part, has the requisite country accent, and doesn't mince his words. He called a public-housing complex in Boligee the 'incubator' because young black girls on welfare 'made babies' there. He pointed to black youths in flashy cars outside the store and called them crack dealers. In both instances he was probably right. He recalled seeing three black men lynched as a boy in his native Mississippi and regularly used the N-word. 'You know what that there black dog's called?' he'd ask. 'Nigger dog!' But he insisted he used the term affectionately.

'I was raised on a cotton plantation and they was niggers then and they'ull always be niggers to me,' he said. 'When my daddy used to call a man an ol' nigger it was someone he cared about.' I witnessed him bantering happily with several blacks during the day. For twenty years he had enjoyed their support at election time. He did not exude hate like John Howard, the owner of the Redneck Shop back in Laurens, South Carolina. Buddy was a character who refused to conform to the demands of these politically correct times and had paid the price.

Before I left he drove me to the sites of the arsons. Where there had been charred timbers and ashes on my previous visit there were now three splendid new churches entirely built with the money and labour of white well-wishers from across America. A huge police and FBI investigation had failed to find the arsonist. Buddy was more convinced than ever that a black hand may have been responsible. I had absolutely no idea who the culprit was, but this time I was less inclined to dismiss his allegation out of hand. I was beginning to learn that in places like Greene County nothing was just black and white.

11

Winners and Losers

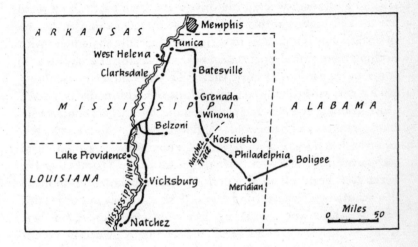

'Even Mississippi, on some remote tomorrow, may reach the estate of Poland between the Two World Wars,' wrote the journalist H. L. Mencken in 1956. I crossed into the Magnolia State past a sign that said 'Welcome to Mississippi – Litter Free by 2003', as if litter was its greatest problem. I stopped at the Welcome Centre where ladies behind the counter almost demanded that you accept free Cokes or coffee. I read a message from Kirk Fordice, Mississippi's governor, modestly welcoming visitors to 'the most captivating locale in the known universe'. This was a state clearly bent on shaking its age-old reputation for coming 48th, 49th or 50th by whatever standard you wished to measure it, Mississippi's only serious rivals being Louisiana and West Virginia.

I checked into a Days Inn in Meridien and studied my map. I wanted to drive the length of the Mississippi Delta, a region that Jesse Jackson, the civil rights leader, once labelled 'America's

Ethiopia'. Should I take Highway 61 from south to north and then head westwards across Arkansas, or from north to south and then cut across Louisiana? It made not a jot of difference, so I plumped for the latter and the next day drove 240 miles up to the north-western corner of Mississippi.

I love these long drives. Whenever possible I avoid interstates and stick to back roads where I can drive at my own pace. Often these are the old highways that have been rendered redundant by the interstates but run parallel to them, and I usually share them with nothing more than the occasional buzzard pecking at squashed possums or armadillos. I love the space, the endlessly changing landscapes, the little towns each with its own distinctive character. I love stopping at diners and petrol stations for brief encounters with utter strangers and being told – almost ordered – on leaving: 'Yew come back and see us agin, yew hear?' There is always something to see – a swamp, some river twice the width of the Thames that I've never even heard of, an abandoned shack, a boarded-up motel, a derelict drive-in cinema. Land is in such short supply in Europe that sites like those would instantly have been redeveloped, but here there are great tracts of untamed land seemingly owned by no one and used for nothing.

I usually stop and read the historical markers – which tell me, for example, that Demopolis, Alabama, was founded in 1817 by exiled Bonapartists who tried but failed to grow grapes and olives. I play little games like seeing how many miles I can coax from an $11 tank of petrol – my record is 423. I collect the admonitions posted outside the multitude of little churches – 'The Smallest Deed is Better than the Greatest Intention' or 'Where Are You Going – Heaven or Eternal Hell?' I stop to read the gushing inscriptions to 'Our Heroes' that you find on the Confederate war memorials in every town square in the South. 'Love's Tribute to the Noble Men who Marched 'neath the Flag of the Stars and Bars and were Faithful to the End,' read one. 'On Fame's eternal camping ground their silent tents are spread, And Glory guards with solemn round the bivouacs of the dead,' read another.

Down here it is sometimes easy to forget that rebellious Dixie was crushed in the Civil War and lost more than a quarter of a million men. Southerners have thoroughly romanticised both the conflict and their leaders. They are still convinced of the justness of their cause which was not slavery, they insist, but states' rights. They still refer to it as 'the War Between the States', 'the War of Northern Aggression' or even 'the late unpleasantness', but definitely not the Civil War. Mark Twain once wrote that 'in the South the war is what A.D. is elsewhere: they date from it'.

I was the first writer I could recall to travel through Mississippi when it was anything other than 100 degrees and steamy. It was certainly sunny, but so cold there was ice on the cypress swamps and catfish ponds. I went through Philadelphia, a town where three civil rights workers were arrested for 'speeding' in June 1964, taken to the local jail, and released late at night to be chased by Klansmen along the country roads. They were caught and shot, and their bodies were hidden in an earth dam. Eight Klansmen served short sentences for conspiracy, but none was ever charged with murder. On this particular day – a Sunday – I found the good folk of Philadelphia coming out of church, and the town seemed a model of tranquillity, but it will be decades before the South can erase such memories.

I crossed the Natchez Trace, the old trail by which traders who floated their goods down the Mississippi to Natchez or New Orleans returned to the Tennessee or Ohio River valleys. In the National Park Service visitors centre I was given a hand-drawn card from a pile produced by children from the local elementary school. Mine was from a girl called Marissa, had coloured crayon scribblings on the front, and inside it said 'Howdy ya'll'. I passed through Kosciusko, which proudly proclaimed itself the birthplace of Oprah Winfrey, through Winona, Grenada and Batesville, past a hundred little churches with overflowing car parks. With the possible exception of Ireland, America is the most religious land in Christendom, with fully a third of its adults claiming to be born-again Christians.

Finally I left behind the rolling hills and forests and found myself crossing a land of flat, black, alluvial earth that stretched far away to distant lines of skeletal trees. This was the start of the Delta, a swathe of former flood plains 200 miles long and 60 miles wide that flanks the Mississippi from Memphis to Vicksburg. Often referred to as 'the most southern place on earth', the Delta boasts the richest farmland but the poorest and blackest people in America.

Before the Civil War the owners of the Delta's cotton and rice plantations grew fabulously wealthy thanks to armies of slaves and the incredible richness of the soil. After slavery was abolished those blacks and many poor whites continued to work the fields for a wage, or as sharecroppers, while the landowners strutted around the ornate lobby of the magnificent old Peabody Hotel in Memphis. Not coincidentally the Delta was the birthplace of the Blues, the soulful laments of the black cotton pickers.

After World War Two came an agricultural revolution that largely dispensed with the need for human labour. The landowners began mechanising and using pesticides. Today rows of tractors and giant combines stand outside their handsome farms, and irrigation pipes on tall, spindly wheels each stretch for half-a-mile or more across their cotton, corn and soyabean fields. Blacks went from being a necessary nuisance to an unnecessary one. In a migration comparable to that of the 'Okies' moving from Oklahoma to California during the Dust Bowl era, tens of thousands of blacks left to search for industrial jobs in booming northern cities like Chicago and Detroit. Those left behind sank ever deeper into poverty. After generations of actual or *de facto* serfdom they lacked the ability to help themselves. More than ever the Delta became a land of the very rich or very poor with practically no one in between.

I was heading for Tunica County, which borders the Mississippi a little below Memphis. Throughout the 1970s and 1980s it enjoyed the dubious distinction of being the poorest place in the entire United States, with half its dwindling population living below the poverty line. But what did I find? Brand new roads slicing across the vast plain, gleaming new motels and petrol stations, giant billboards promising untold riches. Beyond all this, stretched out along the eastern bank of the Mississippi River and brilliantly illuminated against the darkening sky, was a circus big top, an Irish castle, an old Wild West town and numerous other casinos decked out in fantastic guises. Mark Twain could never have imagined such creations. From being America's poorest county Tunica had, thanks to legalised gambling, acquired almost overnight the fastest growing economy in America.

It is an extraordinary story. In 1990 legislation permitting riverboat gambling on the Mississippi slipped almost unnoticed through the state legislature. DeSoto County, which stands between Tunica and Memphis and is relatively wealthy, held a referendum and rejected riverboats. In struggling Tunica there was no such opposition. In the autumn of 1992 two brothers named Ron and Rick Shilling floated a barge down from Kentucky to Mhoon Landing, an old dock near the town of Tunica, and opened a small casino called Splash. It was an instant sensation. Gamblers poured down the narrow, bumpy road from Memphis, queued for hours and happily paid a $10 entrance fee in order to play the slot machines. 'It shocked the gaming world,' Ken Murphree, Tunica County's administrator, told me.

The big boys in Las Vegas suddenly realised the possibilities. Unlike other states, Mississippi's legislation, a carbon copy of Nevada's, had no limits on bets. Tunica was within a few hours drive not just of Memphis but of Atlanta, Chicago, Nashville, St Louis and a huge mid-western market. There was also a wonderful loophole in the Mississippi law. The riverboat casinos were allowed to be on the Mississippi River or its 'navigable tributaries'. In no time the major casino companies were building giant ponds a safe distance from the turbulent Mississippi, connecting them to the river with trenches, floating in huge flat-topped barges, and then refilling the trenches. On those barges they constructed their 24-hour gambling halls which were seamlessly joined to the casinos' hotels and restaurants. They still insist on calling the casinos 'boats'.

Tom Dashiell, a vice-president of Fitzgeralds casino, actually took me down through a trap door to show me the barges on which his establishment was unquestionably floating in a pool of murky green water. He also pointed out the hydraulic pumps that kept the casino level when several tons of coins were removed from the 'boat' each day.

The casinos went up at a dizzying pace, each new one

leapfrogging northwards past the others in order to be nearer Memphis, surreal monuments to extravagance and self-indulgence in a land of poverty and deprivation. Even at 8.00 a.m. on a Monday morning in January, I found scores of people – drawn almost exclusively from the third of the American population that is seriously overweight – mindlessly shoving quarters into fruit machines on the floor of Fitzgeralds. Revenues from 'gaming', as it is euphemistically called, have soared to nearly $1 billion in just five years. Tunica has swiftly become the biggest gambling centre between Las Vegas and Atlantic City. The ten casinos have created more jobs – 12,000 – than there are people – 8,300 – in the county. The number of hotel rooms has rocketed from twenty in which, as Mr Murphree tactfully put it, 'you wouldn't want to stay', to 6,000.

The county, which receives four per cent of the casinos total proceeds, has seen its annual revenues balloon from $3 million to $28 million. 'It's phenomenal. It's beyond anyone's comprehension who lived here and saw the county as it was,' said Mr Murphree, a sober public servant in his early fifties who was born and raised in Tunica. He is building new schools, new roads, a new jail, new community centres. He is planning golf courses, shopping malls, a Blues museum, even a botanical garden – all this in a place that was until very recently the epitome of hopelessness.

For Tunica at least there is no obvious downside. Unemployment in the county has plummeted, wages have soared and for the first time in memory the population is growing. A few local people have lost their shirts but they would probably have lost them in any case in midnight poker games. Mr Murphree and his wife invited me home for dinner that night. 'Like a lot of folk raised in the South and the Bible Belt I don't think gambling is good for society,' Mr Murphree confided over the chicken casserole. 'But if you ask me if it's good for Tunica the answer is undoubtedly yes . . . Tunica was no smarter than any other county around here. We were just more desperate.'

Thirty miles north of Tunica in the tiny town of Walls (population

300) I met the director of a Catholic charity called the Sacred Heart League that does missionary and welfare work in northern Mississippi. Roger Courts deplored the new casinos. Walls lies just off the new four-lane highway between Memphis and Tunica County, and Mr Courts told me its bank had been held up three times, and its post office once, by gamblers who had lost all their money at the tables. Others had turned up desperate on the League's doorstep. In his own way, however, Mr Courts was also a gambler. He was a man who, with one spectacular roll of the dice, had generated nearly $3 million for the deprived children of the Delta.

Though he'd had no relevant experience he'd been convinced he could make a successful commercial movie, backed that belief with $6 million of the League's money, and pulled off one of the most unlikely triumphs in the history of the film industry. I sat in his comfortable office as this tall, soft-spoken, highly-articulate man in his early sixties explained how.

Back in the 1970s, Mr Courts, who has given nearly forty years of his life to the League, became convinced that it would become steadily harder to raise funds through conventional means and 'there had to be a way to get funding other than always begging for it'. He conceived the idea of making a movie. In 1983 he commissioned a feasibility study that said making a full-length feature film was 'very risky, but doable'.

He persuaded his board to back him and paid a well-known writer $60,000 for a screenplay. It proved unusable. Undaunted, he turned to Warren Stitt, a Californian producer who had made advertisements for the League, and Mr Stitt began soliciting scripts. These did not have to be religious, but they did have to be uplifting and reflect Judeo-Christian values. Two hundred scripts and four years later Mr Courts was still searching. 'Everybody knows what's a good story, what's gripping,' he said. 'We were just not going to give an inch till we got the right one.'

In near-desperation Mr Stitt finally introduced Mr Courts to Lee David Zlotoff, a successful television writer who wanted to break into feature films. They met in Hollywood. 'I said we want to make a film that's life-affirming, that espouses a value system people

can emulate, that can help people work out their lives,' Mr Courts
recalled. Mr Zlotoff was enthusiastic but warned: 'I am not a little
Jewish. I'm a lot Jewish.' No problem, said Mr Courts, and paid him
$10,000 to come up with three story concepts.

Three weeks later Mr Zlotoff flew to Memphis to pitch the first
to Mr Courts over dinner at the Peabody Hotel. It was about a
young woman who is released from prison, moves to a small New
England town to start afresh as a cook in a diner called the Spitfire
Grill, and wins redemption through tragedy. 'I immediately said:
"That's it, that's what I've been looking for". I was very moved by it.
I was very teared up,' said Mr Courts.

Mr Courts persuaded the League to invest a further $4 million,
employed a low-cost cast and production team, and had the film
shot in just thirty-six days in a small town in Vermont. There were
numerous setbacks, including the last-minute expenditure of an
additional $500,000 on a new musical score, but Mr Courts was
convinced he was doing what God intended.

'We are supposed to figure out what's God's will for us,' he said.
'You don't do that by a blinding flash. It doesn't come that way. It
comes through a community of people trying to discern what they
should do and spending time thinking and praying. Did I ever get
scared about this? I couldn't count the number of times I woke up
in cold sweats, but my God would tell me through people or events
that we were doing the right thing.'

In January 1996 *The Spitfire Grill* was selected for screening at
Robert Redford's prestigious Sundance film festival in Park City,
Utah. When the film ended a cinema full of Hollywood types gave
it a five-minute standing ovation. A young executive from Castle
Rock Entertainment ran to the nearest telephone, called her company in Los Angeles, and within twenty-four hours it had offered a
record-breaking $10 million for the distribution rights. Mr Courts
flew back to Walls with a profit of at least $2.5 million with which
the League plans to build a new school in the Delta. Its cafeteria will
be called the Spitfire Grill.

In Mr Courts' office pictures of the film's three female stars jostle
for position with those of his many grandchildren. He had been

warned that making a movie was 'the equivalent of rolling craps to build a school', but he had disagreed. It was simply a question of finding the right script, setting a low budget and sticking to it. Like winning gamblers, he has developed a taste for moviemaking. He now heads Gregory Productions, an offshoot of the Sacred Heart League, and is working with the actor Nick Nolte on a new film called *The Best of Enemies* about racial reconciliation in South Carolina.

From Walls it was downhill – and downriver – all the way. I crossed over the broad, chocolate-brown Mississippi into Arkansas, though the Delta is a region with such a strong identity that states are of secondary importance. I wanted to visit West Helena, a town of 10,000 people whose government had been paralysed for over a year because its four black aldermen were boycotting all its meetings. The mayor and the four white aldermen had been solemnly turning up each month, but having to adjourn after sitting around for thirty minutes for lack of a quorum.

Eddie Lee, one of the rebel aldermen, explained that he and his three colleagues had adopted this rather extreme tactic because they believed the council had for far too long lavished funds on the white parts of the town while neglecting the black parts. 'What's the point of going?' Eddie asked. 'If I can't get any groceries why go to the store?'

Eddie, a forty-nine-year-old former electronic technician who now seems to do nothing in particular, gave me a guided tour of West Helena. He certainly seemed to have a point. The white streets were clean and well-paved. There was a pleasant wooded park with a floodlit baseball field, some tennis courts and a whites-only private golf club. The black area – the far side of the Martin Luther King Boulevard – was filthy and run-down, though the residents hardly seemed to be helping themselves.

There were few pavements, just deep ditches filled with water, litter and assorted junk including one dead cat. There was a flat, bland, dismal little park. Most dramatic was the contrast between the adjacent white and black cemeteries. The first was immaculate.

The second was diabolically awful. It was a field of mud with some graves standing in pools of frozen water and others so carelessly covered with earth that you half expected to see limbs or the corners of coffins protruding from the sunken pits. To be fair, a black contractor was responsible for this appalling state of affairs, but Eddie's point was that the town council was doing nothing about it.

'You look at the black cemetery and the white cemetery and you say, "Am I living in the United States or under South African apartheid?",' said Eddie in disgust. 'We don't run nothing but our mouths.'

I crossed back into Mississippi and stopped in the town of Clarksdale. In a legendary local diner called The Ranchero I had an excellent lunch of fried chicken, mashed potatoes, beans, cabbage, cornbread and apple crumble for a mere $4. The walls were covered with photographs of local high school classes and football teams, but interestingly they almost all pre-dated desegregation. I chatted to one of the waitresses. She echoed what several other whites had told me in this overwhelmingly black region – that the white minority is now discriminated against. In almost the same breath she told me she had another job at a white-only country club. Two blacks had tried to join, she said with a grin, but both were blackballed.

The civil rights era is now history, but race still bedevils almost every aspect of Southern life. I read later of a high school in the town of Hernando, Mississippi, that has had two principals – one black and one white, two class presidents, two homecoming queens and two of virtually everything ever since desegregation in 1970.

I wandered round Clarksdale's Delta Blues museum, then continued south on Highway 61, past Alligator, to the little town of Mound Bayou that was founded by blacks, for blacks, more than a hundred years ago and remains all black to this very day. Having now seen it, I find it hard to understand why anyone would want to live there.

Mound Bayou actually began life rather gloriously. In 1887 a freed slave called Isaiah Montgomery and his cousin, Benjamin Green, bought a few thousand acres of wilderness from a railroad company that had just built a line down through the Delta from Memphis to Vicksburg. They moved there with six hundred followers, cleared the land, set up a sawmill and began building a town where they could be their own masters.

By the early 20th century Mound Bayou was a thriving community of about 4,000 people and a sanctuary for oppressed blacks. It had its own railway station which was something of a regional hub. It had its own utilities, bank, hospital and telephone company – the man who installed the exchange and trained its operators was the only white to live there and he only stayed a few months. It had a weekly newspaper called *The Demonstrator*. Montgomery set a high moral tone and there was little crime. In 1907 President Theodore Roosevelt paid Mound Bayou the compliment of stopping his train there during a hunting trip and giving a ten-minute speech in which he called the town 'an object lesson full of hope for colored people.'

Those are not the words that spring to mind today. The town's decline began in the 1920s with a slump in the price of cotton and Isaiah Montgomery's death. It has continued ever since. Mound Bayou is now just another dying community on the great plains of the Delta but all the more poignant for its history. It was probably the saddest place I'd seen since Middlesboro, Kentucky.

Its population has fallen to little over 2,000. The railway line has been ripped up, leaving a great gash through the middle of the town. The main street is lined by failed businesses and abandoned stores. The once-fine hospital is a derelict eyesore, and the two-storey brick building that housed the bank is falling inwards on itself. The only elegant house left is a brick mansion of twenty-one rooms that Montgomery built for himself in 1920, four years before his death. The town has no industry, is heavily in debt, and will soon be by-passed by a new highway.

I wandered into the town hall to see if the mayor was around. It was late afternoon and the place was practically deserted. I found an elderly woman, who I took to be a secretary, sitting all alone in a small square office and doing nothing in particular.

'Could you tell me where I'd find the mayor?' I asked.

'I'm the mayor,' she replied.

Her name was Nerissa Norman. She was a retired teacher who'd been pressed back into service. She was a friendly soul and we sat and chatted for a while. She liked to refer to her term in office as 'this administration', much as President Clinton might, though her annual budget totalled all of $400,000. No descendants of Montgomery or Green still lived in Mound Bayou, she told me. Outsiders were much more interested in the town's history than the people who lived there. She admitted that white visitors had not been welcome in the past, but insisted they were now. In fact three white people were now living in the town – two Catholic sisters who taught at the school, and a white woman who was married to a black man. She glossed over Mound Bayou's transparent malaise. 'We've had our off periods, but we've bounced back,' she insisted. The mayor glanced at a clock on the wall. It was five o'clock. 'Time to go home,' she declared with evident relief.

I thought Mound Bayou was pretty desperate, but there was worse to come. The next day I crossed the Mississippi again and drove across bleak plains in lashing rain to Lake Providence, Louisiana, which has inherited from Tunica the title of America's poorest town.

Precise figures were hard to come by. In fact the whole place seemed pretty defensive about the dubious distinction that had been conferred upon it. Suffice it to say that the average household income was well below $10,000, compared to a national average of more than $30,000. There were only 5,300 people left in a town that once boasted 15,000. Of those, two-thirds were black and well over half were living below the official poverty line. 'We are basically a welfare town,' admitted the mayor, a flamboyant character named James Brown who taught sports at the junior high school.

I was taken around by the Reverend Emanual Jones, a lovely man with five children, who had returned to his home town after college and the army because that was where he believed God wanted him to work. 'God is an awesome God,' was the slogan on his number plate, but the Lord was certainly working in mysterious ways in Lake Providence. I think I've only once had a more depressing tour, and that was during President Clinton's official visit to Belarus in 1994, when we were shown in quick succession land contaminated by the Chernobyl nuclear explosion, a forest where Stalin massacred hundreds of Polish officers, and plains over which rival European armies had swarmed and fought for centuries.

The main street looked like somewhere in Bosnia or Chechenya. The end nearest the levee that protected the town from the Mississippi River had been abandoned altogether and was simply falling down. As for the rest, closed or burned-out businesses outnumbered those still open by about three to one. A single television set sat in the window of an abandoned electrical appliance store. The odd box sat gathering dust on the shelves of what had once been Galanty's haberdashery. The Amazing 99-Cent Store, Dress for Le$$, and an old barber's shop with a stripy pole, still struggled on, as did the Ole Dutch Bakery, but the windows of the Hong Kong Palace restaurant, the Wilson Grocery Market and the Teen Club were all dark.

Opposite the office of the *Banner-Democrat*, the local newspaper, was an expanse of wasteland where a cinema, library, bus station and drugstore had stood until the early 1980s, when the drugstore owner apparently put a match to his property in the hope of collecting the insurance. 'When I was growing up,' recalled Emanual, 'you couldn't drive down here and find an empty parking spot. On a Saturday you'd have to park four or five blocks away and walk back. There were stores everywhere.'

He drove me up Gould Street where young black drug dealers loitered outside a convenience store called the Key Station. Drugs were no longer solely an inner-city problem. 'If you were here at night you'd hear shots right over the town,' said Emanual. He drove me past hovels so wretched you thought they'd been abandoned until you saw a young black kid sitting on the stoop. We visited Vickey Hicks, a white woman who ran a day-care centre for 158 infants and had to provide extra big meals on Mondays because its children were famished after two days at home.

The senior high school was impressively new, but only because two former students had burned down the old one in the early

1990s. We chatted to the principal but the school's student counsellor refused to talk to me.

'If you can't fix Lake Providence I don't want to talk to you,' she said.

'I wonder if anyone can fix Sodom and Gomorrah,' the principal remarked quietly as she left.

Lake Providence has no swimming pool, no cinema, no shopping mall. It has no Wal-Mart, McDonald's or major supermarket. Its sheriff (white) was awaiting trial on money laundering, fraud and bribery charges, and was being detained in prison for improperly approaching one of the prosecution witnesses. Its former police chief (black) was also in jail having been convicted of fraud.

I'm being unfair, of course. North of the pretty lake that gave the town its name were many fine and pleasant homes standing amid trees with well-kept lawns and boats in their driveways. This was, however, an area exclusively for whites. The children went to the private Briarfield Academy, and their parents belonged to the all-white country club. I asked Emanual what would happen if he applied for membership. 'I'd probably have some visitors in the night,' he replied.

Lake Providence suffers from the same problems as most other Delta towns, only worse. It is tucked away in the extreme north-east corner of Louisiana, cut off by the Mississippi to the east and on the way to nowhere. Its wealthy white farmers have traditionally resisted any industrial development that might drive up wages, but they themselves now employ only a fraction of their former workforce. The *Banner-Democrat* had just three job advertisements, one for a car mechanic and two for weekend help at nursing homes. The nearest factory jobs are 30 miles north in Eudora, Arkansas, or 45 miles south in Vicksburg, Mississippi. Any high school graduate with any sense was catching 'the quickest thing leaving here,' said Emanual, and so the town was caught in a vicious downward spiral.

I met lots of good people full of fine intentions, but nobody had any real idea how to save the place. I found Don Boyett, an evangelical white pastor, building an expanded stage in his outsized church and he invited me to join him and various volunteers for a lunch of venison, beans and cornbread. 'We don't have a whole lot of concrete plans because we're so busy trying to keep our heads above water,' he admitted. But he was convinced God had something 'wonderful' planned for Lake Providence because in a destitute place like this the glory would be all the greater. The answer, he insisted, was for the town 'to come together and to pray and fast as a community'.

At the high school I met an idealistic black student, seventeen years old, called Myra Grey who was determined to train as a teacher and return to Lake Providence because this was where she could do most good. She acknowledged, however, that of the eighty-five students in her year she was 'the one per cent that wants to stay' and her friends all thought her 'crazy'.

Mayor Brown sat in his office, wearing a long black leather coat, black scarf and too much aftershave, and refused even to admit that Lake Providence was America's poorest town. He was sure that there were communities in West Virginia, or some town in Texas full of penniless Mexicans, more deserving of that title. He flashed gold-toothed smiles, waved his remarkably long, slender hands around, and airily insisted that, 'With God's help this town will eventually be a model for other towns to come and see'.

'Do you really believe the town has a future?' I asked.

'Definitely,' he said. 'I don't think the good citizens of this town who are well-off enough will stand to see this community rot and go to pieces.'

'Would you stay in Lake Providence yourself if you were just leaving school?'

'Nooooo,' the mayor admitted with a long and heartfelt laugh.

From Lake Providence I drove back across the river into Mississippi and continued zigzagging down the Delta. The towns were mostly struggling, but the wind-whipped winter landscape was huge and clean and in its own way rather wonderful. There was a tremendous sense of light and space. On either side of the raised road the ploughed black earth stretched away like giant sheets of corrugated iron. Lines of telegraph poles tapered to mere dots on the horizon.

Distant water towers on the skyline betrayed the remote little communities they served, and at night you could spot the headlights of approaching cars a full ten minutes before they reached you. Shortly before I reached the town of Belzoni, however, the fields gave way to ponds – endless rectangular man-made ponds of ten or twenty acres that covered the land like a giant quilt. I was entering Humphreys County where cotton is king no longer and catfish are the new cash crop. Indeed this is the self-proclaimed 'Catfish Capital of the World'.

Catfish in their natural state are hideous, bewhiskered creatures who scavenge for food in the detritus on the bottom of lakes and swamps. They have long been a staple of poor Southerners, especially blacks, who could afford nothing better. But in the mid-1960s, when the price of rice plummeted, a few local farmers decided to experiment with commercial catfish farming. They built a couple of ponds. They developed a floating feed so the fish would come to the surface to eat and lose their muddy flavour. The experiment was such an astounding success that Humphreys County now has 35,000 acres of ponds. It produces fully a third of the 500 million pounds of catfish raised in Mississippi each year, and Mississippi produces seventy per cent of America's total. At any one time there are roughly 400 million catfish in Humphreys County, and just 10,000 humans, so one rather hopes the catfish never rebel.

These underwater factories have rescued the county from the poverty afflicting so many of its neighbours, and it is duly grateful. Belzoni now hosts an annual World Catfish Festival featuring a Catfish Eating Contest, a Catfish Queen and the world's largest fish fry. It has even built a Catfish Museum to which, I noticed, I was only the thirteenth visitor in two weeks. There, a young man named Gene Luster waxed lyrical about what a low-fat, high-protein and incredibly versatile food the farm-raised catfish is, and how Northerners love it if they can only be persuaded to eat it. He pressed cookbooks on me full of recipes for dishes like Catfish Brie Soufflé and Catfish Pasta Primavera, then sent me 7 miles up the road to the Confish plant in the little town of Isola which processes more than 150 tons of catfish daily.

The plant manager, a young man named Lee Parker, gave me a guided tour beginning with the 'flavour checker', a man who samples 300 catfish daily. He rejects any with a taste, muddy or otherwise, because the blandness of catfish is apparently one of its greatest selling points. That way people can use seasoning or marinades to give the meat whatever flavour they want.

We watched tankers unload rivers of squirming green-black catfish on to conveyor belts. We watched them being stunned by electric rods as they were whisked inside the plant. Amid a tremendous din, machines swiftly decapitated, skinned and filleted them. Within forty minutes of its arrival at the plant the average catfish had been reduced to fresh, frozen or marinaded fillets while its head, bones and guts were on their way to the animal food factory.

Though the process was fascinating, the workforce interested me more. Every manager I saw was white, and every one of the five hundred or so women on the production lines was black. They barely earned the statutory minimum wage, but it probably still beat working in the cotton fields.

Before leaving Humphreys County I thought I should sample some of its most famous product. I was directed to a little diner half a mile from the Confish plant called Peter Bo's which advertised itself as 'Keeping the Taste of the South Alive'. Peter Bo was a big, round, cheery black man with a shiny bald head whose real name was Robert Birkenhead. He fixed me up with a massive plate of catfish fried in his secret batter, chips, coleslaw and little balls of deep-fried cornmeal known as hush puppies. The fish was fine, good even, but Peter Bo must be putting something in that batter. Its allure transcended race. Blacks and whites were sitting side by side and gobbling down his catfish. It was the first time I'd seen blacks and whites doing anything together since I'd left Tunica's gaming tables.

I carried on down Route 61, passing through the town of Onward where, in 1902, Theodore Roosevelt had refused to shoot a helpless bear and thus inspired a New York toy manufacturer to create the teddy bear.

Just after my car completed its 70,000th mile, beside a roadside shack, I saw a life-size blue rhinoceros, a green dinosaur and a yellow giraffe all made from scraps of metal. Out of curiosity I stopped and knocked.

'Come in,' said a voice. I stepped out of the sunshine and couldn't see anybody in the gloom.

'Here,' said the voice. A young man was sitting behind the door, a crossbow in his hands. I started. He grinned and said, 'I'm only cleaning it.' He told me the sculptor had long since moved away but left the animals behind. People stopped all the time. He offered me some of the canned spaghetti he was eating. Fortunately I was full of catfish.

'What's the name of this place?' I asked as I turned to go.

'Egremont,' he replied. 'Don't ask me how to spell it.'

At mid-afternoon something extraordinary appeared in the distance. It was not high, but it was most definitely a hill. There were more behind it, and they were forested. I was leaving Delta country and was soon in Vicksburg, an old Confederate stronghold overlooking the Mississippi that resisted weeks of bombardment by Union forces before finally surrendering on 4 July 1863. Parts of the town looked as if they had not recovered yet, but there was a fine museum in the old court house. I particularly enjoyed the story that appeared beside a bullet known as a 'minnie ball':

> During the battle of Raymond, Mississippi, in 1863, a minnie ball reportedly passed through the reproductive organs of a young rebel soldier and a few seconds later penetrated a young lady who was standing on the porch of her nearby home. The story was written 11 years later by Dr LeGrand G. Capes of Vicksburg for the American Medical Weekly. Capes claimed that he tended the wounds, that the girl became pregnant from the fertile minnie ball, that he delivered the baby, introduced her to the soldier, that the two were married and had two more children by the conventional method.

Outside the museum was another of those riveting historical markers. It recorded how the Mississippi Dental Association was founded in Vicksburg on 21 April, 1875, by Dr J. B. Askew and Dr J. D. Miles. I would naturally have liked to learn more but a still greater attraction was awaiting me in Natchez, 70 miles further downriver. I had a long-standing invitation to stay at the Monmouth Plantation, a magnificent old antebellum mansion that was now one of America's most exclusive private hotels. It was necessary to research all sides of plantation life, I told myself. In any case, after weeks of soulless cheap motels I reckoned I deserved it.

The Monmouth did not disappoint. I slept in a giant four-poster bed that had once belonged to General John Quitman, a former Mississippi governor and hero of the Mexican War. I woke to birdsong, not to the sound of traffic thundering down some highway. I walked out of my room into a brick courtyard with a tinkling fountain, scented air, and views of a lawn, lake, magnolias and ancient oaks – not acres of tarmac. Dinner was an elegant five-course candlelit affair served by two delightful black waiters, Otis and Roosevelt – not a hamburger and chips gobbled down in the car.

Yes, I thought. To have been a rich Southern planter before the Civil War must have been even better than life as a sahib in the British Raj.

12

The Incarceration Station

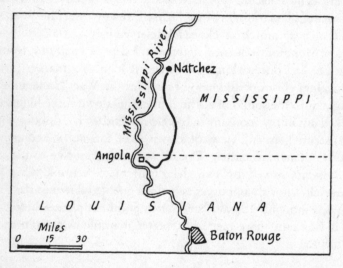

After visiting so many dead or dying Delta communities I finally found one that was quite the opposite. It is clean, green and spacious, occupying 18,000 acres of former plantation land within a loop of the Mississippi River. It boasts a prize-winning newspaper, a lively radio station, a small college, a popular annual rodeo and a quality arts and crafts show. It grows its own food, has no unemployment and minimal crime. It enjoys a constant influx of newcomers, most of whom stay for life, but the funny thing is that not one of its inhabitants lives there voluntarily. This is, after all, a maximum security prison that houses 5,000 of Louisiana's most violent criminals and the state's Death Row.

To reach the Louisiana State Penitentiary, commonly known as Angola, I rather reluctantly left my rarified perch in Natchez early one morning and drove an hour south on my old friend, Highway 61. Shortly after leaving Mississippi for the last time I turned sharp just with the physical, but if you deal with the moral the physical becomes easy because moral people are not violent, and that's exactly what we do.'

America locks up more of its citizens than any other country, and the conservative South – with 487 inmates for every 100,000 residents – more than any other region. Mr Cain considers Louisiana's 'life means life' law 'ridiculous' because it precludes the possibility of redemption, but he has to work within that limitation. He seeks to persuade the many inmates destined to die in Angola, either naturally or by execution, that there is still 'light at the end of the tunnel', that they can still go to heaven and that perhaps God intends them to do his work inside a prison just as other missionaries worked in Africa or China.

Mr Cain also insists on treating the prisoners like human beings. He has improved their food and recreational facilities. He has introduced proper funerals with graveside prayers, flowers and an inmate choir instead of the previous perfunctory affairs. The prison officers are mostly unarmed and forbidden to swear at inmates. Convicts wear jeans and T-shirts, not prison uniforms. The compliant are made 'trustees' and awarded various privileges including dormitory accommodation – instead of cells – and better jobs (the best job of all, to my way of thinking, was that of the prison angler whose task was to keep the warden supplied with fresh fish). 'We're as good as they let us and as mean as they make us,' said Mr Cain.

He claimed there were as many as 1,800 born-again Christians among the 5,000 inmates. There was no way of checking this, but today's Angola is certainly a far cry from its infamous predecessor. There has not been a killing or suicide in nearly two years. Drugs are rare. The place seems as happy as a prison can be – so much so that the inmates held a farewell dinner for the previous warden and inner-city school kids come for visits during which the prisoners lecture them on the importance of being good. When Cathy and I walked unprotected through several iron gates into the very heart of the 'Big Yard', the main prison complex, we did not feel remotely threatened even though half of Angola's inmates are convicted killers.

If Mr Cain sets the prison's moral tone, *The Angolite*, its news magazine, is its conscience and we were on our way to meet its celebrated editor, Wilbert Rideau, a convicted murderer who has spent all but nineteen of his fifty-five years in Angola. When I'd asked the previous week if I could meet him, Cathy had chuckled and replied: 'No problem. Wilbert's not going anywhere.'

The Angolite's office is a long breeze-block room painted light green and crammed with files, papers, computer screens, telephones and a dozen stacked cases of soft drinks. It could be the office of any smalltown newspaper were it not in the heart of a top security prison. Rideau himself is a wiry man and, like seventy-seven per cent of Angola's inmates, black. He is not particularly likeable. He has a hard face and an aggressive manner, but he also has a compelling personal story and has achieved, I must admit, far more as a journalist behind bars than I have as a free man.

Aged nineteen, he robbed a bank in Lake Charles, Louisiana, took three of its employees to a swamp outside the town and shot them. He cut the throat of one and stabbed her in the chest. The other two survived. He spent eleven years on Death Row, but his sentence was commuted to life imprisonment when the Supreme Court temporarily halted the death penalty in 1972.

Rideau began reading voraciously while on Death Row, and subsequently started to write. When he joined the general prison population he was refused a job on the all-white staff of *The Angolite* so he started a rival newsletter – *The Lifer* – and wrote a weekly column from his cell for a black-owned chain of Southern newspapers. The authorities shut *The Lifer* down, but in 1975 a new warden called C. Paul Phelps took charge of the penitentiary. He had read and admired Rideau's columns. He offered him not only the editorship of *The Angolite* but his full protection – so long as he wrote the truth – and the right to question prison officials. Mr Phelps believed honest reporting of prison affairs could do much to avoid misunderstandings and reduce tension.

The new warden was as good as his word, his successors followed the same policy, and over the past twenty years Rideau has built *The Angolite* into a formidable tool for justice and reform. It is a thick, bi-monthly news magazine that contains not only death notices, sports news, prisoners' poems and religious announcements, but highbrow investigative articles about all facets of prison life.

It has won the release of old, disabled or forgotten prisoners who should have been freed years earlier. 'This *Angolite* has got more inmates out of prison than the biggest law firm in the United States,' Rideau boasted. It ran pictures of burn marks on an executed prisoner that helped to persuade the state of Louisiana to switch from the electric chair to lethal injection. It highlighted the low pay of prison employees, and engineered the removal of the swaggart who had long been Louisiana's official executioner with an interview in which the man claimed that executing people bothered him about as much as 'goin' to a refrigerator and getting a beer'. The executioner 'might have been a law-abiding citizen,' Rideau told me, 'but he was more offensive and obscene as a human being than a lot of the people I live with. He usually got his man, but this time we got him.' A long and particularly powerful essay by Rideau entitled 'The Sexual Jungle' exposed the vicious world of homosexual rape and sexual serfdom in prisons and gained national attention.

The Angolite and its six-man team has won several prestigious national journalism awards, though Rideau has never been able to accept them personally. It has 3,500 subscribers around the country including many in the national media. 'We have helped shape stories,' said Rideau. 'We've been able to influence the public's perception. They had never seen the public texture behind the statistics, numbers and names. What we did was put a face on all of that and show that these numbers and names live, eat and breathe. We got rid of a lot of the myths and misconceptions that cripple prison populations everywhere.'

The one thing Rideau has been unable to achieve, however, is his own release. The thirteen men on Death Row when he first arrived back in 1961 are all now free, and nearly 700 other murderers have left Angola in that time. He has been a model prisoner – indeed *Time* magazine once dubbed him 'the most rehabilitated prisoner in America'. He has many prominent supporters, including Angola's past and present wardens, and parole boards have four times recommended his release, but each time the state's governor has refused. It doesn't help that he is a black man who killed a white woman, or that one of his victims still has thirteen bullet fragments lodged in her neck, but Prisoner 75546 mostly blames his own high profile.

'I did too good,' said Rideau. The rule in prison was 'don't attract any attention, remain anonymous. When you roll up and say "give me parole, give me clemency" you don't have anyone opposing you . . . It's a hell of a system when you punish productivity and reward mediocrity and anonymity.'

Rideau talked and talked. Time was no object to someone in his position. Cathy and I finally escaped for a lunch of turkey, beans and cornbread cooked by prisoners in the dog pen dining hall (where the toilets are marked 'Personnel' and 'Inmates'), and then visited another extraordinary feature of Angola – the only federally-licensed radio station in America operating from a prison.

It is officially called KLSP, unofficially the 'Incarceration Station'. It occupies a small studio in one of the administrative buildings and broadcasts daily from 12.00 p.m. till 2.00 a.m. It has a priceless collection of long-playing records, but as yet few compact discs. It used to be financed in part by prisoners selling blood until AIDS killed the plasma programme.

We arrived to find 'Goldie', a black disc jockey whose real name was Prentice Robinson, crooning into the microphone.

'This is "Down by the Riverside" by Bobby Powell,' he purrs. 'Just go on down by the river, study war no more, and call God precious. Look outside. It's a beautiful day. It's a beautiful day God has given us, one you'll never see again. But know this, know this: you are blessed.'

The music takes over, and Goldie swings round in his chair to chat. Prisoner 75065 is a big man of forty-five with a short beard and gold-capped teeth. He seems a warm, good-natured fellow and it is hard to believe he's a convicted rapist who has served twenty-four years of a life sentence. For the first seventeen of those years he refused to repent, he says, but 'there comes a time when you sit back and take an inventory of your life and where you're headed, and the Lord put a blessing on me to teach the gospel'.

In 1993 he was ordained as a Baptist minister and is now

occasionally allowed out to preach in Louisiana's churches provided he spends the nights in local jails. He has also married a prison visitor, though the marriage necessarily remains unconsummated.

That must be hard, I suggest.

'Tell me about it,' he replies with a grimace. It had been equally hard watching his son by his first marriage grow up into a twenty-five-year-old soldier who fought in the Gulf War. Would he ever be released? 'I don't believe God brought me this far to leave me languishing in prison,' he replies. 'I've done a lot of things in my life I'm not proud of but I'm remorseful and repentant of the wrong I've done.'

The Incarceration Station has a heavy religious bias, with several hours set aside for mandatory gospel music and sermons, but each of the four DJs has his own distinctive style. Goldie offers 'oldies, blues and love' – music designed, he admits, to bring back memories and induce a certain melancholy in his listeners. He gets a lot of requests from Angola's sixty-three Death Row prisoners, he says, and on execution days he will preach and pray on air. He also likes to talk about particular prisoners so they feel like somebodies.

Suddenly he invites me to address his listeners. I can hardly refuse, but what do you say to 5,000 incarcerated killers and rapists? That you hope they have a good day? That you just love their prison? I introduce myself and explain how I'm travelling across America, free as a bird, writing about whatever takes my fancy. Only after I finish do I realise how that must have sounded to men who have spent most of their adult lives locked up in tiny cells.

There were yet more surprises in Angola – the After-dinner Speakers Club, the group of inmates that travels around the state teaching mouth-to-mouth resuscitation, the bands it sends out to play at carnivals. There is the rodeo stadium where every Sunday in October the inmates stage 'the wildest show in the South' for some 15,000 spectators from the outside world. This includes a couple of events not found in conventional rodeos. In one, 'Convict Poker', four inmates sit at a table playing cards while a bull is let loose behind them. The last to flee wins $50 – a lot of money when the maximum prison wage is 20 cents an hour. In another, called 'Guts

and Glory', dozens of inmates pack the ring and try to snatch a
$100 chit from between the horns of a raging bull. For its more
senior prisoners, the prison stages an annual 'elderly Olympics', and
the stadium also hosts revival meetings by visiting evangelists and
concerts by the likes of Linda Ronstadt.

By the main gate a museum is being built. The prize exhibits are
the oak electric chair in which seventy-seven men died before
Louisiana switched to lethal injections in 1991, and the leather
mask put over the prisoners' heads so their eyes would not pop out.
Finally, of course, there is Death Row itself and the actual execution
chamber. It seemed nothing was out of bounds, so off we went.

Death Row is housed in a two-storey cream-and-red building
with ducks waddling across its neat front lawn and vending
machines in its lobby. We were admitted through one barred iron
gate, turned right down a brightly-lit corridor and went through a
second gate, turned left and passed through a third. Before I had
really braced myself we were there, standing amid a bunch of burly
guards and facing two dark brown sliding steel grills marked 'Tier A'
on the left, and 'Tier B' on the right.

Cathy told me not to speak to any of the prisoners and temporarily relieved me of my notebook. A guard slid back the grill to
'Tier B' and walked me quickly to the far end and back. On one side
of the narrow passage were mounted television sets, all showing the
same soap opera, and windows looking out on to the prisoners'
tiny exercise cages. On the other side were fifteen six-by-eight-foot
concrete cells with bars across the front. Each contained a bed, a
steel toilet, a steel basin, and a first-degree murderer who was confined in that tiny space for twenty-three hours of every twenty-four.
One of the men was reading a girlie magazine. Another was reading
a cheap novel. Several lay motionless on their beds. The rest stared
out at us like beasts from cages, one or two nodding, some scowling,
but none saying a word. Some were white, some black, but all
looked haggard and haunted. We were in there for no longer than a
minute, but that was long enough for me.

On the day of their execution these men are taken to Camp F
next to the Wildfowl Refuge on the far side of the penitentiary

There they are put in one of four cells in what is called the Death House. There is a telephone box from which they can make unlimited calls, a shower and air-conditioning. Mr Cain has relaxed the rules so relatives can spend most of the day with the condemned man, and once even sent a car to fetch some, but at 6.00 p.m. they must leave. The prisoner then eats his final meal, which can be whatever he wants.

Antonio James, the last man executed, in March 1996, chose a seafood buffet, pecan pie and Coke, which he ate with Mr Cain in an adjacent cafeteria. James, who killed a sixty-nine-year-old man for money to buy drugs in 1979, had since turned to God, and the two men had spent a lot of time together preparing for that day. 'We had talked about his soul,' Mr Cain recalled. 'He wanted to know how it was going to be. He thought his spirit would be in limbo. I said a band of angels was coming to take him off, God was waiting for him.'

Shortly before midnight the condemned man is escorted by six officers from his cell through the dining room and into the death chamber, a surgically-bright white room with a plate-glass window down one side so a dozen witnesses, including the victim's relatives, can watch the execution. Apparently hundreds of people write in asking to be witnesses. There is a microphone on a stand through which the prisoner can deliver a last message. James said nothing, though he'd given a final interview to *The Angolite*. On the wall opposite the plate-glass window are two red telephones through which Louisiana's governor or the secretary of its Corrections Department can inform the warden of a last-minute stay of execution using a pre-arranged code word. Incredibly, one of the telephones rang while we were in the chamber but it was a wrong number. I tried to imagine the trauma had that happened during an execution.

In the centre of the room is a black padded gurney with two outstretched arm rests on to which the prisoner is strapped, face up. In James' case the medical officers had trouble finding a vein, so they had to unstrap him again so he could help. Everyone but the warden then leaves. In an adjoining room, watching through a one-way window that is the modern-day equivalent of the executioner's black hood, is the anonymous volunteer who turns on the intravenous drips when the governor gives the signal. This room is painted dark red and used as a general storage room, but the intravenous drip stand and a medical trolley were standing there in readiness, and there was a hole in the wall for the tube to pass through. Three chemicals are administered in quick succession. The first, sodium pentathol, puts the condemned man to sleep. The second, pancuronium bromide, stops all muscle activity including breathing, and the third, potassium chloride, stops the heart.

Mr Cain had only presided over two executions during his time at Angola. The first time, he said, he used a downward motion of his hand as his signal, but realised afterwards that Nero had used a similar gesture to dispatch Christians to their deaths. In James' case he simply nodded his head.

'I reached out and held his hand,' Mr Cain recalled. 'He looked at me and said "bless you", and the last words that came out of his mouth were "bless you" to his executioner. It took two minutes to stop his breathing. All the time I was talking to him and telling him "God is waiting for you. You're going to ride away on a chariot. Your time has come." He just kept on holding my hand, really hard, then he relaxed his grip. I wish I could have done that for his victim, but there was no one to hold the victim's hand. If I could have held their hand I would.'

It was late afternoon, and time to return to the outside world. As I left Angola I tuned my car radio to KLSP 91.7 FM. Goldie was still going strong. 'Right now we have the Bright Stars from Flint, Michigan,' his disembodied voice announced from the far side of the fence dividing the free from the imprisoned. 'I tell you that Jesus is real, and I tell you that between now and 2.00 a.m. I'm going to give you oldies, love and blues. You know Jesus is real . . .' A few miles down the road the signal faded.

13

Gators, Coons and Mudbugs

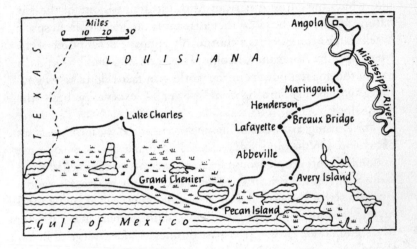

It is daybreak in the middle of America's largest swamp. The rising sun is setting the topmost tips of the trees aflame, and I am skimming through the chilly mist below in a flat-bottomed steel boat, just me and a complete stranger armed with a rifle, a pistol and a large machete. This was really not where I had intended to end up after leaving Angola.

The following day I had continued south on Highway 61 until I saw a sign pointing westwards to a ferry across the Mississippi. That sounded a much more romantic option than a bridge and so I followed a little country road 7 miles to where it ended at the water's edge. A couple of old black women were selling peanuts. Two abandoned cranes were rusting away just up the shore. I sat in the warm midday sun and watched a tug steering a huge flotilla of barges slowly down the great flood while the ferry returned from the far bank.

I had been curiously unaware of this mother of all rivers during my journey down the Delta, probably because it is lined by high levees on both sides and is therefore rarely seen. Surveying it now, at water level, as millions of gallons of turbulent brown water swept down towards the Gulf of Mexico, I realised what I'd been missing. This was the river that divided a continent, the mighty channel into which the entire American Midwest drained, one of the few natural features of the globe that astronauts can identify from space. Weeks later I came across a thoroughly apposite description of the Mississippi by Abraham Lincoln. 'The London *Times*,' he said, 'is one of the greatest powers in the world – in fact I don't know anything which has much more power – except perhaps the Mississippi.'

The crossing cost a dollar, making it one of the cheapest pleasures of my trip. On the other side I entered Acadiana, the home of some 700,000 Cajun people whose French ancestors were expelled from Nova Scotia by the British in 1755 and eventually resettled in southern Louisiana. 'Le Grand Derangement,' they called it. I found myself meandering through villages with names like Labarre, Maringouin and Grosse Tete, past businesses like Gineaux's Pizza, Picard's Auto Parts and Dupuis Memorials.

I had planned to drive straight through to Texas because, I believed, the Cajuns had been discovered, thoroughly commercialised and turned into tourist fodder when there was really little left to distinguish them from any other Americans save their stubborn pursuit of the Napoleonic code instead of English common law. I was reinforced in this belief by billboards inviting me to 'Paint the Town Rouge' and to 'Laissez Les Bons Temps Roulez', and by tourist brochures offering visitors helpful phrases like 'Merci (mare see)' and 'Joie de vivre (jhwa da veev)'. But then I got on to Interstate 10 which runs for 20 miles on stilts across the million-acre Atchafalaya River basin.

That watery world looked quite bewitching and I began to waver. Halfway across, on impulse, I took an exit signed for the Whiskey Bay boat ramp. Three sportsmen were just hauling a sleek new powerboat from the water. Were there any old timers left, I asked them? Cajuns who lived off the bayous? Take the next exit off the interstate, they advised. Go to Henderson and ask around. I did so, and behind the inevitable service stations and Cajun gift shops massed around the intersection I found a complete fishing village some 60 miles inland from the Gulf of Mexico.

Standing around at the Breaux Brothers bait shop, chatting in archaic Cajun French, were men who harvested the swamp for fish and men who harvested it for that great staple of Cajun cuisine, the crawfish or 'mudbug', but it was when one of them mentioned Curtis Robin – pronounced 'Roh-bahn' – that I knew I'd found my man. Malcolm Landry, a jovial culler of crawfish, led me in his pick-up to a small wooden house on the edge of town where he introduced me to one of the few authentic fur trappers left in Louisiana, indeed one of the last practitioners of a long French tradition of fur trapping in North America dating back to the 17th century.

Curtis was a slight, diffident, mild-mannered fellow in his early fifties with prematurely silver hair, a handsome weather-beaten face and smiling green eyes. He and Malcolm exchanged greetings in Cajun. I asked if I could spend a day on the water with him. Of course, he said in an accent that was probably the French equivalent of the Elizabethan English brogue spoken by Chesapeake Bay's Smith Islanders. And so it was that we set off early the next morning for a day's trapping on the swamp.

Curtis had seventy traps in a wildlife refuge covering several hundred thousand acres north of the Whiskey Bay boat ramp. The sun soon burned off the mist to reveal a magical world of brown bayous and tangled light-grey woods set off by clumps of bright green palmettos, sprays of red berries and a vivid blue sky. We spent the day weaving our way around that aquatic wilderness, nosing up narrow channels, ducking under fallen willows, manoeuvring around submerged logs and the stumps of ancient cypress trees. We saw kingfishers, woodpeckers, cormorants and great blue herons. There was a hint of spring in the warm air, and the first yellow-bellied turtles of the year were sunning themselves on branches protruding from the water, but once we'd left the main channel we saw not another soul. Twice we heard hunters' distant rifle shots. The only other reminders of humanity were the remains of an old oil well and the occasional shells of long-abandoned cabins.

Had I been by myself I'd have been lost in minutes, but Curtis knew his way around this maze like a cabbie knows the streets of London. He'd worked these waters all his life. He was one of the last frontiersmen. Like so many men in the American boondocks he had no health insurance, no pension plan, no security whatsoever. He lived by his wits, surviving from day to day off what he caught, trapping all winter and fishing in the summer. He could sell an otter's pelt for $30, a mink's for $13, a raccoon's for $10 and a nutria's – or giant rat's – for $3. Surprisingly, he said, there was no longer a market for beaver.

You would never have spotted Curtis' traps unless you knew exactly what you were looking for, and probably not even then. They consisted of single sticks stuck into the mud about a foot out from the bank with two pieces of fish nailed to them. At the foot of each stick, concealed beneath the water and a layer of mouldering black leaves, was a small iron trap sprung when animals stepped on it. We visited all seventy traps, and I confess to feeling a certain tingle of anticipation each time Curtis manoeuvred our boat into some little backwater to see what, if anything, he'd caught.

Five times that day we found bedraggled coons the size of cats splashing around in the water, one leg caught in iron jaws. Most froze in terror as we approached, staring helplessly at us with their round black eyes. One tried to swim towards the boat as if sensing rescue. Curtis dispatched all five with single shots, and, as the blood from their twitching bodies turned the brown water red, he reset the traps and pinned fresh fish to the sticks. Occasionally, he said, coons chewed their own feet off in order to escape.

In other traps we found a dead possum, which he chucked away, three big black crows, one of them dead, and, in one of the very last traps, a magnificent hawk whose beating wings and fearsome beak made it difficult for Curtis to release. The great bird finally flew off, one broken talon dangling visibly below it.

Five raccoons was a poor return, barely sufficient to cover the day's costs, but Curtis didn't grumble. He was a man as contented as Dwight Marshall on Smith Island. He loved the swamp and the way it was constantly changing with the seasons. In the spring, he said, he could work all day and not see the water beneath all the flowering hyacinths. In the summer the swamp became a hot, dark jungle infested by snakes and alligators. His four children and five grandchildren all lived close to Henderson. He'd never travelled beyond the states immediately surrounding Louisiana and had no desire to.

'People born in New York and Chicago and places like that live and die and never get out of the city,' he said. 'They never see anything but cement and skyscrapers.' He visited Louisiana's cities only if he absolutely had to, and regarded New Orleans as decadent and dangerous.

Like Dwight Marshall, though, Curtis was also one of a dying breed. His language was vanishing – while his eighty-eight-year-old father spoke only Cajun and he was himself bilingual, his sons spoke English only. Like the Gullahs of the Sea islands, they had been taught that Cajun was a backward language, something to be ashamed of. Curtis' way of life was also disappearing. No young men became trappers nowadays. The traps and equipment were too expensive, the anti-fur brigade had severely damaged the market, and fur farms were taking over. Not for the first time on this journey, I felt I'd arrived just in time.

That night I ate a spicy chicken gumbo in a diner in the Cajun capital of Lafayette that tasted all the more delicious after weeks of bland fast food. I was beginning to enjoy Acadiana. It really was different. It had its own speech, its own cuisine, and a refreshingly *laissez-faire* attitude compared to the unbending social conservatism of the South in general. Here you found bars and lounges on the back roads instead of ubiquitous little churches. Here you found people sitting round in backrooms playing cards for money. Here the people had elected four times as governor a roguish fellow Cajun named Edwin Edwards whose boast was that he was defeatable only if caught in bed with a live boy or dead girl.

I revised my plans accordingly. I decided that instead of driving straight to Texas on Interstate 10, I would head still further south then follow a minor road westwards through Louisiana's vast coastal marshes – nearly two million acres in all – that border the Gulf of Mexico.

I had an introduction to one Paul McIlhenny and visited him on the private estate, Avery Island, where his family have manufactured Tabasco Sauce for well over a century. Although technically an island, Avery is really a patch of dry land in a sea of marsh. He gave me lunch in his wood-panelled boardroom, drove me around the landscaped island which included the highest point – 150 foot – on the entire Gulf coast, and showed me the factory where the fumes alone gave me a sneezing fit.

It struck me that Paul's great-grandfather had stumbled on one of the simplest means of making a fortune I'd come across. All you do is pick ripe red peppers, put them in oak barrels with salt, and after three years drain off the liquid. You then put that liquid in much bigger oak casks with vinegar and after thirty days you're done. The factory produces 350,000 bottles a day of this fiery red concoction and sells it in more than a hundred countries.

That afternoon, beyond Abbeville with its 'Hotel de Ville', I found myself driving past what looked like flooded rice fields except that there were crawfish pots clearly protruding from the water. I saw some men erecting a shed in a pleasant green pasture dotted with farm machinery, boats and ancient oaks, so I stopped to inquire. The farmer was an affable, middle-aged Cajun named Raywood Stally with an accent so thick I could scarcely understand him.

His friends called him T'neg, Cajun for 'little nigger', he said, and he was certainly swarthy. He explained that he grew rice from March to September, then flooded the fields and raised crawfish through the winter. Where else, I wondered, could you find agricultural land that yielded both fish and vegetable in a single year?

Raywood turned out to be a man of many parts. He had begun life as a trapper, but over the years had amassed 600 acres of land on the edge of the marshes. Aside from rice and crawfish he also raised cattle and bred horses, but the core of his business nowadays was contained in a dozen grey, windowless steel sheds on one side of the pasture. He took me over and opened the door of the nearest. I was hit by a truly revolting hot, moist stench. There was a tremendous splashing and flopping from the dark interior. We ducked inside and there, piled up against the furthest wall and divided from us by a pool of putrid black water, were a hundred little alligators.

One was lurking just to the left of the door. Raywood put a large white gumboot firmly on its back, picked it up carefully to show me, then threw it back in the water where, with a single flail of its tail, it soaked the pair of us.

Raywood had started raising alligators as a sideline just six years earlier, but now had 14,000 of the creatures. Early each summer he chartered a helicopter and scoured the marshes for the mounds of dry, brown grass that were alligator nests. He dropped tall white plastic poles to mark them, then went back with airboats to collect the eggs, frightening away the mothers by knocking them on the head with poles. There would be thirty or forty eggs in a nest, and in a single day he and his men could easily collect 3,000, for which he would pay the landowners about $6 each. He incubated and hatched the eggs, put the baby alligators into his heated sheds, fed them a high-protein diet, and within a year they were three feet long. He then knocked them out, killed them with a knife through the back of their heads, and skinned them.

In another shed he showed me about five hundred identical hides, all scraped, salted and neatly piled, that would soon be shipped off to a tannery in France and turned into handbags, boots and belts. Each skin would fetch about $80, the meat about $20, and the heads about $1.50 from tourist shops. In other words Raywood's 14,000 alligators would fetch roughly $1.4 million, minus his expenses. Not bad for a man who left school at sixteen and admitted he could barely read or write.

Alligator farming, I later learned, was Louisiana's equivalent of catfish farming in Mississippi. Since the mid-1980s, when the farmers were first permitted to collect eggs from the marshes, it had ballooned into a $20 million industry. The state now had eighty-five farms producing about 125,000 alligator skins a year, making it the world's biggest supplier by far, and since the farmers were required to return roughly twenty per cent of their animals to the marshes the wild alligator had also made a spectacular recovery. By the early 1970s there were less than 150,000 of the overhunted creatures left and they had joined the endangered species list. Today there are well over 600,000 – as many as there were at the beginning of the century – and hunters are allowed to kill nearly 30,000 a year. That was yet another of Raywood's sidelines – taking people alligator hunting. It was not the most challenging of sports. You simply put a chicken on a large hook attached to a long rope and left it suspended above the water. The next day you came along and hauled your catch in until it was close enough to shoot in the head.

The road through the marshes was deserted and lovely. It was slightly raised, giving me a fine view over the watery grasslands. A few alligators and turtles basked in the unusually warm January sun. Blue herons and white egrets stood motionless in the shallows, waiting for unsuspecting fish. Anhingas, wet from diving, perched on stumps and hung out their broad black wings to dry. Coots, cormorants and ducks floated on the water and teals swooped and wheeled overhead. I passed tiny fishing communities with names like Pecan Island and Grand Chenier, and the occasional hunting camp, but all too soon the road turned north. After a final seafood gumbo at the Cajun Seafood Restaurant in an obscure little village called Creole, I rejoined the interstate and was soon crossing a bridge high above the Sabine River which divides Louisiana from Texas, the South from the West.

14

Matters of Life and Death

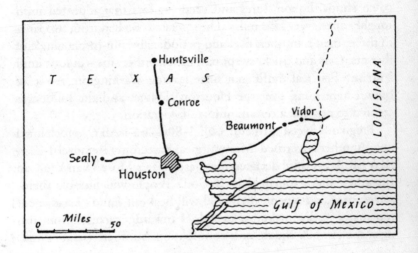

I'd not chosen the most attractive route into the Lone Star State. The first place I passed was Vidor, a blue-collar town renowned as one of the last redoubts of the Ku Klux Klan. What caught my eye, however, was a large red-and-yellow billboard proclaiming: 'This is Orange County, City of Vidor. Here you get by with brutally murdering a woman.'

A few minutes later I passed a row of smaller billboards by the interstate. Put together, they read: 'With the buddy system . . . You can get by . . . With murder in Vidor . . . May 14 1991 Kathy Page . . . Brutally murdered beaten strangled . . . Raped while dying no arrest.' Just beyond the last one was a sign pointing to a tourist information centre, but I somehow doubted that many people availed themselves of its services. I certainly didn't.

A little later, in Houston, I met a woman who told me how she'd once pulled off the interstate to fill up with petrol in Vidor. Four white teenagers had swaggered up to her to show off tattoos on their forearms of black men hanging from nooses.

Beyond Vidor the road was bordered by giant refineries and petrochemical plants from which clouds of smoke and fumes billowed skywards. Fully 25 miles from downtown Houston the last fields and trees vanished beneath a sequence of motels, gas stations, pawn shops, liquor stores and used-car lots that repeated itself roughly once every four miles. The interstate swelled from two lanes to three, then four, then five, and periodically split into a tangle of flyovers. Cars and trucks swept past me on either side – at least until I hit my first real traffic jam since leaving Washington. A visible brown haze hung over the Houston skyline, and the billboards seemed to bespeak a certain human desperation.

'Pregnant? Need a friend? Call 1-800-264-BABY', proclaimed one. Another advertised 'Microsurgical Vasectomy Removal 1-713-REVERSE'. A third declared that 'Jesus Cares More Than You Can Imagine', and a fourth that 'If God's People will humble themselves, pray and repent, then God will heal our Land'. I had spent too many weeks in the backwoods. I inwardly recoiled from this ugly, soulless 500-square-mile conurbation, but there was no avoiding it.

I'd always heard how Friday-night high-school football was like a religion in small-town Texas, so I'd telephoned Scott Kaiser, the *Houston Chronicle*'s high-school football correspondent to find out where to watch some. He had directed me to Sealy, a town of 5,000 people an hour west of Houston, whose team had won the all-state championship for mid-sized high schools two years running and had once again reached the regional play-offs. I quickly discovered that such information did not come free, for Scott subsequently wrote an article about me in the *Houston Chronicle* headlined: 'English Author to Feature Sealy's Friday Night Heroes'.

'Interest in high-school football always peaks when the state play-offs begin,' Scott's story started, 'but one observer this week is bound to have an eye-opening experience . . .' How right he was. What I learned was that Bill Shankly's famous description of English soccer applied equally to Texas football, even when played by seventeen- and eighteen-year-olds. The game was not 'a matter of life and death' the legendary Liverpool soccer club manager once said. It was 'much more serious than that'.

Sealy is a pleasant little town with stockyards and feedstores in the fertile east Texan countryside. It is the sort of place we journalists habitually label 'sleepy', except that on this occasion there was clearly something afoot. 'Sealy Tigers – District Champions', announced a sign at the shopping centre, and in every shop window along the Main Street were large messages proclaiming 'Go Fight Win', 'Tiger Territory' and 'We Love You, Tigers'.

I spotted the stadium before the school. In fact 'Tiger Stadium' almost completely obscured the school. Its stands were not only capable of seating the entire town but frequently did. At the far end was a suite of offices and locker rooms housing the school's football department and there, in his inner sanctum, I found the coach, T. J. Mills. He was a hulking man with short grey hair and a grey moustache that aged him beyond his forty-two years, and that unique characteristic of former football players – a neck thicker than his head.

T. J. was on the telephone, so I perused the mementoes of his eleven years at Sealy that plastered every wall. There were plaques, medals, newspaper clippings and a signed picture of Eric Dickerson, a former Sealy player who had gone on to play professionally for the Los Angeles Rams. A framed text defined a football player as 'Courage in Cleats, Hope in a Helmet, Pride in Pads and the best of young manhood in moleskins'. Another proclaimed:

It is not the critic who counts; not the man who points out how the strong man stumbled, or where the doer of deeds could have done them better. The credit belongs to the man who is actually in the arena, whose face is marred by dust and sweat and blood . . . who, at the best, knows in the end the triumph of high achievement, and who, at the worst, if he fails, at least fails while daring greatly so that his place will never be with those timid souls who know neither victory nor defeat.

*

T. J. finally put down the phone, stood up and stuck out a great paw. 'Coach Meealls,' he announced in broad Texan.

'Martin Fletcher,' I replied in constipated English.

I explained I wanted to be a fly-on-the-wall for thirty-six hours. 'Sure,' he replied, but warned that he'd be somewhat preoccupied because it was going to be a tough game the next night. Sealy had drawn the Cuero Gobblers – bitter rivals who the Tigers had narrowly beaten before 15,000 fans in the Houston Astrodome in last year's all-state semi-finals.

'We kicked their butts right up the field,' he chuckled.

T. J. was raised in the docklands of Pasadena south-east of Houston. He was a blunt, slightly intimidating fellow with a very thick hide, and as the Tigers' coach he needed one. Like most Texan high-school coaches he was the most exposed and vulnerable man in town. If his team was losing he could expect to find vituperative letters in the local newspaper, 'For Sale' signs stuck in his front garden, and his family's life to be made miserable. Fortunately that was not a problem he'd yet faced. Under his firm hand the Tigers had won forty-one of their last forty-two games. They had recently lost the game that would have given them the most consecutive victories in Texan history, but winning a third consecutive state championship would more than compensate. First, though, they had to beat the Gobblers.

T. J. took me next door where several assistant coaches, clad in shorts and 'Sealy Football' T-shirts, were intently studying videos of the Gobblers' recent games. He had twelve assistants in all – this in a school of just 667 students – but insisted he could still use a couple more.

The players began drifting in from their afternoon classes – forty muscular hulks for whom football was a commitment that required hundreds of hours of training, weightlifting and mental application. For the most talented, particularly the black ones from poor or broken homes, it also offered the chance of a golden future unattainable through any other means. At least three Sealy players stood a chance of winning lucrative college scholarships, while in Isaiah Joiner, a young black streak of lightning who had only just turned fifteen, T. J. saw another Eric Dickerson capable of earning millions as a pro. Given the stakes, it is small wonder that some high-school players elsewhere in Texas resort to steroids.

T. J. took the players out on the field for a final rehearsal of their various plays, bellowing at those who fell short of the clockwork precision he demanded. On the night, he told me, he would decide each 'play' and relay his decision to two assistant coaches through their headsets. One assistant would then tell the players what to do through an elaborate series of hand signals from the sidelines. The other would simultaneously make dummy signals to confuse the Gobblers' coaches. No detail, it seemed, was too small to be overlooked.

That evening the school staged a pep rally in the gym. The cheerleaders did their flips and cartwheels, the band struck up, and hundreds of supporters roared as the players marched in. Afterwards I found T. J. back in his office, having his blood pressure taken by the team doctor. He looked tense. He was tense. 'You cain't help it,' he said. 'This is how I gauge my success in life, by whether I win or lose.'

On the day of the game Sealy awoke to some truly shocking news. Four people had been found shot to death in Raccoon Bend, a cluster of homes a few miles out of town. There had been no break-in and nothing taken, and there was no obvious motive. No one in Sealy could remember such a wanton act of carnage, but not even a quadruple murder could stand in the way of football.

At J. W.'s petrol station 'Blue' Schroeder, a 6-foot 8-inch giant of a man with a half-chewed cigar hanging from his mouth, confidently predicted a 20-point Tigers' victory in the slowest Texas drawl I'd ever heard. 'Ain't nothin'' in Sealy to compare with the excitement of football, he informed me.

Down the road at Toni's Restaurant a bunch of good ol' boys sat round a table recalling great plays of the past. There was the final game of 1950 when Sealy, without a win all season, beat their undefeated neighbours, Belleville, thanks to a 60-yard run in the final minute by Marvie Sens. Then there was Dickerson's astonishing

75-yard dash past seven or eight tackles to win the 1978 state championship.

These people didn't give a damn about the nearest professional team, the Houston Oilers, but they never failed to watch the Tigers. That night's game was to be played on neutral territory, in another small town called Lockhart, a hundred miles westwards, and it seemed all Sealy was preparing to make the journey. 'If I was to rob a bank this would be the time to do it,' joked Herbie Kollatschny, the veteran sportswriter of the *Sealy News* who had not missed a Tigers' game in thirteen years.

T. J. spent the morning performing the elaborate sequence of superstitious rituals he went through every game day. He said goodbye to his wife and carried his lucky clothes to his pick-up truck. He visited his daughters' old babysitter who hugged him and carefully placed a penny, heads up, in his palm. This he would keep in his trouser pocket all day. He and his assistants then gathered in his office to eat Mexican tacos, though it was only mid-morning. Later, in his pick-up, he would listen to a particular Creedence Clearwater Revival tape. When one of his assistants told me he would, as usual, be slicking down his hair with gel before the game, I made the mistake of laughing at all these superstitions. 'You dance with those that brung you,' T. J. retorted. 'You don't abandon things that work.'

It was the second *faux pas* of my visit. The previous evening he'd invited me home for dinner with his charming wife and daughters, and I'd casually mentioned soccer, which is beginning to threaten football's long supremacy in some parts of America. 'Don't say that word,' T. J. had snapped.

At 2.00 p.m. we drove out to a country club where the players sat outside in warm sunshine and ate huge barbecued steaks, turkey drumsticks and baked potatoes. We then returned to the school to find an army striking camp. When I was at school in England we would climb into a minivan (guaranteed to induce carsickness) with bags of kit and muddy football boots slung over our shoulders, and that was more or less that. Here a small mountain of equipment was being loaded into a large truck – blackboards, benches for taping the players' ankles, electric cables for the coaches' headsets, a public address system, camera equipment to film the game, nets for kicking practice, bags of towels, cases of cold drinks and chests of medical supplies.

There were two buses for the team. There were three more and another equipment lorry for the team's marching band – a uniformed force of a hundred and ten that included a nine-strong flag corps, a six-strong rifle corps, two baton twirlers, two drum majors and three full-time directors.

Also preparing to depart was the eight-strong cheerleading squad, the cream of Sealy's girlhood. These nubile young creatures attended summer cheerleading camp. They practised their drills for weeks on end. Their duties included painting giant posters for the games and sticking messages of encouragement on the players' lockers. It was a role whose attractions escaped me, yet Texans kill to become cheerleaders – almost literally. In one celebrated case a few years earlier, a woman in a small town the other side of Houston hired a hit man to murder the mother of her daughter's rival for a place in their high school's squad. Things aren't quite that bad in Sealy, but in order to avoid bitter parental recriminations the school does employ three independent judges to select their cheerleaders.

By late afternoon a mighty convoy began rolling down Interstate 10 towards Lockhart. The team bus was full, so I found myself leading the way in a police car along with the school's assistant principal who chewed tobacco and regularly disgorged the results into a spittoon. In the buses behind us the players were watching Arnold Schwarzenegger in *Eraser* because, said T. J., it was full of 'gore, blood and killing'. Behind them, strung out for miles along Interstate 10, were thousands of supporters in a fleet of pick-ups, cars and chartered coaches.

Viewed from an aeroplane that evening, Lockhart's floodlit stadium, standing alone on an empty plain, would have seemed a tiny spot of intense light in a sea of blackness. Inside, as kick-off time approached, it was a cauldron of energy and excitement. Sealy's black-and-gold draped fans packed one stand, a green-and-white army from Cuero filled the other, and the rival bands and cheerleaders were whipping both sets of supporters into a veritable frenzy. 'Go Big Black. Beat those Gobblers,' the leggy young girls from Sealy chanted through their megaphones.

Inside the Sealy locker room there was a deathly silence. The crew-cut adolescents were grimly strapping on the bulky padding that transformed them into vast-shouldered giants. They knew that if they lost that night's knock-out game it would almost certainly be the last they ever played, because only the most gifted players went on to play college football. Indeed it was quite probable that nothing else in their lives would ever compare to the exhilaration of playing high-school football. After so much intensity and adulation, after being treated as demi-gods for so long, I wondered how they would cope with being mere mortals for the rest of their days.

T. J. had spent the past hour pacing around, head thrust aggressively forward, defying anyone to speak to him, but now he was sitting in a corner with his face in his hands as if in silent prayer. An assistant coach then abruptly turned on a tape recorder, filling the room with the rasping voice of General George Patton addressing his troops during World War Two:

> I want you to remember that no bastard ever won a war by dying for his country. He won it by making the other poor bastard die for his country . . . Americans will not tolerate a loser. Americans play to win . . . The Nazis are our enemy. Wade into them. Spill their blood. Split them in the belly . . .

Patton's speech lasted six minutes. When it ended the players whooped and hollered. T. J. barked out last-minute instructions. He made them kneel around him in a circle, each player with his hands on another's shoulders. Until recently one boy had been included in the team purely because he was good at saying prayers, but he'd been dropped because of poor academic grades so T. J. had another of the players invoke God's blessing. Together the team shouted out the Lord's Prayer.

'Play your hearts out,' T. J. ordered.

The pumped-up players slapped and thumped each other. 'Let's go,' they bellowed.

The coaches solemnly shook hands, and the might of Sealy charged out on to the floodlit field to a tremendous roar from their supporters.

Over the next three hours the Tigers carved the Gobblers up. They destroyed them with ruthless efficiency. They were an unstoppable machine flawlessly executing the plays they'd rehearsed all year. Isaiah Joiner twice ran half the length of the field for touchdowns, another young black kid named Jaron Dabney scored two more, and the quarterback, Jeff Gaston, added a fifth to give Sealy a thumping 35–0 victory. I watched from the sideline, dazzled by the speed, intensity and sheer brutality of the game.

When it was over I, the journalist voyeur, instinctively headed across the field to where the Gobblers' coach had gathered his devastated team around him. 'I'm sorry it had to end like this,' he was telling them, 'but hold your heads up high. You have nothing to be ashamed of.' The players embraced their families, their girlfriends and each other, and as they trudged miserably towards their locker room – and the beginning of the rest of their lives – many were openly weeping.

At the far end of the field T. J. had called the victorious Tigers together. Once more he made them kneel, recite the Lord's Prayer and give thanks to God. Then, as they ran over to bask in their supporters' adulation, he finally allowed himself a smile. It was the briefest of respites. An hour later he was back at work. As the Tigers headed in triumphant convoy back to Sealy, this time watching an Eddie Murphy comedy, T. J. drove off westwards into the night to pick up videos of Sealy's next opponents.

Astute readers may have spotted my little chronological detour. I had actually flown down to watch the Sealy Tigers the previous November, knowing that the season would long be over by the time I arrived by car. In fact I didn't visit Sealy at all this time. I did arrange to meet T. J. in Houston, however, and the man who walked into the Cadillac Bar with his wife on his arm was scarcely recognisable as the man I remembered pacing the Lockhart touchline so anxiously three months earlier.

He was relaxed and funny. Over steak and beer he recounted how the Tigers had romped to the regional championship, won the all-state semi-final 31–14, then clinched their third successive all-state title with a 36–27 victory over the Tatum Eagles before 14,000 spectators at the Houston Astrodome. Back in Sealy the Tigers had received heroes' welcomes with fireworks in the stadium and parties that lasted till dawn. Two players won college scholarships. The Tigers were named the Texas high-school team of the year and T. J. was named high-school coach of the year.

As we finished dinner, I asked T. J. how he could maintain his motivation through yet another season. He leant forward, and the old intensity suddenly returned. The Tigers were only the fourth team ever to win a Texas high-school championship three times running, he informed me. None had ever won it four times in a row. 'Someone is going to do it, so why not us? Why else would I be allowed to win three? This,' he solemnly declared, 'is our destiny.'

The next day, in Houston, I had the car checked because it was making various discomforting noises. I ended up paying $285 for new brake pads and bearings, which was preferable to having a rear wheel seize up in the middle of some western desert.

There was also a second person I wanted to see before leaving the city – one even more intimately acquainted with matters of life and death than T. J. His name was Clarence Brandley. He was a black man who was framed by the white establishment of the small Texas town in which he lived, and spent nine years, five months and twenty-three days on Death Row for a murder he did not commit. He once came within two weeks of execution, and on another occasion within five days – so close, in fact, that he'd actually been moved into a holding cell and written his final will.

Mr Brandley's story is brilliantly chronicled in a book called *White Lies* by another British journalist named Nick Davies. It is worth retelling because it reveals the darkness that still lurks behind

the peaceful and pleasant façades of some small American towns –
the racism, the cronyism, the frontier justice mentality. No black has
been physically lynched in America for nearly half a century, but
Brandley was unquestionably the victim of a legal lynching.

In 1980 he was twenty-eight and head janitor of the high school
in Conroe, a town of about 30,000 people 50 miles north of
Houston. One Saturday that August a sixteen-year-old white girl
named Cheryl Fergeson was raped and strangled during a volleyball
tournament at the school. Term was beginning ten days later and
the authorities were desperate to catch the killer. Mr Brandley had
found the body and reported it. He had taken and passed a lie
detector test. The police nonetheless homed in on him as the only
black amongst the five white janitors, one policeman allegedly
telling him that 'Since you're the nigger you're elected'.

The town's district attorney, judges and law enforcement officers
all then conspired to secure Mr Brandley's conviction, despite
having not a scintilla of hard evidence against him. Vital facts were
suppressed, including the discovery on the victim's body of
Caucasian pubic hairs. Routine procedures such as taking hair and
blood samples from the other janitors were never conducted. Key
exhibits including the semen sample were 'lost', destroyed or with-
held from the defence. Prosecution witnesses perjured themselves.
Defence witnesses were intimidated. Leads that did not point to Mr
Brandley were ignored. The prosecutors and four consecutive
judges – all requiring popular support for re-election – secretly col-
luded and rigged the proceedings.

Mr Brandley's first all-white jury split 11 to 1, the lone hold-out
being branded a 'nigger lover' by his fellow jurists. A second all-
white jury convicted him, and the date for Mr Brandley's execution
was reportedly set for the court clerk's birthday to give her something to celebrate. It took seven years and two fruitless appeals
before one of the janitors cracked, other witnesses with uneasy con-
sciences began recanting, and a proper hearing was held well away
from Conroe before a judge with no links to the town.

That judge, Perry Pickett, declared that in thirty years he had
never encountered 'a more shocking scenario of the effects of racial

prejudice, perjured testimony, witness intimidation, an investigation the outcome of which was predetermined, and public officials who, for whatever motives, lost sight of what is right and just'. The investigation had been conducted, he continued, 'not to solve the crime, but to convict [Mr Brandley]'. The colour of his skin 'pervaded all aspects of the State's capital prosecution against him'. He had been 'denied the most basic fundamental rights of due process of law, and did not commit the crime for which he now resides on Death Row'.

The likely murderers, Judge Pickett concluded, were another janitor, Gary Acreman, and a former janitor, James Robinson. Two years later the Texas Court of Criminal Appeals, relying heavily on Judge Pickett's report, overturned Mr Brandley's conviction. He was finally freed on 23 January, 1990, and became the pastor of a makeshift church called God's House that occupied a former car-parts warehouse in the middle of a bleak black ghetto in south Houston.

I'd interviewed Mr Brandley for *The Times* in 1995, but the telephone numbers he had given me then were now disconnected so I drove out to the church. It was an unnerving experience. Black men on the pavements turned and stared as they spotted my white face. Cars with tinted windscreens slowed as they passed me. I gave silent thanks that I'd had the car repaired as this was no place for a white man to break down. Alas, my journey was fruitless for God's House had been ousted by a strip joint called the Equal Justice Nite Club whose outsized bouncer had no idea where Mr Brandley had gone. A large pawn shop was still in business across the road, I noticed, and it was now offering free weddings to purchasers of diamond rings.

I called various opponents of capital punishment (yes, there are still a few left in America). They too had lost track of Mr Brandley but I got talking to one, Jim Marcus, executive director of the Texas Defender Service, who offered me an interview with one of his Death Row inmates in Huntsville. Naturally I accepted. I finally found Mr Brandley through Mike DeGeurin, a high-powered Houston defence lawyer who had helped him win his freedom. He got Mr Brandley on another line, and I was soon heading back down a freeway to south-west Houston.

Mr Brandley, a large, slow-moving, sad-eyed man of forty-five met me on the forecourt of a Texaco petrol station and led me back to a tiny apartment where he introduced me to his fiancée and her two young children. His personal life had never been easy to follow. Prior to his imprisonment he had had five children by three different women, only one of whom was his wife. Following his release he had married a woman who had campaigned for his freedom, but that marriage was also now finished, he told me.

It was mid-afternoon, and we sat and chatted in the darkened living room while a huge television in the corner showed cartoons. He had grown a beard, shaved his head and shed some weight, but he remained a sad figure. His church had folded because of trouble with the landlord. His $120 million lawsuit against Conroe's white officials had collapsed because they enjoyed immunity from prosecution. He had received neither an apology for his wrongful imprisonment, nor a penny in compensation, and the state of Texas had actually threatened to sue him for more than $20,000 in child support payments that he had patently been unable to make during his long incarceration. No attempt had ever been made to prosecute Acreman and Robinson.

Mr Brandley now had a night job servicing Houston city buses and earned just enough to make ends meet. Yes, he was bitter, he said. None of Conroe's 'good ol' boy network' had paid any penalty and many were still in office. 'I was put through living hell for almost a decade yet still, to this day, no one will admit what took place was wrong,' he protested. He would never live in a small town again 'because I know how they function, how they operate, and what they are apt to do'. As I left, he asked for payment for the interview so I gave him $20.

The next day was warm and sunny, and I headed north towards Dallas on Interstate 45. For once I was delighted to be on an interstate, if only because it was carrying me rapidly away from Houston and back into the country. It took me an hour to reach Conroe which seemed, at first glance, a most attractive town on the edge of the Sam Houston National Forest.

There was a tranquil town square built around the imposing

courthouse, a fine old theatre where the Crighton Players were performing *Last Days at the Dixie Grill Café*, and an impressive new
library whose two copies of *White Lies* had, I was pleased to discover,
been taken out seventy-nine times since 1991. Cars stopped to let
you cross the road, and a man hurried over to help when he saw me
perusing a map.

Scratch the surface, however, and you very quickly discovered
that the same old racial divisions persist. Most blacks still live in
shacks on one side of the railway line, whites in considerable com-
fort on the other. Just two of the *Conroe Courier*'s eighty staff are
black, though the paper's new young editor said he was trying to
change that. Most of the whites I spoke to in Bob's Barber Shop and
elsewhere continued to insist that Brandley was guilty. An exclusively white establishment still runs the town, and it still includes
several of the officials who persecuted Brandley.

I wandered into the courthouse in search of Jim Keeshan, the
arch-villain of *White Lies* who, as district attorney, spearheaded the
drive to send Brandley to his death. Far from suffering for his conduct, Keeshan had been elected a judge. I found him sitting in a big,
red leather judge's chair, an elderly man in long black robes benignly
releasing divorce petitioners from unhappy marriages and looking
the very model of decorum. During a break in the proceedings, I
accosted him outside his chambers. He was perfectly friendly until
I raised the subject of Clarence Brandley.

His smile vanished. In fact he positively bristled. 'On that subject
I have been questioned and interrogated and tortured enough, so I
am going to decline to talk about it,' he declared with a note of distinct self-pity in his voice.

'Was Nick Davies' book accurate?' I persisted.

'I don't think he wrote it,' the judge replied coldly. 'I think it was
written by the defence attorney. I didn't recognise it as being con-
sistent with the facts of what happened here.'

Another court official from the Brandley era, who asked to
remain anonymous, had already assured me that *White Lies* was
'extremely accurate'. As I left the courthouse I recalled what Mr
Brandley told me the previous day. 'Conroe is just a typical little

town,' he said. 'Just because you don't see them with sheets on their heads doesn't mean they're not racist. They've got smarter now. They wear three-piece suits.'

The town of Huntsville, another 30 miles up Interstate 45 from Conroe, has two claims to fame, the first of which is that it was the home of Sam Houston, the general who won Texas' independence from Mexico in 1836 and twice served as the new republic's President before it joined the United States in 1845.

The people of Huntsville are determined you should know this. A 67-foot Soviet-style statue of the great man towers over the interstate. There is a Sam Houston university, a Sam Houston memorial museum, a Samuel Walker Houston cultural centre and the Sam Houston gravesite. On one corner of Huntsville's pretty town square I found a historical marker that read: 'This corner was a favourite site where General Sam Houston sat in a chair to whittle small objects and talk with customers at the general mercantile store.' On the opposite corner there was another that read: 'General Sam Houston is credited with having sat on this corner to whittle and tell stories to groups of listeners who gathered around him.' I dutifully checked the third and fourth corners, but it seemed the general had whittled in neither.

Huntsville is also famous for being America's capital punishment capital, a place where nearly three times as many modern-day criminals have been executed as anywhere else in the country. Texas' Death Row, which has more than 450 inmates, is in the Ellis Unit, which sits in open country a few miles out of town. The execution chamber or Death House, however, is a mere stone's throw from Huntsville's town square. It is housed in the Walls Unit, a hideous red-brick fortress with 30-foot high walls topped by watch-towers that is incongruously surrounded by pleasant tree-lined residential streets and a Dairy Queen ice-cream bar.

The town makes no effort to conceal the gruesome death-and-incarceration industry in its midst. In fact it positively broadcasts it. The Chamber of Commerce publishes a 'prison driving tour' that guides tourists around no less than eight different prisons in the

Huntsville area and finishes at the Peckerwood Hill cemetery where the unclaimed bodies of more than 900 inmates are buried. It directs visitors to the bus station where some fifty prisoners are released each day, and invites you to 'excite your senses' by listening for the periodic whistles from inside the Walls Unit that mark the completion of prisoner counts.

There is even a Texas Prison Museum amongst the town square's antique and gift shops which sells 'I Did Time in Huntsville' T-shirts. Its star exhibit is 'Old Sparky', the electric chair in which 361 prisoners died between 1924 and 1964, but I personally preferred two other exhibits.

One was an extraordinarily long and detailed hand-written list of what Prisoner 321, a man named Morrow, wanted for his last meal. At the bottom the condemned man wrote: 'This is my last meal and damn it I want it served hot and on however many plates and bowls it takes to keep from mixing any of it up and I want it served at one o'clock this afternoon.'

The other was a letter written to Henry Ford by Clyde Barrow, of Bonnie and Clyde fame, from behind bars. He congratulated Mr Ford for making such a 'dandy car' and continued: 'I have driven Fords exclusively when I could get away with one. For sustained speed and freedom from trouble the Ford has got every other car skinned.'

I got rather carried away by all this levity. I called David Nunnelee, the Texas Criminal Justice Department's spokesman, who agreed to show me the Death House itself which is in the north-east corner of the Walls Unit.

We approached it along a red-brick path bordered by rose bushes and two narrow strips of grass hemmed in by towering walls – the condemned man's last glimpse of the world. There is a row of holding cells like those in Louisiana's Angola prison, but the execution chamber itself is much grimmer. It is a small room with grey doors and woodwork and brick walls painted a darkish blue. In the middle, beneath a dangling microphone for the prisoner's last statement, is a steel gurney with a white mattress and six thick leather straps. The world's first execution by lethal injection took place on this gurney in 1982, and since then more than 125 other men have died on it, including one the previous evening. Figuratively speaking, it was still warm.

Mr Nunnelee, a slight, dapper man, told me he found the executions clinical, unemotional affairs, though they were often cathartic for victims' families. He was a man seemingly unafflicted by doubts, and he acknowledged a certain distaste for 'arrogant' British journalists who came to Texas and criticised its system. Innocent men were never executed, he insisted, but sometimes guilty men escaped because 'our system is so thorough that any one little thing can get somebody off'. In the latter category he unhesitatingly placed Clarence Brandley.

The next day I visited Dorsie Lee Johnson, the Death Row inmate whose lawyer, Jim Marcus, had offered to set up an interview.

The Ellis Unit has none of the redeeming features of the Louisiana state penitentiary. It is a cheerless brick edifice tightly ringed by watch-towers and two high mesh fences topped with tightly coiled razor wire. I was ushered into an equally cheerless visiting hall where I awaited Johnson's arrival. He had spent ten years on Death Row, had exhausted his appeals process, and even his lawyer believed he would shortly be executed. On the face of it, I could see little reason why he shouldn't be.

Johnson had not been framed like Mr Brandley. His guilt was not disputed, and his crime was pretty grisly. Aged nineteen, high on drugs and alcohol, he and a girlfriend had walked into a convenience store in the west Texas town of Snyder one night in 1986, shot dead the man behind the counter, and made off with $161.92. Two weeks later he had robbed another store, shooting the storekeeper in the face but not killing him. I naturally expected to be interviewing a monster, but I was mistaken.

The guards led in a black man in a white prison uniform who was just 5-foot 2-inches tall and looked much younger than his thirty years. They placed him in a steel cage on the far side of a screen of glass and thick wire mesh, then removed his handcuffs through a slit in the cage's door. Johnson had a pleasant, boyish face and a diffident smile. I was allowed to buy him a drink from a vending machine behind me, and he asked for a Pepsi. I suggested he start by telling me why he shouldn't be executed, and over the next ninety minutes I found myself quite won over.

Johnson said what you'd expect him to say. He argued firstly that he was a mere adolescent when he committed the murder, and secondly that he was now a completely reformed character who could make a positive contribution to society. He had begun reading voraciously in prison. He had found not Jesus, though his father had been a Baptist preacher, but Allah. He now 'strove emphatically to do what's right' and had worked 'extremely hard to bury that person that committed those things in the past, to slay that person that was driven by carnal desires'.

It made not a blind bit of difference whether I believed him or not, but as it happened I did. He spoke slowly and softly. He thought hard before answering my questions. There was nothing remotely aggressive or threatening in his manner. He had no record of violence during his eleven years in prison, and when I asked myself if I'd happily leave this person alone with my children I concluded that I would. As a small test I asked what he was currently reading. 'A book called *Freemasonry, Ancient Egypt and Islamic Destiny*,' this high-school dropout replied without a moment's hesitation.

I could hear other prisoners further down the hall loudly protesting their innocence to visiting reporters, but Johnson never sought to excuse what he had done and refused to blame his crime on drugs. He said he had consciously chosen a lifestyle of drugs, alcohol, women and fast cars because he wanted to be seen as a 'tough person in the neighbourhood', because 'it was to me exciting. It was to me everything that could be desired'. He even admitted that he'd committed other serious crimes and got away with them. When I asked if he regretted what he had done he corrected me. 'Regrets were a ball and chain,' he said. There was nothing you could do about them. They drove you mad, made you suicidal. What he had done was repent, because to repent meant 'striving to become a better person'.

Another reason I found Johnson convincing was that he seemed disinterested in trying to avert his approaching execution. He had given the subject little thought, he insisted. His faith had enabled him to banish fear. He was more concerned with helping his fellow inmates, and believed that if Allah wanted to save him, he would. Johnson had only reluctantly let his lawyers file a clemency petition with George W. Bush, the Texas governor, because he believed it was a fruitless exercise in the present political climate and did not want politicians exploiting his execution.

During the 1990 gubernatorial race in Texas, a former governor named Mark White had actually broadcast commercials boasting of all the criminals he'd sent to their deaths, while a rival, the then-attorney general Jim Mattox, responded with advertisements declaring that he'd personally attended thirty-two executions. In the official press release announcing Johnson's execution, Dan Morales, the state's present attorney general, noted that Johnson would be the eighty-ninth criminal put to death since he took office.

Johnson professed to be a much happier man now than he was when free because he had 'atoned spiritually' and discovered in Islam 'a sure foundation for joy, peace and happiness'. Freedom meant more than simply not being confined. 'Freedom is something spiritual, and I feel I've reached that level of freedom within this environment,' he said. He had also recently received a letter that had added greatly to his happiness. It was from his victim's son. The son wrote, said Johnson, that 'he forgave me for what had happened because he himself had been in prison and had hurt many people in the past but he had now found Jesus and Jesus had become a part of his life'.

There was no chance of Texas forgiving Prisoner 850, however. There was no chance of the state opting to proclaim his rehabilitation a triumph for its prison system and commuting his sentence to life imprisonment. Four months after my interview Johnson was driven to the Walls Unit in his prison whites, strapped down on that steel gurney, and had his young life extinguished by a cocktail of lethal chemicals.

In a written final statement Johnson insisted that with Allah's help he had rid himself of 'an immoral, unprincipled and ignoble state of being', and that 'I can say with much confidence to the twelve individuals who made up my jury that they were without a doubt or contradiction wrong when they said in 1986 that a young nineteen-year-old man of African descent could and would never change.' His last words before his execution, delivered in a quiet voice from the gurney, were: 'Tell my family that I love them and always be strong and keep their heads up and keep their faith in Jesus.' He said nothing to his victim's family.

In his final minutes Johnson's faith in Allah seemed to serve him well. He appeared calm, composed and displayed no emotion. As the chemicals began to flow and Johnson gasped, his brother, Gary, ran sobbing to the back of the witness room and was let out. The victim's wife and daughter watched impassively and said nothing but could hear Johnson's family weeping.

Johnson was one of two men executed in Huntsville that night, and one of four that week. It was still only June, but with his execution Texas equalled the record of nineteen executions by a single state in one year that it had itself set in 1995. Indeed executions have become so routine in Texas nowadays that they attract minimal media attention and no more than a handful of protestors. Watching a conveyor belt soon becomes tedious whatever commodity it may be carrying.

15

Living in Hope

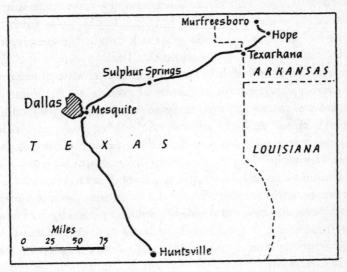

A couple of evenings later I found another irrepressibly cheerful man dwelling, like Dorsie Johnson during his Death Row years, in the most miserable of circumstances.

His name was Robert Richard. He lived all alone in a giant truck stop bounded by roaring freeways and unbelievably squalid motels. His job was to preach God's word to rough, tough truckers who could scarcely be less interested. Mr Richard radiated happiness, but I was thoroughly dejected. It was Valentine's Day. I was missing my wife and children. I was in what was surely one of the vilest spots in America, and the night got progressively worse as it went on.

Truckers are the sort of men who would have been cowboys a hundred years ago. They are a solitary, hot-tempered, macho breed. They roam the country for days or weeks on end, talking to colleagues on their CB radios. Their steeds are massive, long-nosed 18-wheelers that weigh as much as 40 tons when fully loaded and have 200-gallon fuel tanks. Instead of laying mats out by a camp-fire they sleep on bunks in the back of their cabins, and they ride into truck stops like cowboys rode into old Wild West towns. There they rest, eat, shower, watch movies, wash clothes, call home, change money, buy provisions, do repairs. The truck stops have other attributes of old frontier towns as well – prostitutes, thieves, violence.

Mr Richard lives and works in a truck stop in Mesquite, east of Dallas, that services 1,200 trucks a day. I arrived late in the after-noon and found 300 of these chrome-and-steel monsters lined up in rows across a concrete apron the size of a small airport. There was every sort of truck you could imagine – 'rooster cruisers' (produce haulers), 'tanker yankers' (oil tankers), 'bed buggers' (removal lor-ries), 'stick haulers' (furniture deliverers). Because most had their engines running to keep their sleeping drivers warm there was a low but constant roar and a pervasive stench of diesel fumes.

One truck was painted white and set well away from the others. It had the words 'Spirit of the Road' emblazoned in large red letters along its side and, in smaller writing, 'Jesus said: "I have come that you might live more abundantly."' Even its mud flaps proclaimed: 'Jesus carries my load.' This was Mr Richard's mobile chapel. Halfway along the trailer were some steps up to a door on which was yet another little notice reading: 'Jesus loves you so much that it hurts.' Inside were two padded benches and four panels of stained glass stuck up on the walls to look like windows.

I found Mr Richard cooking beans on an electric ring. He was a far cry from the beefy, bearded truckers outside. He was in his mid-forties, looked frail and pale having recently completed a forty-day fast, and had a nervous disposition. He was dressed in a white shirt and black trousers with a baseball cap labelled 'Chaplain'. He seemed delighted to see someone. 'I love Jesus and I hope you do too,' he told me by way of greeting.

Mr Richard's story was by now becoming rather familiar. He was born and raised in Louisiana although, he quickly added, 'I con-sider my citizenship is in heaven now.' He drifted from job to menial job. He married, divorced, married again. When he was twenty-eight his second wife abruptly left him. That same weekend, when he was at his lowest ebb, 'the love of God flooded my soul' and his life was filled with a joy that it seemed no setback, however serious, could quench.

He married a third time, this time to a 'Christian girl', but she too divorced him, apparently suffering from a surfeit of religion. 'She'll come back when God restores her faith,' Mr Richard assured me. 'If she doesn't, I'll be content to go to heaven and marry Jesus.' He went to work as a security officer for Jimmy Swaggart Ministries until the televangelist was found cavorting with a prostitute, but that didn't shake him either. 'When the rug was pulled from everyone's feet I ended on the rock because I never followed Jimmy Swaggart. I followed Jesus.' In 1994 he went on a two-week missionary trip to Russia during which, he said, 'God set me on fire for souls. I've been on fire ever since and I don't plan on going out. I plan on getting hotter and hotter.'

Mr Richard was ordained in 1996 and heard that the Association of Christian Truckers was looking for a preacher to man one of its two mobile chapels. The competition for this unpaid post was evidently not very stiff for he was appointed on the spot and dispatched immediately to Mesquite. He had by now spent nine months living in the truck, which has a tiny bedroom at one end of the chapel and a minute kitchen at the other, and surviving on what people gave him. 'I'm fishing for souls, and that's very rewarding,' he told me. 'I try to lay my treasure up in heaven and bring as many people with me as I can.' After all, the Second Coming was imminent – certainly less than five years off.

Mr Richard's only company was a cat called Buddy but he insisted he was never lonely. 'I have Jesus, I have Buddy, and I have visitors. When I don't have visitors I read the word and I find that very fulfilling.' Once, he said, a prostitute had pursued him into his chapel, but he'd told her that either she left or he would.

Shortly after 5.00 p.m. Mr Richard pulled on an old anorak and set off on his rounds. He worked his way down every line of trucks, knocking on cab doors and climbing on to footplates as the surprised occupants wound down their windows. 'Hello, I'm the truck stop chaplain,' he shouted above the roar of engines. 'We have a service at 6.30 this evening and you'd be very welcome to attend.'

The truckers looked down at him with a mixture of amusement and amazement. Just as I was thinking how thoroughly dispiriting Mr Richard's job must be he turned to me. 'I think I enjoy this bit more than anything, even though most of them don't come,' he remarked cheerfully. 'Some tell me to get lost. I just love them. One guy said to me "I'm an atheist". I told him "The God you don't believe in loves you all the same".'

I surveyed our bleak surroundings – lines of trucks, acres of floodlit concrete, high wire fences, billboards advertising oil changes and all the steak you can eat for $10.99.

'Don't you ever long for fresh air and green fields?' I asked him.

'Never,' he replied. 'The Lord has made this place a spiritual oasis for me.'

Mr Richard completed his rounds with an announcement over the truck stop's public address system, and by 6.00 we were back in his tiny mobile chapel. 'Every now and again I wonder what I'm going to do if everyone shows up,' he said with a grin. He need not have worried. We waited, and we waited, and we waited. Just before 6.30 a single trucker arrived – a forty-nine-year-old fellow named Lawrence who had thick glasses and a hearing aid and was driving from Wyoming to Louisiana via Taos, New Mexico. He was as smitten as the chaplain. 'A lot of times I'm on the road seven days a week, but a good part of those days are devoted to praising the Lord,' Lawrence told me. 'I'm a bit accident prone, and when I look back on the accidents I've had it's because I hadn't said my prayers in the morning.'

By this time I too was silently praying – that others would turn up to dilute our little gathering. I'm British. I'm reserved. I cringe at such intimacy, but my prayers went unanswered. At 6.45 Mr Richard decided it was time to start. 'I'm going to sing a song,' he announced. It was one he had written himself and we were apparently being treated to its inaugural performance.

'I've learned how to do this without being intimidated,' he confided. 'I close my eyes and focus on Him.'

He stood, switched on some background music and began singing into a microphone, eyes closed, one hand held aloft, his foot and Lawrence's stamping out the rhythm on the floor of the mobile chapel. The words had something to do with adjusting one's 'spiritual receiver' to thwart the 'great deceiver'.

That, in retrospect, was the high point of the evening. When Mr Richard finished he put on a video of a slick, blow-dried televangelist named John Bevere preaching in some Florida megachurch. Mr Bevere was profoundly obnoxious. He was an arrogant, self-important young man who demanded humility and selflessness. He screamed and shouted at his audience, berating them for their sins, for professing their faith without really practising it. 'I didn't come here to make you happy tonight,' he declared as the camera picked out tearful members of his congregation. 'You can throw stones at me. I don't care. I'm going to preach it.'

He launched into what he absolutely insisted was a true story. In the old Soviet Union three KGB officers burst into a secret Christian meeting. They gave the worshippers sixty seconds to leave, and most did. The KGB officers then threw down their Kalashnikovs. 'We are believers too,' they told the Christians who'd stayed, 'but we only wanted to worship with the true ones.' Believe that if you will.

Mr Bevere boastfully related how he had banished homosexuals and transsexuals from his church to teach them the error of their ways. On and on he went, periodically cupping his hand to his ear and saying 'I can't hear you' if his audience was not responding with sufficient enthusiasm to his diatribe. Finally, mercifully, his marathon monologue reached its climax. He ordered the sinners in his audience to rise and come forward. Men and women poured from the pews. He told them he hesitated to pray for them lest that offer them temporary relief. He demanded they shout out their sins in unison, and with tears pouring down their cheeks they obediently did so.

The video lasted ninety minutes and was accompanied by frequent 'amens' from my two companions. Its sole redeeming feature was that it did not require my active participation. When it finished Mr Richard appeared all ready to launch into a long sermon of his own, but by that stage even Lawrence seemed anxious to be off. It was nearly 9.00 p.m, and he would be driving out of the truck stop at 3.00 a.m. He made his excuses and I was left alone with Mr Richard.

I asked if he was disappointed that more truckers had not shown up. He'd have liked more, he conceded, but 'some evenings I don't get anybody to come. They've hardened their hearts to the point where they think they don't need anything.'

Following Jesus was not an easy road, Mr Richard conceded, 'but He never said it would be. He said, "pick up your cross and follow me".' Nothing could dim the man's enthusiasm. He whipped out a record book. To date, he said, he'd achieved 'ten first time conversions and fourteen or fifteen rededications', and tomorrow would bring a whole fresh crop of truckers for him to work on.

I got hopelessly lost going back to my motel that night. I could actually see it across the tangle of freeways and feeder roads, but whichever one I took whisked me off in completely the wrong direction. It took me fully an hour to negotiate that nightmarish concrete maze, and when I did eventually reach my room I found a truck parked right outside and its driver kept the engine running all night long.

The next morning I made the mistake of studying my map. I had planned to head directly west across Texas, but the name of Hope, Arkansas, jumped out at me, a mere two inches back in the opposite direction. How could I write about rural America and not visit President Clinton's birthplace? As an extra inducement, if that's the right word, I could also stop *en route* in Texarkana, home town of Ross Perot, the diminutive Texas billionaire who ran for president in both 1992 and 1996. And so I set off eastwards up Interstate 30, vaguely trying to calculate the chances of two men born thirty miles apart twice running against each other for the presidency of a nation covering 3,618,774 square miles.

Texarkana proved an unexpectedly rich source of amusement. For one thing, as the name suggests, it straddles the Texas-Arkansas border. This means that it has to have two of everything – two mayors, two councils, two police forces, two fire services, two court systems – one for the Texas side of the city and one for the Arkansas side.

The Arkansas side of State Line Avenue, the road that runs down the border, is lined by liquor stores because the Texas side of the city is dry. Towards the bottom of State Line Avenue the road splits and goes round either side of an ornate post office building which was deliberately built half in Arkansas and half in Texas. There is no state income tax in Texas, so Arkansas has had to exempt residents of its side of the city from paying its income tax lest they move *en masse* across the border. The city's slogan is 'Texarkana is Twice as Nice.'

Downtown Texarkana is dominated by a nine-storey brick edifice that was once a grand hotel. Today it is abandoned and derelict, a haven for tramps and junkies. The great ground-floor ballroom windows are boarded up. Flaps of curtain still hang in the broken upper windows. Peer through the hole someone has obligingly punched in the front entrance and you can see mattresses and scraps of broken furniture littering the floor of the ornate lobby. I mention this because huge signs on the front and roof of this pitiful place still proclaim its name. It is called – I kid you not – the Hotel Grim.

What amused me most, however, was the true story about the rather handsome red-brick bungalow on Olive Street in which Mr Perot was raised. A subsequent owner painted the house white. In 1979 the billionaire bought it back and had every brick turned inside out so the house looked exactly like it used to. Still chuckling, I drove on in warm sun to Hope.

Back in 1873, when Colonel James Loughborough, a lawyer for the Cairo and Fulton Railway Company, named this little whistlestop town in the remote south-western corner of Arkansas after his four-year-old daughter, he could have had no idea what a boost this would give to an aspiring presidential candidate 119 years later.

Mr Clinton constantly invoked Hope during his triumphant campaign to defeat George Bush in 1992. He repeatedly portrayed the town as a humble repository of the finest American values of faith and family. He claimed to have learned in his grandfather's country store 'more about equality in the eyes of the Lord than all my professors at Georgetown, more about the intrinsic worth of every individual than all the philosophers at Oxford, more about the need for equal justice under the law than all the jurists at Yale Law School'. It was a town he immortalised in the emotional climax of his 1992 Democratic convention speech: 'My fellow Americans, I end tonight where it all began for me: I still believe in a place called Hope. God bless you, and God bless America.'

I found, alas, that the real Hope does not quite live up to the mythical Hope of Mr Clinton's rhetoric. It is a town of about 10,000 people that sits in pleasant, wooded country just off the interstate and is periodically cut in half by a mile-long goods train rumbling through, horn blowing, on its way to Dallas or St Louis. It certainly has its good points. It boasts a wonderful coffee house called the 'City Bakery' where old-timers gather to gossip every morning. It stages an annual watermelon festival that gives the town its motto – 'A slice of the good life' – and in 1985 produced a whopping 260-pounder watermelon that made the *Guinness Book of Records*. It still supports a lively local paper, the *Hope Star*, and an outfit called the 'Dear Old Town Club', and it does seem to have a certain civic pride. The Saturday I was there bevies of teenagers were out sweeping the streets to raise money for the high-school band and there was a parade marking African-American history month. It is also 'dry', which is a good thing or a bad thing depending on your point of view.

What Mr Clinton omitted to mention was how the ugly sprawl of businesses strung out along the interstate has sucked the life from the old town centre where, despite a recent facelift, every other storefront remains dark. He said nothing about how Hope, in common with so many other small towns, is now afflicted by drugs and gangs, or how its 3,000 blacks mostly still live in dilapidated shacks on the wrong side of the railway line. That same Saturday I found members of the militant black Nation of Islam organisation actively recruiting on the streets.

Mr Clinton also played down the fact that he and his family actually left Hope just after his seventh birthday. His formative years, right up to the age of eighteen, were really spent in Hot Springs, a racy gambling and resort town ninety miles to the north-east where the Clintons enjoyed a comfortable middle-class existence. There is no way he would have invoked Hope so fulsomely had the town not been so fortuitously named, and had the political imperative not been to portray himself as a man of exceedingly humble origins running against an East Coast patrician. Hot Springs simply did not fit the Bill, if you'll excuse the pun.

The President's rhetorical elasticity has caused Hope a bit of a problem. The town attracts roughly 20,000 tourists a year, but there is precious little for them to see. The old railway station has been turned into a visitors centre that features some black-and-white photos of a distinctly chubby little boy, and a sickly-sweet ten-minute video in which Bill waxes lyrical about Hope, Hillary waxes lyrical about Bill, and Chelsea waxes lyrical about her parents.

Sandwiched by a railway line, an underpass and a shopping mall is the modest white wooden house in which baby Billy lived with his grandparents while his newly-widowed mother trained as a nurse in New Orleans. This had become a dilapidated squat by the time Mr Clinton became President, and he'd begun his second term before it was restored. There is also the nondescript bungalow in a nonde-script residential street into which the future president moved with his mother and her new husband when he was four, but this is closed to the public.

There are the singularly unmemorable buildings that were once Mr Clinton's kindergarten and elementary school, and his parents' modest graves, but that is about it unless you want to see the new by-pass which has been named 'Bill Clinton Drive', or the William Jefferson Clinton primary school. The hospital where he was born has been torn down and replaced by the new Brazzel Oakcrest funeral home. No one seems quite certain which building housed his grandfather's famous store, and anyway it is in the black part of town. Morbid political aficionados can search out the grave of Mr Clinton's childhood friend, Vincent Foster, the deputy White House counsel who mysteriously killed himself in 1993, but it certainly doesn't appear on the tourist maps. Add ten minutes to visit one of the two or three souvenir shops and you can easily see the whole lot in an hour.

The other thing that struck me was the general indifference, even here, towards America's amorphous, reactive, scandal-plagued 42nd President. There was none of the obvious affection the people of Plains clearly felt for Jimmy Carter. The foundation that had restored Mr Clinton's first home had found it hard to raise the necessary money. An assistant in the town's book-and-music shop said he'd sold numerous copies of the many books attacking Mr Clinton, but just two or three of the President's own slim volume – *Between Hope and History* – published during the 1996 campaign. 'No one likes him down here,' the young man confided. 'He's been messing around with us for long enough.'

The most exciting thing about Mr Clinton's presidency, several people told me, was having Barbra Streisand come to Hope for his mother's funeral.

This antipathy was not universal, of course. At the Western Sizzlin' restaurant I bumped into Falba Lively, a distant cousin of the President's who was working behind the till. 'I think he's just precious. I just love him to death,' she told me. 'It's really hard to keep from crying when you hear the things they say about him because I don't believe any of them.'

Hope's dearth of presidential attractions actually proved – for me, at least – a blessing in disguise. It gave me time to search out a place I'd once been told of that proved far more interesting. It was a beautiful spring-like day, so I followed a series of winding back roads about 30 miles northwards until I reached the foothills of the Ouachita Mountains near the tiny town of Murfreesboro. There, in the middle of a pine forest on the banks of the Little Missouri River, I found thirty-six acres of ploughed earth across which I counted around two dozen small figures scrabbling around in the mud.

These people were not actually mad, though a few were perhaps a little crazed. They were there for much the same reason that tens of thousands of level-headed Americans threw up everything to join the great 19th-century gold rushes. They were, with varying degrees of seriousness, chasing that elusive dream of instant wealth, for this was the Crater of Diamonds state park, the only place in North America where anyone can come and hunt for diamonds and take home those they find.

This 'field of dreams' covers the top of a vertical volcanic pipe through which diamond-bearing magma erupted roughly 95 million years ago. More than 70,000 diamonds have been found since it was first discovered in 1906, some worth tens of thousands of dollars. The biggest, Uncle Sam, weighed 40.23 carats and is the largest diamond ever found in the United States. The Kahn Canary, weighing 4.25 carats, was worn by Hillary Clinton for her husband's two inaugurations. Nine hundred and twenty-three diamonds were found in 1996 alone and the earth is reploughed every month to freshen the supply. Whenever a new one is dug up the wardens blow a siren.

Most of the people there that day were amateurs like myself, wandering around in the vain hope of spotting a diamond glinting in the sun. Occasionally it happens. But there was also a hard core of serious diggers – men like Francis LaRiviere, a middle-aged plumber from Little Rock who gets up at 4.30 a.m. most Saturdays and drives three hours to be at the park when it opens.

He and his wife spend the day extracting gravel from mud until they have two bucketsful to spread out and minutely examine on their kitchen table during the course of the following week. That way they had found four small diamonds over the previous two years and Mr LaRiviere admitted he was now 'hooked, totally addicted'. He was in the midst of telling me how he would retire and become a full-time diamond hunter the moment his teenage kids were off his hands, when he abruptly strode off across the mud. He'd seen something sparkle in the earth about fifty feet away. It turned out to be nothing, but he offered me some advice. If you see a glint drop everything, don't lift your eyes and march straight to it.

Mr LaRiviere was what you might call a semi-professional. The real pros were much further from the visitors centre and largely invisible as they were in the bottom of deep holes that they'd dug that morning and would have to refill before they left that night. They were looking for layers of grit. They reminded me of how, as a boy, I'd repeatedly tried to dig down to Australia.

Richard Cooper, a former sawmill operator who'd moved down from northern Arkansas so that he could come here every day, reluctantly interrupted his digging to tell me he'd found about 250 diamonds over the past six years, the biggest worth about $3,000. He'd once found twenty-two in one hole. 'There ain't no secret,' he assured me. 'Jus' a lot of hard work.'

No one had found more diamonds, however, than James Archer, a canny old black man who had been coming here six days a week for as long as anyone could remember. On Sundays he went to church.

I trudged over to where he was sitting, chewing tobacco, on the lip of his hole. He was a wonderful sight with his mud-spattered spectacles, yellow rubber overalls and a red baseball cap worn backwards. He had great gnarled hands from so much digging, and when he smiled he revealed a small gold star set in one of his front teeth. He had reputedly extracted a small fortune from the field, enough to put several children through college, but was admitting nothing. 'I quit countin' five years ago,' he said. 'It's jus' a hobby. I don' gamble, don' drink, don' run women. Ah had to find sumthin' else ter do.'

'What's the secret?' I asked him.

'Lot of it's skill,' he replied, directly contradicting Mr Cooper. 'Knowin' what yer lookin' fer and where ter dig. I know this dirt pruddy good. There's not diamonds all over the field. They're jus' in places.'

Four white men had paid Mr Archer the tacit compliment of digging a hole right next to his. It was so deep they needed a ladder to climb down into it. In the bottom, splashing around in ankle-deep water and furiously shovelling out mud, was a wild-looking man with a long beard and flowing hair. His name was Jim Walker. He spent his summers prospecting for gold in Alaska, and his winters looking for diamonds in Arkansas.

'Found a big one yet?' I shouted down to him.

'Not as big as the one I want,' he yelled back. 'We're going to stay till we find one big enough to choke a chicken!'

Mr Archer cackled. 'There ain't one that big,' he said. 'If there were, it 'ud quickly be a pruddy dead chicken!'

I slogged back to my car, my feet gathering more and more mud with every step. Perhaps this was what Paul Simon meant when he sang about diamonds on the soles of shoes.

16

Cow Patty Bingo

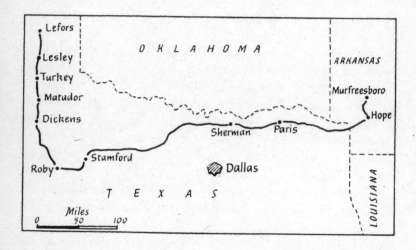

I was amazed how suddenly the South ended and the West began when I crossed from Arkansas back into rural Texas. Antebellum homes and black faces almost instantly disappear – Mexicans are the cheap labour here. The men really do wear stetson hats, cowboy boots and skin-tight jeans. The barbecue restaurants are invariably 'famous', as in 'Tommy's Famous Barbecue'. The diners all advertise 'home cookin'' and serve a uniquely Texan dish called chicken-fried steak – a piece of pounded, breaded, deep-fried beef that comes smothered in creamy white sauce. Texans eat an estimated 800,000 of these daily. At its best it is a very tasty way of giving yourself a coronary. At its worst it has the consistency of shoe leather.

I spent the next four days meandering across the northern half of Texas, driving virtually the length of England every day and considerably expanding the split that had developed in the plastic cover of my driving seat. The first day, I arrived in a little town called Muenster about 90 miles north-west of Dallas and was greeted by a sign saying not 'Welcome', but 'Willkommen'.

I drove down the main street past Rohmers Restaurant, Hamrich Menswear, Gehrig Hardware, Klement Ford and Wimmers Diesel Services. The supermarket, Fischers, sold Dusseldorf mustard, Pils beer, riesling wines and umpteen different sorts of German sausage that were made on the premises. In Bayers Kolonialwaren und Bakerei, where I ate a delectable apple strudel, the girl behind the counter told me the town was founded by German Catholics, for German Catholics, and that even today ninety per cent of the town's 1,500 inhabitants were German Catholics.

It was a bank holiday Monday, so the mayor – Henry Weinzsapfel – was not in his office, but I did find Father David Bellinghausen, the Benedictine pastor of Muenster's Sacred Heart church. He sat me down in the front room of his rectory and gave me a potted history of the town.

It was founded in 1889 by the brothers Flusche, a remarkable trio who spent much of their adult lives establishing settlements for German immigrants to the New World. They had previously founded communities called Westphalia in Iowa and Kansas, but there was already a Westphalia in Texas so they'd named this one after the cathedral city of their home province. They brought in Benedictine monks to take charge of Muenster's spiritual life because they spoke German.

One hundred and eight years later there are still numerous Flusches living in the town and the people remain thoroughly Teutonic in their outlook. They work hard and hoard their money – at the height of the oil boom in the 1970s there were said to be a hundred millionaires in Muenster. They flock to mass on Saturdays and Sundays. They go in for big celebrations, including an annual spring 'Germanfest', that features mountains of food and drink. 'In Heaven there is no beer. That is why we drink it here,' says a sign in one of Muenster's restaurants. Remarkably, many of the older inhabitants still speak German as their first language, and the only reason more of the young ones don't is that it became decidedly rash to speak German or flaunt one's German-ness in America during the two World Wars.

Muenster had an air of comfortable bourgeois prosperity about it, but that, as I soon discovered, was exceptional in rural Texas. I drove on through empty country dotted with cattle, occasional steel windmills for raising water and the odd pumpjack slowly nodding above an oilwell. The towns grew further and further apart until, in a place called Breckenridge, I saw a sign warning: 'Next McDonald's 120 Miles'. This was becoming seriously remote. I also began to detect a pattern in these small communities – cotton gins, cattle pens and feedstores on the fringes, a few pick-ups parked outside a single café, and a once-fine town square whose pretty old western storefronts were mostly boarded up. Settled when the railroads came through in the late 19th century, these towns had taken root and briefly prospered, but almost all had now fallen on hard times. The cities of Texas may be paved with gold, but its small rural towns are mostly littered with the rubble of shattered dreams.

At first sight Roby, which straddles a slight ridge on rolling plains some 200 miles west of Dallas, is a prime example of the latter. A roadsign announces that its population is precisely 616, making you wonder whether the sign is changed every time someone dies or gives birth. As you drive in across Cottonwood Creek the main street is a pitiful sight – abandoned homes, closed shops, derelict petrol stations, a boarded-up cinema and long-defunct ice plant. There is one blinking traffic light at the only real junction, and in one of the old petrol stations someone now sells 'good used clothes 10c–$1'.

What a casual visitor would never guess is that Roby probably has more millionaires per capita than anywhere else in America. I met one in the convenience store, two more in the cotton gin, another in the Silver Star Café. The place was positively riddled with them. A few months previously – on the eve of Thanksgiving Day – forty-three of its citizens had won a $50 million jackpot in the Texas state lottery and literally saved the town from extinction.

For the first half of this century Roby was a thriving cotton town with five grocery stores, three car dealerships, two drugstores, two motels, two dry cleaners, a cinema and a population twice its present size. It survived the 1930s Dust Bowl, and on Saturdays in the 1940s 'there'd be so many people in town you couldn't stir them with a stick,' recalled Roby's mayor, Cecil King, as we sat in the sunshine in his garden. What began the town's collapse was the advent of mechanised cotton harvesting in the 1950s which destroyed hundreds of jobs. Since then, agriculture generally has been in decline, and over the previous five years a severe drought had pushed the town's remaining farmers – including those who had diversified into cattle – to the brink of bankruptcy. If they went under so would the businesses in Roby that had extended them so much credit.

In desperation the town had tried to attract quail hunters. It had even staged domino tournaments in an effort to generate some money. Nothing had worked and there seemed no way out. 'You were talking about a big bust,' said Mr King, who had owned the town's only bank until he retired in 1996. For all practical purposes, he agreed, Roby would have been finished off. The *Dallas Morning News* had even used the town to illustrate the drought's devastation, raising the possibility that 'Roby and other already thinning Texas communities will eventually disappear inside the constant, wind-driven dust.'

Some in this God-fearing town call it divine intervention, others just extraordinary good luck. Down at the cotton gin Peggy Dickson, the middle-aged bookkeeper, had noticed how none of the farmers smiled any more. After several weeks without a winner the prize in the state lottery had risen to $50 million, so she decided to have some fun and organise a pool. She asked anyone who happened to drop by the gin to buy a $10 ticket. She called one farmer who was out in his fields on his mobile phone. Some people bought tickets for their wives and children. She was going to the dentist in Sweetwater, the nearest big town, and bought the tickets in Sweetwater's Longhorn Liquor Store because she'd heard it was a lucky place. The store's owner purchased a couple more tickets, making forty-five in all.

At 10.00 p.m. on Thanksgiving eve the news came through. The pool had won. 'It was all over town within thirty minutes,' said Mr King, whose daughter was amongst the winners 'The place exploded. People couldn't believe it. It was like everybody was in a dream. It affected so many people it was really unbelievable. That so many people in a town this size were going to get so much money was mind-boggling.'

As I said, you would never know Roby was a town full of millionaires. After tax, the winners will each receive $39,082.82 every November for the next twenty years. There are a few new pick-up trucks in town, but thirty of the winners were farmers and almost all are using this bonanza to ease their debts.

One, Mike Terry, a big, burly farmer, had bought tickets for himself, his wife and his three sons, and his mother and two sisters were also winners. He was still beaming when I found him in the back office of the cotton gin. His sole treat, he told me, had been to buy himself a new camera. The only other thing he now needed was rain, but that he couldn't buy.

From Roby I turned north up the Texas panhandle. I stopped for the night in a cheap little motel in a one-horse town called Dickens. It was inevitably run by an Indian family, for Indians own motels in America like Pakistanis have corner shops in England. In fact their dominance is such that some non-Indian motels now trumpet the fact that they are 'American-owned and operated'. On the whole, I found these Indian-run establishments no more or less depressing than any other motels, but this one was an exception. I woke at 5.00 a.m. to do some writing but the water was too cold to shower and the electric sockets were so ancient that I could not plug in my laptop.

I packed and left in a temper that was soon allayed by a glorious sunrise over a distant ridge of hills and – 30 miles up the road in Matador – a substantial breakfast of ham, eggs, hashbrown potatoes and limitless coffee in Billy Jean's café. These cafés are still the focal point of tiny western towns; where men in old checked shirts and baseball caps gather before work each morning to smoke, drink coffee, crack ribald jokes and flirt with the frowzy waitresses. A sign on the wall of Billy Jean's summed up the general atmosphere: 'Wanted – Good Woman. Must be able to clean, cook, sew, dig worms and clean fish. Must have boat and motor. Please send picture of boat and motor.' Outside, on one of the pick-ups, I spotted a bumper sticker that read: 'It used to be wine, women and song. Now it's beer, the old lady and TV.'

Another 30 miles north I stopped in Turkey to make a telephone call, and it was lucky I did. I smelled burning. I lifted the bonnet and found that I'd forgotten, in my anger, to replace the engine cap when I'd topped up the oil before leaving Dickens. That could well have been the end of my jalopy.

The land here was tremendous. I had stunning panoramic views across wild, rolling grasslands riven by gulches, mini-ravines and red-earthed creek beds. When I stopped the car the air was scented with juniper and I could hear nothing but the whistling of the wind. In the midst of this splendid isolation I drove through a place called Lesley that appeared to have been completely abandoned. Strung out along the road were a rickety old store and gas station, a large cotton gin that was beginning to fall apart, the shell of an old schoolhouse and a few derelict homes. Then I spotted an elderly man in blue overalls tinkering with his tractor on a patch of grass. I stopped the car. He looked up as I approached, put down his tools and held out his hand. He was a genial old soul called Arthur Clark.

'What's happened to this place?' I asked.

'Used to be a hundred and five people living here,' he replied, 'and now there's two – me and my sister. The old people died out and the young'uns went to the big towns.' Arthur was seventy-four, and his sister eighty-four.

It was a poignant story. His father was one of many homesteaders who had settled in and around Lesley at the beginning of the century. Like Roby, the town prospered for half a century. 'We had a gin, three churches, two grocery stores, a barber's shop, a café and a blacksmith's shop and a coloured town of thirty families three or four hundred yards down there,' said Arthur, pointing.

In those days a family could make a living from two or three hundred acres of wheat and cotton, but then mechanisation turned agricultural economics upside down. One by one the smallholders gave up. Arthur survived only because he had inherited a slightly larger farm from his father. As his neighbours moved away he bought up their land. With the help of ten tractors, five cotton-stripping machines, two nephews and four full-time labourers who drive out daily from the nearest town, he now farms 10,000 acres that would, in the old days, have supported the entire town.

'I've seen the place built up and gone,' he said. 'I was here when it was at its best and now at its worst.' He and his sister had probably seen 500 people die in Lesley, he reckoned.

Arthur walked me round what remained of Lesley. There were still a couple of old petrol pumps outside the store, and a well-weathered bench on the porch. Through the windows we could see a few cans on the shelves and a broom left lying on the dusty floor. The owner, a man named J. O. Adams, had been Lesley's last inhabitant besides Arthur and his sister, but he had died three years ago and was found to have amassed a million dollars.

Next door was the old garage, unlocked and empty, a summer haunt of rattlesnakes, and beyond that were the overgrown foundations of the blacksmith's shop. Across the road were the remains of an old rabbit farm and the white, two-storey house where the gin manager had lived until 1989. Its windows were broken and its roof was coming off. 'I'd nearly give it to a man to tear it down and move it,' said Arthur.

A couple of miles across the fields there was a perfectly habitable house where an old lady had lived until a few years back. Arthur reckoned you could probably buy it for $3,000. Nobody would, of course. 'The winters'll come, hailstones will knock the winders out, no one'll fix it and that'll be the end of it.'

As we talked, a car came slowly along the road – the first in half an hour. This almost amounted to an event, especially when it stopped and a young woman got out. She had a flat tyre, she explained, so we helped her put on the spare – three strangers momentarily united on a vast and empty plain.

Arthur didn't mind living in a ghost town. His sister cooked for him and he looked after her. He loved the wide-open land, the rich, red earth and the contours of the distant ridges. He and his sister would both die there, and soon after that there would be nothing left to mark Lesley's brief existence.

My ultimate destination that day was Lefors, a small town high in the panhandle that had attempted to reverse its declining fortunes not by entering a lottery, like Roby, but by staging one. The prizes were free land for anyone prepared to settle in the town, but what Lefors discovered was that in some parts of rural America nowadays it is hard even to give land away.

Lefors was founded in the 1880s as a cattle town. It was bypassed by the railroads, and usurped as the county seat, but in the 1920s it was found to be sitting right in the middle of a huge oilfield. Oilmen moved in. The town boomed, and for a few decades it was a place where, in the words of an old song, 'oil wells flow and millionaires grow'.

At its prime Lefors boasted more than a thousand inhabitants, several grocery shops, a couple of liquor stores, two or three bars, a cinema, a bowling alley, a pool hall and even a brothel. In 1975, however, a tornado demolished much of the town. The oil was beginning to run low and many of the people who lost their homes moved away for good. In the 1980s the oil price slumped and the major companies pulled out. Today you approach the place across barren plains dotted with pumpjacks, but almost all are idle and most of the wells are plugged. Lefors has lost its *raison d'être*, its population has dwindled to barely 600, and it is one of the most soporific little places I've ever come across.

It occupies a shallow valley formed by the north fork of the Red River, which has long since silted up, and is shaded by cottonwood trees. It sits just off a little-used highway that leads nowhere in particular. Most of its streets are just dusty tracks because no one has ever got round to paving them, and strangers seldom visit for there is no earthly reason why they should. There is a petrol station that doubles as a grocery store and café, a post office, a garage and a hairdresser. The school has a football stadium, but can no longer raise a team to play in it. There is one part-time marshall, crime being nonexistent. The biggest event of the year is 'cow patty bingo' which involves turning a cow loose on the baseball field and placing bets on where it will do its business.

It is the sort of place where, as a reporter from *USA Today* once wrote, 'watching a good thunderstorm blow across the rolling plains always makes for an entertaining afternoon'.

It was the school's declining numbers, and its threatened closure, that finally roused Lefors from its lethargy. Town officials realised they had to attract new people, so the school superintendent and the mayor dreamed up the idea of a lottery with fourteen vacant plots as prizes. The winners would have six months to start building a home, and would have to stay five years, but apart from that the land would be theirs for nothing.

The town did not exactly sell itself hard. Its letter to prospective residents described Lefors as 'just a small, used-to-be oilfield town. Not a whole lot happens here'. It pointed out that the town was now dry, and conceded that 'the job market here in Lefors is zero'. It was 'just a good small town to live in, where everyone knows practically everyone, even on a first name basis'. The lottery nevertheless attracted more than five hundred entries from as far afield as Canada and Bermuda.

I arrived four months after the grand draw, which was conducted by the county judge. It was the middle of the day, the town hall was closed, and there was not a soul in sight. It was warm and sunny, so I ambled off on a fruitless search for half-built new homes. By the time I returned, Virginia Maples, the city secretary, was back from lunch. She was, she admitted, 'kinda disappointed'. In the event only four of the twenty-eight winners and runners-up had accepted the plots, she told me, and none of those had yet started building. Another of the plots had been given to the city superintendent, who presently lived outside Lefors, and she was in the process of contacting all the losing entrants to try to find more takers.

Weeks later, long after the six-month deadline had passed, I telephoned and was told that building had started on just two of the fourteen plots, and that even the city superintendent had surrendered his as he had resigned and moved away.

Nobody I spoke to in Lefors seemed terribly concerned by the lottery's apparent failure. The town's decline would continue, but at least there would be no great influx of newcomers disturbing the peace. Over at the garage I found an old-timer in his seventies named Curly Callaway tinkering with a car. 'I guess I'm kinda selfish,' Curly told me, 'but I like a nice quiet place to live, and this is the quietest place to live in the entire United States.'

17

Richard the Lionheart

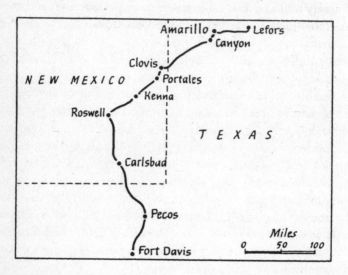

After Lefors the city of Amarillo seemed relatively bustling and prosperous. I sat in the Big Texan restaurant to eat steak and take stock. Billboards on the road into town had offered me a free 72-ounce steak but there was, of course, a snag. The steak was the size of a telephone directory. To get it free you had to eat it in an hour, along with a baked potato, a shrimp cocktail, a salad and a roll. If you failed, your bill was $50.

Since 1963, when the restaurant first made the offer, 23,342 people had tried and 4,619 had succeeded, 642 of them women. Two people had managed to eat two of the giant steaks in an hour. One man had eaten his raw. Several had subsequently asked for desert. A fat ten-year-old boy had done it, and so had a petite sixty-three-year-old woman. I debated whether – in the interests of research and economy – I should try it myself, but fortunately two hefty fellows from Illinois were already engaged on the attempt so I let them be my guinea pigs. Both gave up after fifty minutes having eaten only about as far as the letter 'P'.

I needed to take stock because my plans had gone awry. I had hoped to stay in a monastery for a couple of days. This was not just any old monastery, but a Benedictine establishment called the Monastery of Christ in the Desert that was hidden away in a canyon in the mountains of northern New Mexico. Just as their predecessors illuminated medieval manuscripts, so these monks earn their keep by designing intricate Web sites. I had sent an e-mail to Brother Andre, keeper of the monastery's guest house, asking if I might visit, but he had sent a polite e-mail back declining my request. 'We need to have a sense of peace and quiet to maintain our life as monks,' he explained. 'I'm sure you understand.'

I decided to implement Plan B. Down in the south-western corner of Texas, a bunch of armed rebels had holed themselves up in the mountains and declared Texas an independent republic. I studied my map and found that the most direct route there would take me through the south-eastern corner of New Mexico via Roswell where, as everyone knows, aliens crashed in 1949, and Carlsbad, where the government is planning to dump oodles of nuclear waste in a giant underground cavern.

The next day I drove 20 miles south to the town of Canyon where the Ten Commandments are painted on a wall opposite the courthouse for the edification of miscreants. There I lunched off chicken-fried steak in a diner called 'Village II' with some old friends, Gene and Betty Morrison, and I had to take back the rude things I'd said earlier about that exquisite dish.

I then set off for New Mexico, passing *en route* an appropriately Ozymandian epitaph to my tour of smalltown Texas. It was a historical marker planted between the road and a railway line. 'Site of Parmerton,' it read. 'In 1907 the Parmerton Townsite Company bought 20 acres of farm and laid out a town that was designated the county seat that same year . . . When in late 1907 Farwell was elected the next county seat, Parmerton's citizens departed taking homes and other buildings with them.' Featureless flat fields stretched away into the foggy distance and not a trace of the place remained.

The railway ran parallel to the road, and before I reached the border I'd overtaken a mile-long goods train. I'd seen lots of these since leaving Washington, all moving at a snail's pace, but I'd never spotted a hobo and rather assumed the practice of jumping trains had died out with the Great Depression. Not at all, I was told by an official with the Burlington Northern Santa Fe railroad company some weeks later. In his company's Seattle depot alone the railway police, or 'yardbulls', had caught 627 men 'riding the railroad' during the previous nine months. 'It's a terrible problem for us,' he admitted.

I felt the same sensation when crossing from Texas into New Mexico as I had when crossing from Arkansas into Texas – and not just because the border town here was called, needless to say, Texico. The border was an arbitrary line on a map, but the ambience changed instantly. Suddenly the people and architecture were predominantly Hispanic. The fast food of choice was tacos or burritos. There was a faint air of seediness and neglect.

I hurried through Clovis and Portales – which advertised itself as the 'Home of 12,000 friendly people and two or three old grouches' – and before I knew it I was on the loneliest, most forlorn road yet. I later learned that the sun shines 345 days a year in southern New Mexico, but I'd managed to pick one of the wet and dismal ones. For fully 90 miles between Portales and Roswell the land was flat and bleak and utterly devoid of human or any other sort of life. This was not the mountainous, forested New Mexico that entranced Georgia O'Keefe and D. H. Lawrence. It was not the place where Henry Miller once exulted 'Nature has gone Gaga and Dada.' Had I been an alien landing here I'd have taken one look through my saucer's porthole and flown straight off again, which may be what they did.

There was a place called Kenna marked on my map some 30 miles beyond Portales but it consisted of a single general store and post office – closed. About 15 miles beyond that a large white building loomed out of the fog, proclaiming itself a bar, but that too was shut. I meant to stop in Elkins – the only other place marked on my map – to ask why anyone would open a bar in the middle of absolutely nowhere, but I must have blinked at the wrong moment for I never found it. Eventually a large cinema and Walmart Superstore heralded my arrival in the World's UFO capital. I checked into the Hacienda motel, but the name and adobe architecture made not a jot of difference. It was still run by an Indian.

Roswell deserves some credit. It is an unprepossessing town of 50,000 people in the middle of the desert, 200 miles from the nearest big city and riven by a hideous commercial strip. It has little going for it, but it certainly has an eye for the main chance. One night back in July 1947, something fiery crashed out in the mesquite-covered desert. The *Roswell Daily Record* led its front page with a report quoting the local army base as saying it had captured a flying saucer. Within twenty-four hours the military disowned the story, insisting that what had really crashed was a high-altitude weather balloon.

There the matter rested until the late 1980s when 'ufologists' began claiming there had been a cover-up, that the military had spirited away a spacecraft and its occupants. Americans are deeply distrustful of their government. They are also highly suggestible when it comes to extraterrestrial matters, having been reared on movies like *2001: A Space Odyssey, ET, Alien, Close Encounters of the Third Kind* and *Star Wars*. The story rapidly gained a life of its own. 'Witnesses' stepped forward with highly-embellished accounts of what they had seen or heard or been told by someone who knew someone. A New Mexico congressman called for an official investigation, which in due course reiterated that a balloon had crashed, albeit one used for monitoring Soviet nuclear tests, but the report merely fuelled speculation by disclosing that records from the Roswell base between 1946 to 1950 were missing.

Movies like *Roswell* and *Independence Day* further fanned the flames, and by mid-1996 a *Newsweek* poll showed nearly half of all Americans believed the government was concealing evidence of alien spacecraft. In 1994 Roswell elected a new young mayor called Thomas Jennings. He spotted the commercial possibilities, and on these flimsiest of foundations the town has now built a flourishing tourist industry worth an estimated $5 million a year.

The grandly-named UFO Museum and Research Centre occupies the old Plains Cinema on Main Street and probably attracts more visitors daily than Belzoni's Catfish Museum does in a year. It features large numbers of newspaper clippings that speculate about the speculation, and a model of an alien body on a hospital bed, beside which you can be photographed for $2.50. Its gift shop is crammed with alien merchandise including lollipops that glow in the dark and an amazing selection of publications with titles like *UFOs and How to See Them, Alien Contacts and Abductions* and *Countdown to Alien Nation*. The museum's president, Glenn Dennis, a retired mortician, tells you how he received an order from the military right after the crash for several hermetically-sealed child-sized caskets, and how a military nurse, who told him she'd worked on the alien bodies, was swiftly transferred from Roswell and never seen again.

On the edge of town is a rival establishment, the UFO Enigma Museum, which displays a large fibreglass model of the flying saucer with dead aliens draped across it and a military policeman standing guard. The *Roswell Daily Record* sells thousands of reprints of its famous front page each year for a few dollars each. And 30 miles to the north Hub and Sheila Corn will guide you – for $15 – to the rocky bluff on their ranch where the spacecraft is said to have crashed, although the UFO Museum insists the real site was 53 miles west of Roswell in the middle of a national forest. Both places were identified by the late James Ragsdale, a former truck driver who was 'buck naked' with his girlfriend in the back of his pick-up when, he claimed, he saw the actual crash.

I called the mayor's office. Mr Jennings answered the phone himself. Could I come and see him, I asked. 'Sure,' he replied, 'if you come right now.' That was one of the great things about life away from big city America. You could see people without having to make an appointment sixty-eight days in advance.

Mr Jennings was a laid-back fellow with longish hair who punctuated every sentence with 'man'. His office resembled the museum gift shops. There were alien T-shirts and a framed copy of that famous front page pinned up on his walls. Alien teddies were scattered around on chairs. A flying saucer hung from the ceiling fan, the doorstop was shaped like an alien's head, and an alien's face stared out at me from the stone in the mayor's Mexican bolo tie. He showed me the town's new saucer-shaped logo he'd had designed, and even the watermark on the city's official stationery now bore it.

The previous mayor had had little truck with all this saucery, fearing Roswell would be branded a town of nutters, but Mr Jennings has no such compunction. He has a marketing degree. He reckons Roswell should be more than a mere pitstop where travellers refuel themselves and their vehicles and then drive on. Something occurred back in 1947, though he has no idea what. 'It happened, man, so we are going to take advantage of it. This is America. This is a capitalist society.' Besides, he added, 'This is fun, and the rest of my job sucks.'

Back at the UFO Museum, I conducted my own highly unscientific survey by quizzing about a dozen visitors. Not all believed it was an alien spacecraft that crashed near Roswell, but not a single one accepted the government's version of events. 'I don't believe anything the government says. They've covered up too many things before,' said Jerry Cotten, a pony-tailed postman from Albuquerque.

I realised it was time to leave when a museum volunteer named Dennis Balthaser began rebuking me for being flippant. He was a wiry, intense, bearded fellow with a toothpick sticking from his mouth. He was a certified UFO investigator, he informed me, and a fully-fledged member of MUFON – the Mutual UFO Network. He had moved here from Texas to pursue his research. 'This is serious business,' he insisted, but I was already halfway out the door.

You make money where you can in this barren, arid region. Roswell makes it from UFOs. Carlsbad, a town of about 27,000 people 80 miles further south, makes it from nuclear waste.

Back in the 1970s, when the Department of Energy was searching for a site for a subterranean nuclear dump, Carlsbad actively lobbied to have it built beneath a 16-square-mile patch of desert east of town. The competition was not exactly fierce. Work began in

1981, and the vaults were ready to receive their first consignment by the late 1980s. The regulatory battles were far from over, however, and the scheduled start of operations slipped from 1988 to 1990 and then to the end of 1997. During all this time the project has been Carlsbad's largest private employer. It has provided 1,000 well-paid jobs and pumped hundreds of millions of dollars into the local economy, and will continue to do so until the dump is filled and closed in 2033. Paradoxically, opposition in New Mexico to the 'Waste Isolation Pilot Plant' or WIPP, as the dump is known, grows stronger the further you are from Carlsbad.

Early the next morning I added to my growing list of great American diners with a breakfast of ham omelette, hashbrown potatoes, toast and limitless coffee for a mere $1.95 in the Deluxe Café. Then, as the tourists headed off to the famous Carlsbad Caverns national park, I drove 25 miles eastwards through the sagebrush and mesquite with Ralph Smith, WIPP's institutional programmes manager, to explore this entirely different sort of cavern.

From the surface all you could see was a large brown rectangular building sitting in the middle of nowhere and surrounded by high wire fencing. We were welcomed by Jay Lees, WIPP's press officer. We put on helmets and goggles, went through some elaborate safety and security procedures, and took a steel-mesh lift half a mile down into the earth to where, some 225 million years ago, the evaporating Permian Sea had deposited a layer of salt 2,000 feet thick. We stepped out into a warm, dry, muffled subterranean world unlike anywhere I'd been before. A golf cart was waiting for us, and we set off into an 11-mile rectilinear warren of dimly-lit tunnels with crystalline walls and great vaults as long as soccer fields. One day these modern-day catacombs would hold 6.2 million cubic feet of waste from America's nuclear weapons programme stored in hundreds of thousands of 55-gallon drums.

We spent two hours driving around this intestinal maze, and I found my guides' enthusiasm quite contagious. Salt was elastic, they explained. It moved. In the 100 years after the dump was sealed the walls would envelop the drums like putty and the catacombs would disappear. The shafts to the surface would likewise heal. Moreover the layer of salt was so thick that no water had permeated it for more than 200 million years. It would take 240,000 years for the nuclear waste to lose its radioactivity and that, by comparison, was a 'mere hiccup in time'.

The only real danger, as these men saw it, was if future generations inadvertently breached this toxic capsule by drilling or mining, and the Department of Energy was making some remarkable plans to prevent that happening.

For a century after the dump was sealed the site would be closely guarded, but two panels of independent experts had also dreamed up ways of warning men thousands of years hence of the radioactive waste buried 2,150 feet below the surface. The site would be ringed by a 33-foot high earthen barrier, 98-foot wide at the base, with radar reflectors and magnets buried inside it. There would be granite monuments, extending 22 feet below the earth and 25 feet above it, inscribed with pictograms and warnings in seven languages. Two 'information centres' with detailed stone-carved messages would be left at the site, one above ground and one buried in case our descendants were tempted to excavate. Discs made of various durable materials and carrying warnings about the location of the waste would be randomly buried in the area, and detailed records would be stored at locations around the world.

I found these measures a little disconcerting. They implied that our present civilisation might not survive. That may seem unthinkable, but then New Mexico is littered with the abandoned pueblos and cliff-dwellings of Indian cultures that doubtless thought they would last for ever.

As Mr Smith and I drove back to Carlsbad, along a road that in the heat of summer would be carpeted with basking tarantulas, he told me how deeply any federal official was distrusted in the West nowadays. To work for the government, he said, was 'like having a five-hundred pound albatross tied round your neck . . . you have to build your credibility from the bottom'. It was the same theme I'd picked up at Roswell, and it was one I was to encounter time and again as I travelled ever further into the huge open spaces of the

West, where Americans have traditionally gone to escape the reach of government.

South of Carlsbad was another hundred miles or so of empty desert. It was an agoraphobe's worst nightmare, a place where spotting a jackrabbit was a noteworthy event. It was so vast and empty that soon after crossing back into Texas I found a historical marker next to a turn-off to Mentone that read:

> Mentone: Only town in Loving County, last-organised and most sparsely populated county in Texas . . . With a population of 42 Mentone has no water system (water is hauled in). Nor does it have a bank, doctor, hospital, newspaper, lawyer, civic club or cemetery. There are only two recorded graves in the county.

I later discovered that Loving County covers no less than 664 square miles.

The light is so clear here that I could see my destination, the Davis Mountains, from 50 miles away. An hour later I finally left the desert and began following a tumbling river lined by cotton-wood trees up into rugged hills topped with sheer red bluffs. In the evening light the scenery was breathtaking. I doubt one American in a thousand has even heard of these mountains, but in England they would unquestionably be a national park. Thirty ecstatic miles later I drove into Fort Davis – the highest town in Texas at 5,000 feet – that was just as enchanting.

The town's old frontier fort, built to protect westbound settlers and gold-seekers from the Apaches and Commanches, has been tastefully restored. In the middle of the town square is a fine, silver-domed courthouse surrounded by lawn and ancient cottonwoods. Scattered around the square's four sides are stone buildings dating from the early 1900s, including a four-cell jail that now serves as the public library and a marvellous old limestone establishment called the Hotel Limpia where I found a blazing fire in the lobby. There was no traffic, the crisp mountain air was scented with woodsmoke, and as night fell a million stars lit up the heavens.

I awoke the next morning to a brilliant sunny day, ate an excellent egg, cheese and potato burrito for breakfast at an original 1911 soda fountain in the Old Texas Drugstore, and set off across a great grassy plateau dotted with cacti and fringed by distant mountains. Someone had erected a plaque on the side of a boulder honouring 'the stage drivers who travelled this route, fearless heroes of frontier days. By their courage the west was made'. The country reeked of the old Wild West. It even had its own resident outlaws – a group of armed men led by an erstwhile carpenter and failed vintner named Richard McLaren – that was the latest perverted manifestation of America's long tradition of dissent.

This group had been holed up for three months in these hills, insisting that Texas was an independent nation and fighting a bizarre, almost comical, war against the US government and its Texan 'stooges'. Two warrants had been issued for McLaren's arrest, but he was threatening 'World War Three' if the authorities sought to arrest him, and the forces of law and order, singed by their deadly raid on the Branch Davidians' Waco compound in 1993, were not exactly rushing in.

McLaren, the Republic's 'chief ambassador and consul general', had told me over the telephone how to find him. Ten miles west from Fort Davis I turned on to a dirt track and rattled five miles into the hills past the Paradise and Lazy Shade ranches. There I waited, with some trepidation, at a tiny country store until two men arrived to collect me in a big brown pick-up.

They were actually rather friendly. One introduced himself as Chris Leonard, a thirty-five-year-old former window cleaner from Lubbock, Texas. He explained, with a perfectly straight face, that he had been the Republic's district commander in Lubbock until the previous October when the 'secretary of defence' had promoted him to 'major' and sent him here to guard the headquarters. He was now, he proudly informed me, head of security.

The other was a sixty-three-year-old trucker called Melvin Kriewald who had recently chucked in his job to become San Antonio's district commander. 'Freedom. Everything we do is for freedom,' he told me. 'The school system is beyond repair. The government is beyond repair. Even our state government is beyond repair.' Sewn on Kriewald's baseball cap was the lone star emblem of the 'Republic of Texas Defence Forces', and slung from his waist was a semi-automatic pistol.

Leonard bought some bread, eggs and milk, spoke conspiratorially into his walkie-talkie, and off we set up labyrinthine tracks that carried us high into the rugged interior. This was the sort of place where loners and misfits came and hid themselves away, and we passed several trailer homes buried in groves of stunted oaks and pinyon trees, and posted with 'Keep Out' signs.

Our first stop was at Leonard's own trailer where he dropped off the groceries and his wife handed him his SKS semi-automatic rifle. He told me his two children were homeschooled, and invited me to photograph the Republic of Texas numberplates on his car. A couple of miles further into this cloud-cuckoo-land the track became impassable. We got out and walked the last few hundred yards. I glanced back and noticed another armed man had stepped out of the trees on to the track behind us.

The Republic's 'embassy' was a peculiar hybrid construction, half caravan and half wooden shack, with a sign saying 'Embassy of the Republic of Texas – Certified Diplomatic Immunity' stuck up somewhat optimistically outside. The door was thrown open by a cheery blonde who introduced herself as Evelyn McLaren, the ambassador's wife. The interior was a kitchen, bedroom and office all in one, an untidy jumble of tables, chairs, beds, filing cabinets, televisions, fax machines and computers with a wood stove crafted from an oil-drum. McLaren jumped up from one of the screens. He was a scrawny, exuberant fellow in his mid-forties with a bald pate ringed by long, flyaway hair that made him look like a mad professor. He seemed genuinely pleased to see me as if my mere presence was conferring international recognition on the Republic. He apologised for the mess. The embassy had just moved here from an empty fire station back down the track. If attacked, he explained, this place would be easier to defend until reinforcements arrived.

There was an Indian named White Eagle, an odd-job man who had come down from Colorado, working on the computers, and we were joined by another woman who McLaren introduced, without a trace of irony, as 'our ambassador to the Middle East'. Her name was Karen Joy Coffey Kosier, a retired and decidedly humourless teacher who hailed not from Texas but Nebraska. McLaren, for that matter, was raised in Missouri. We all sat down, and for the next two hours I was assailed by a torrent of fluent gibberish and eloquent nonsense that made Alabama's creationists seem the epitome of moderation and good sense.

These people were serious conspiracy theorists. It was common knowledge, they said, that the government had blown up its own federal building in Oklahoma City in 1995 in order to destroy incriminating records on the Whitewater scandal, the Waco assault, and the chemical and biological contamination of American troops during the Gulf War. They insisted that the government knew how to produce free energy and make cars run on water, but were suppressing these technologies because oil was a means of control. They had not the slightest doubt that the US and other governments were puppets of a small cartel of Zionist financiers, and that the federal government was a profoundly malign and oppressive institution bent on suppressing the people.

McLaren had come up with what he evidently considered the perfect, foolproof solution. Leaning close to my face, he said he had proved 'beyond a shadow of a doubt' that the original Republic of Texas was illegally annexed by the United States in 1845, and then scurried around the room pulling out hefty legal tomes and ancient congressional records to make his point. For all I know he may be right, but it all seemed rather irrelevant when 18 million Texans – however much they boast of their uniqueness – happily call themselves Americans and have been doing so for a century and a half.

McLaren had nonetheless broadcast his discovery on the Internet. In December 1995 he and more than a hundred other self-proclaimed 'Texians' – as the original Texas republicans had called themselves – had gathered at an old cotton gin near San Antonio for a two-day 'constitutional convention' that had declared Texas an independent nation once again.

Those present elected a 'provisional government' complete with a president, vice-president and full cabinet. That government had 'reannexed' the parts of Colorado, Kansas, New Mexico and Oklahoma that had belonged to the original Republic. It had 'ordered' George Bush, the governor, to step down. It had 'seized' the state capitol in Austin, though it was generously allowing the legislature to continue using it for the time being. It had set up kangaroo courts to 'try' state officials and created a 'corps of engineers' to take over the state's roads, dams, reservoirs and other infrastructure. It had demanded $9,300 billion in 'war reparations' from Washington, and had sent letters to other nations requesting recognition.

McLaren pulled open the bottom drawer of a filing cabinet to reveal a stack of manila files 'for all the countries we're dealing with'. One European state was about to offer the Republic embassy space, he claimed, but unfortunately he could not reveal which until the deal was completed. He even produced a copy of the handwritten document confirming Queen Victoria's recognition of the original Texas Republic in 1840 – a recognition he claimed had never been revoked.

The 'provisional government' had also embraced McLaren's plan for ousting the present 'illegal' government of Texas. Its weapon of choice was not the gun, but the lien – a legal device by which creditors in Texas can put a hold on people's property to prevent it being sold or otherwise disposed of. McLaren and other 'Texians' had now filed hundreds of phony liens against Governor Bush, top state officials, judges, law enforcement officers, the state's banks and countless other Texans. According to McLaren the liens require the recipients to prove within ninety days that the state's assets belong to it and not to the illegally-annexed Republic. They had failed to do that, he said, so ownership of those assets had reverted to the Republic.

Officials in Austin were 'having a heart attack', McLaren continued. They knew they had no way out. Their whole corrupt and rotten edifice was collapsing. The only remaining question was whether the illegal government of Texas would capitulate quietly or resort to violence. The latter would be a terrible mistake, he warned.

At least ten per cent of Texans had guns, hated the government, and would take to the streets if there was another 'Waco'. The Republic, he claimed, had organised military units in almost every county, identified strategic targets throughout Texas for retaliation, and been promised support by citizens' militias from all across America. There would be a 'national military response', he insisted, and once the fighting was over those who had perpetrated the violence would be tried by an international war crimes tribunal. He was, naturally, ready to die for the cause.

McLaren was living in a world of complete fantasy, of course, but he was right in saying that Austin was concerned. He and his followers had cashed hundreds of thousands of dollars' worth of bogus 'Republic of Texas' cheques, and the liens – his 'paper terrorism' – were causing Texan businesses and individuals tremendous legal headaches. A judge had ordered him to desist, but he had ignored that order and three months earlier the judge had issued a warrant for his arrest. The Texas attorney-general's office had also fined him and his followers $10,000 for contempt of court and that fine was doubling daily. The total had now reached $5,764,607,523,034,237,180,000, according to the attorney general's office, or 'in excess of $5 sextillion'.

The day before my visit another judge had issued a second arrest-warrant after McLaren failed to appear in the Fort Davis courthouse to answer a burglary charge. The problem was that no one knew how many men McLaren really had up in his mountain hideaway, and whether they would in fact use their guns. McLaren was certainly not telling me, though he claimed there was at least one unit of thirty-five men with others as back-up. The interview was over. I stepped outside and found half a dozen armed men sitting around in the sunshine. 'Give my regards to the Queen,' the ambassador to the Middle East told me as I departed. 'She's my relative. I know she's no fool. I know she'll rise to the occasion.'

As it happened, Her Majesty was spared the need to rise to the occasion. Three months after my visit, one of McLaren's colleagues was arrested during a visit to Fort Davis. His group responded by kidnapping a couple who lived nearby, whereupon more than a hundred law enforcement officials equipped with armoured personnel carriers swiftly surrounded McLaren's 'embassy'.

McLaren issued 'Mayday' appeals on short-wave radio. He sent out a message in a 'diplomatic pouch' chucked from the front door that echoed Colonel William Barrett Travis' famous appeal for help while defending the Alamo in 1836: 'I pray reinforcements will arrive before they overrun the embassy.'

World War Three did not break out, however. Militias across the country did not rush to help McLaren. No more than a dozen armed men were detained as they tried to reach him. After a week-long siege McLaren finally called an 'international ceasefire' and surrendered, saying he planned to seek diplomatic immunity. The state police killed one member of the group who tried to escape into the mountains and defused about sixty pipe-bombs and booby traps discovered around the 'embassy'.

18

Cowboys and Indians

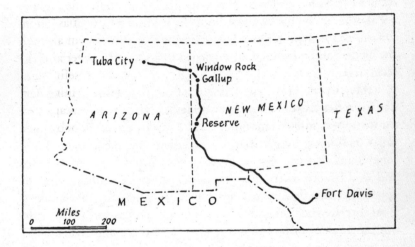

An hour after leaving McLaren's 'embassy' I was instantly converted to his cause. I had come down from the hills and was driving at a leisurely pace along a wide, straight, empty road when I spotted a state patrol car's flashing lights in my rearview mirror. I was doing 60 miles an hour in a 45 mph zone, the officer informed me. I looked around. There was not another vehicle or creature in sight, just one or two tumbledown shacks by the roadside that apparently constituted the town of Valentine. By no stretch of the imagination could I be said to have been driving dangerously. I was momentarily tempted to pull out my newly-acquired 'Republic of Texas' passport and challenge his jurisdiction. I didn't, of course, and resumed my journey $140 poorer and livid.

It was a hot, hot day and mountains shimmered in the distance. For a while I followed a back road along the fertile valley of the Rio Grande, on the other side of which lay Mexico. Everyone spoke

Spanish, most of the signs and advertisements were in Spanish, and with the exception of several border patrol jeeps, the cars were all jalopies that made my own look positively smart. I joined the interstate just before El Paso, a city that has chosen to conceal its undoubted charms behind a truly hideous façade, and kept driving well into the evening until I reached the gentrified old mining town of Silver City in south-west New Mexico. I stopped for the night at yet another motel distinguished only by its utter lack of distinction. One pleasure of winter travel, however, is that you can haggle with the owners and most nights I managed to knock $10 or $15 off the room rate.

I thought the Fort Davis area was beautiful, but early the next day I entered Catron County, a wonderland of gorges, canyons and snow-capped, forested mountains. The county covers 7,800 square miles, making it bigger than Connecticut, but has a mere 2,600 inhabitants. It truly seemed God's own country, a haven of peace and wild beauty where man has all the space he could desire, but appearances are deceptive. Catron County is actually the source of a 'sagebrush' rebellion against Washington that has spread throughout the rural West. It is here that the old West has launched a bitter rearguard action to defend its way of life against a federal government that has adopted the environmental and recreational agenda of America's suburbanites. It is a place whose county commission made headlines in 1994 by passing a resolution calling on every home to arm itself. The issue that has aroused these violent passions is which America – rural or suburban – has first claim on the national forests and other publicly-owned lands that cover three-quarters of Catron County and half the entire West?

I headed north on the only main road and stopped at a cattle ranch just beyond a tiny community called Glenwood. This is one of 175 ranches in Catron County that support three-fifths of its population. It is owned by Hugh McKeen, a lean, brown, square-jawed cowboy with deep-set eyes who would make a good stand-in for the Marlboro Man, and by his brother Bob, who wouldn't. They lent me a horse. The three of us forded the San Francisco River and rode up through scrubby bushes to the top of a nearby mesa from which we surveyed a breathtaking view of rugged hills and valleys.

It was here in the Mogollon Mountains that the Apache chiefs Geronimo and Victorio led some of the last Indian raids on white settlers. It was in the valley immediately below us that Butch Cassidy and his Wild Bunch hid and worked as cowhands between their periodic rampages in the 1890s. It was near Glenwood that Billy the Kid was first jailed, but escaped by climbing up a chimney. And it was to this beautiful but inhospitable corner of America that the McKeens' grandfather had come at the start of this century, when it was still very much frontier territory, to raise cattle and sell fodder to passing wagon trains.

Most of this land was inside the Gila National Forest and therefore federal property, but the brothers' point was this. Their grandfather had settled here at considerable personal risk – his brother had actually been killed by the Indians – and with the active encouragement of a government that believed it was America's 'manifest destiny' to tame the entire continent. For nearly a century he, his sons and now his grandsons had paid fees and raised cattle on that land. If anyone had a right to use it – and knew how to preserve it – it was the McKeens. But now, they claimed, the Forest Service was preparing to force them off in the same way that the US Fish and Wildlife Service had recently destroyed Catron County's second biggest industry – logging – by declaring the Mexican spotted owl an endangered species.

The Forest Service was planning sharply to reduce the number of cattle the ranchers could graze, claiming this was necessary to protect the grasslands. It was planning to double the subsidised grazing fees, and to declare substantial tracts of land off-limits altogether by listing creatures like the willow flycatcher and spikedace minnow as endangered species. It was also planning to reintroduce the cattle-killing Mexican grey wolf. How high were passions running, I asked Hugh McKeen. 'High enough,' he replied, 'that you have people who say that when they come to take away my water rights and grazing rights they're going to have to pass over my 30:30 [gun] . . . There'll be another civil war over this thing if the government doesn't change.'

I drove on to Reserve, the county seat, along a road with so little traffic that other drivers waved as they passed. There I searched out Michael Gardner, the Forest Service's district ranger, who to his credit scarcely tried to deny that government policy was changing. He felt deeply for the ranchers, he told me, but city folk wanted real wildernesses again. They wanted to see wildlife, not cows. 'It's pretty obvious to me that change is coming,' he said. 'These are national forests and rural America has a lot less votes and say-so in Washington than urban America.' Besides, he said, it took more than 600 acres to raise a cow in this arid region of America compared to forty or less in the Midwest.

Proud, independent westerners have reacted with varying degrees of fury to what they see as President Clinton's 'War on the West', to the ever-tighter restrictions being placed on their use of federal lands by a government they consider arrogant and overbearing. In southern Utah locals were re-opening old rights of way through 1.7 million acres of pristine but coal-rich canyonlands in a bid to thwart Clinton's attempt to declare it a national wilderness. Shots had been fired at Forest Service officials in California, and in 1995 a bomb exploded outside the Forest Service's district headquarters in Nevada's Carson City. In Catron County pipe-bombs had been found in the Gila Forest, and there was an aborted attempt to establish a citizens' militia, but so far the county's leaders have chosen to fight within the law.

The county commission has passed ordinances insisting on its legal right to participate in decisions on the use of federal lands within its boundaries and, in effect, threatening to prosecute federal agents violating the civil and property rights of Catron County citizens. Those ordinances have since been emulated by dozens of other rural counties that have joined the so-called 'county supremacy' movement.

The commission has produced its own detailed plan for the use of federal lands whose preamble warns that federal agents 'present a clear and present danger to the land and livelihood of every man, woman and child. A state of emergency exists that calls for devotion and sacrifice'. It has filed lawsuits where it believes federal agencies have failed in their statutory duty to take that plan into account when making decisions. The big question, however, is how the county's ranchers will react if these efforts fail and their livelihoods are directly threatened.

Reserve is a town of less than four hundred people, a cluster of homes, family businesses and the county courthouse high in a mountain valley. I found it bristling with tension. On pick-ups parked along the main street were bumper stickers reading 'Hungry and out of work? Eat an Environmentalist', or 'Due to a shortage of wood and paper products wipe your a** on a spotted owl'. In Bill's Bar, as I drank a beer, I heard a rancher quietly ask his neighbour whether I was an environmentalist. Mr Gardner, the district ranger, had instructed his employees to avoid all confrontations, and elsewhere in Catron County, Forest Service employees had been issued with personal radios.

Shortly after checking into a motel there was a knock on my door and the owner came in to talk. He and his wife were city folk who had moved to Reserve the previous year, he said. He was a nature lover but wouldn't dare admit it around here because 'I'd get in one hell of an argument and would probably lose a lot of business.' He had quickly removed the 'tree hugger' vanity plates from his car, and had dropped plans to offer Forest Service employees a discount in his café. The locals hated change and resented newcomers, he said. Moving here had been a bad mistake. He and his wife would pay off what they'd borrowed to buy the motel then get out, but 'right now, we're pretty much stuck'.

The threat of violence was pervasive. Some of the ranchers sounded like Patrick Henry declaring 'give me liberty or give me death' before the American Revolution. 'A lot of people feel it's better to die than get ruined as a person,' said Bob McKeen. 'If it comes right down to it they will get their gun out and say "leave me alone".' But not many believed they would ultimately prevail.

In Jake's general merchandise store I found a balding, middle-aged man named Danny Fryar behind the counter. His logging business had gone bankrupt thanks to the Mexican spotted owl, and the family ranch was now in danger too. 'I think we'll lose,' he admitted. 'The city folk will probably get their way. They will manage these forests from Washington DC and they will go to hell. No one will take care of them . . . It is heartbreaking,' he said. 'My family moved here to get away from civilisation and now it's caught us here. We've talked about it a lot but there's no other country to go to and no other place in the United States. We don't have any place to go.'

I somehow doubt that Texas will ever achieve independence, Richard McLaren's efforts notwithstanding, but there is already a sovereign nation within the United States. It has a population of nearly 170,000 and is almost the size of Ireland, covering 25,000 square and decidedly arid miles of New Mexico, Arizona and Utah. It has its own capital, parliament, judicial system, police force, taxes, flag, national parks and time zone. It is a dirt-poor third-world country ringed by the richest of the first-world, a neo-socialist welfare state in the heart of capitalist America. Its people have their own language and very distinctive physical features – black hair, brown skins, high cheek bones. I am talking of the Navajo Nation.

I drove the 150 miles north from Catron County to Navajoland in a blinding snowstorm that lent my journey a dreamlike quality. It was as if I had travelled through a long white tunnel and emerged in a completely different continent. I did, admittedly, spend a night in Gallup before entering the reservation – or 'preservation' as President Reagan once mislabelled one of these Indian enclaves – but that only enhanced my sense of entering a foreign land. Gallup is a tatty border town catering to – and exploiting – the less felicitous demands of the Navajo people. It is full of pawn shops, loan companies, liquor stores and bars. I also found in Gallup my cheapest motel yet, though for what I got, $15.95 was quite expensive.

The Sunset Motel was one of several strung out along the old Route 66, and not a penny appeared to have been spent on it since that famous highway was rendered redundant by new interstates several decades ago. My room had subdued lighting courtesy of 30-watt bulbs. Its decor had a hole motif – holes in the bedcover, the shower curtain, the walls. The window was cracked, the grill had fallen off the heater, the paint was peeling and there were damp stains on the ceiling. The basin had no plug – though I have yet to find a motel anywhere with plugs that work. The flannel looked as if it had been used to clean the shower – except the shower had patently not been cleaned because the previous occupant's soap wrapper was still there. It was the sort of room that made you instinctively itch and scratch, and any hope I had of actually sleeping in this motel from hell was dashed by interminable clanking goods trains that arrived unfailingly every time I dozed off.

The next morning I positively galloped from Gallup, earnestly hoping that the sun would soon set on the Sunset Motel, and spent the next day and a half in the Navajo capital of Window Rock, which sits on the reservation's southern edge and is named after the big round hole in one of the great red sandstone cliffs that tower above the town.

Window Rock, with a population of just 3,300, is a miniature version of so many third-world capitals. It is a straggly place that aspires to a certain grandeur and sophistication but falls well short; superficially a modern place where old habits and customs persist. I do not say that disparagingly. After the efficient blandness and impersonality of so many American cities I found Window Rock refreshingly idiosyncratic.

The boulevards are big and wide, for example, but they are pitted with great holes and split by cattle grids. On patches of scrubby grass between the town's many administrative offices horses graze. Right opposite the modern shopping mall is a large expanse of dirt on which vendors peddle hay, secondhand shoes, and 'fry bread' – a deep-fried dough eaten with honey that is the Navajo 'fast food'. Craftsmen wander unimpeded through the government buildings, hawking jewellery or carvings. There is a fine war memorial just beneath the sacred window rock, but the eternal flame had gone out. The tribal museum is doubtless just as fine but was closed for lack of staff.

I was shown round KTNN – 'The Voice of the Navajo Nation' – which seems just like any other American commercial radio station except that it broadcasts in Navajo and plays Native American music. Intermittently, however, the disc jockey announces arrangements for someone's funeral in Houck, that some livestock have been lost near Sheep Springs, or that there will be a pow-wow the next Sunday at Rough Rock. Barely one Navajo home in five has a telephone and the station is the Nation's noticeboard, the only means of rapidly disseminating information to all its widely scattered people.

America's 2.1 million native Indians have the highest rates of poverty, unemployment and disease in the country. Here in the Navajo Nation, the largest Indian reservation, the 1990 census found the average per capita income to be $4,106 compared to $14,420 nationally. Fifty-six per cent of its inhabitants live below the poverty line compared to thirteen per cent in the country as a whole, and less than three per cent have a college degree compared to twenty per cent nationally. Of the reservation's 170,000 inhabitants, barely 30,000 have jobs, and of those nearly half are employed in the public sector. That does not make these red men grey, however. From the radio station I wandered over to the Department of Behavioural Health Services and met an unusually colourful array of characters.

There was the department's director, Stanley Benally, a Vietnam veteran with two braids of long black hair. He spoke with surprising candour about the problem of alcoholism on a reservation that is officially 'dry'. Fifty or sixty per cent of adult Navajos, and as many as nine out of ten males, were alcoholics, he said. There were four or five hundred bootleggers bringing in booze with almost complete impunity. Most of the male population was debilitated by alcohol, and he was 'losing the battle' to control it. Yes, he admitted, he himself was a recovered alcoholic.

Down the corridor I met Tex Joey, another braided civil servant who hardly fitted the Whitehall or Washington mould. He was a genuine medicine man who sought to cure alcoholics through traditional Navajo healing ceremonies, and there is actually an Association of Medicine Men in Window Rock.

Then there was Lenny Foster, a genial fellow in his early fifties who also wore his long grey hair in a braid and had little turquoise ear studs. He was the son of a Navajo code talker, one of the celebrated tribesmen the US Marines used to transmit secret messages in the Pacific during World War Two because their language was so complex. Lenny himself was a fervent Native American activist who had fought for his people's rights by joining the famous occupations of San Francisco's Alcatraz Island in 1969 and Wyoming's Wounded Knee in 1973. He was now a spiritual adviser for the Navajo Nation's corrections project, a job that involved touring America's prisons and persuading them to let him conduct sweat lodge ceremonies for their Navajo inmates. Those ceremonies purified the body and soul, he insisted, and helped prisoners put their misdeeds behind them.

About 5.30 that evening I was back in my room in Window Rock's only hotel, the Navajo Nation Inn, when the telephone rang. It was Lenny. Come right over, he said. Bring shorts or swimming trunks. He was having a sweat lodge ceremony that night.

Lenny lived in one of a row of newish brick bungalows on the other side of town. I found him standing in his muddy garden, throwing layers of blankets and tarpaulins over a small dome, perhaps eight foot across, that he'd constructed from willow branches. His ancestors, he said, would have used buffalo hides. Inside this 'lodge' he'd spread some scraps of old carpet around a central pit. Outside its east-facing door was a small mound of earth – an altar – on which he had placed a drum, a clay pipe and medicine pouches containing various herbs. Beyond the altar, in a straight line running east from the dome, was a blazing fire heating a pile of lava rocks. The line was called the 'corn pollen path' and represented life's spiritual journey, Lenny explained.

We were joined by Lenny's brother, Oree, and a neighbour, John, and not for the first time on my travels I was overcome by a profound sense of unreality. On a dark and bitterly cold night, on a patch of snow-covered mud in a distinctly suburban-looking road in the middle of America, one tall, pale Englishman stripped down to his swimming trunks, crawled inside the little dome, and sat cross-legged and shivering with two brown-skinned Indians as we waited for this spiritual sauna to begin.

John carried seven red-hot rocks across to the pit with a pitch-fork. The first four rocks represented the points of the compass – east, south, west and north, the fifth Mother Earth, the sixth the Great Spirit or 'Grandfather', and the last the five-fingered person or human being. On each Lenny scattered sage and cedar needles that momentarily sparkled and filled the lodge with a sweet aroma. The rocks were literally sizzling. The spirits were talking to each other, said Lenny. John then crawled in and pulled down the doorflap, rendering the dome's interior pitch black.

There is a sudden hiss as Lenny ladles water on to the rocks and the steam scalds my throat. Lenny then starts singing loudly in Navajo and rhythmically beating the drum. The others join in. What, I wonder, do the neighbours think? Lenny pours more water on the rocks, and then still more. The heat becomes so intense I can hardly breathe, and in no time I'm dripping with sweat. On the opposite side of the dome Lenny, still speaking in Navajo, launches into a lengthy prayer. The only words I understand are 'Martin Fletcher' and 'London *Times*'. When he finally ends John takes over with a long speech of welcome and advice in English. Without warning, Lenny invites me to speak. I am momentarily stumped, then mumble thanks for the privilege of attending this sacred ceremony.

'Is that all?' asks Lenny in a tone of faint surprise, and with that the first 'door' ends. John throws open the flap, admitting a shaft of firelight and welcome draughts of icy air.

The ceremony consists of four 'doors', or rounds, four being an almost mystic number to the Navajos. As John brings in fresh rocks for the second 'door', Lenny gently suggests that I speak from the heart not the head, that I shouldn't rationalise my emotions. Damn my British inhibitions! John crawls back in, and we launch into another intimate group therapy session. This time the steam's heat seems even worse. I can't breathe without burning my throat or nostrils. Just when I think I can stand it no longer there is a whoosh as Lenny throws yet more water on the rocks, and then he passes around the clay pipe from which we must all inhale at least four times. I am soaked with sweat. I feel faint and nauseous. There is no escape so I lie down on the muddy carpet, thankful that I'm invisible in the darkness.

Oree, speaking in English, prays long and hard to 'Grandfather'. John does the same, invoking Grandfather's blessing on all those present, on his family, his friends, the tribal leaders, President Clinton and a host of others. Then it's my turn again. This time, in my debilitated state, I find my tongue a little looser. Panting in the heat, speaking in gasps, I suggest my journey across America is a spiritual as well as journalistic quest. I ask, from nobody in particular, for guidance, for help in doing the right thing. As I speak, the others sing softly in the darkness, subtly coaxing me on. I keep going for a few minutes this time, then John throws open the flap once more and I gulp in the cold night air like a man who has nearly drowned.

Between the second and third 'doors', while John is bringing in a fresh supply of red-hot rocks, a traumatic event occurs. John finds he has dropped a stone from the fire on to the drum and burned a hole in the taut hide. Lenny is visibly upset and the tone of the last two 'doors' is far more sombre. He has had the drum for eight years, he explains. It has travelled with him across the country. It was a friend, a living spirit. Now it had sacrificed itself. There was a message in this, a warning. We had to heed it. There was something wrong, something amiss. We had to pray, be humble, ask Grandfather's forgiveness. I found myself thinking that perhaps it was my presence, my agnosticism, that was to blame. I felt almost guilty.

After two hours we stumbled out into the night and rapidly cooled off, the cold mud squishing between our toes. We shook hands. In a funny way we'd bonded by opening ourselves up, by sharing the same intense experience, and I certainly felt physically – if not spiritually – cleansed. We then pulled our clothes back on, went inside and slumped on to sofas in Lenny's sitting room. With cans of ginger ale in hand we watched the girls of Monument Valley high school playing basketball on NNTV, the Navajo Nation's own television station.

*

Early the next morning I descended from the realm of the ethereal to the mire of politics. I had asked to meet Albert Hale, the Navajo president, and was told he would join me for breakfast at my hotel at 8.00 a.m. I put on a jacket and tie for only the second time since leaving Washington, the first being for my encounter with Alabama's governor. At 8.25 a large green Landcruiser with darkened windows pulled up outside the hotel and Mr Hale climbed out, preceded by a bodyguard who turned out to be his brother.

Mr Hale is a tall, slim, good-looking man with longish black hair and a moustache. He wore a dark jacket, neatly-pressed black trousers and, on his wrist, a traditional leader's leather-and-silver bow guard. To his lapel was pinned a little horned toad brooch because that animal was, like the Navajos, a great survivor. He smoothly glad-handed his way through the crowded dining room to a table in the corner where a second aide said a Navajo grace so long that our mutton-and-egg breakfast grew cold.

Mr Hale and I spent an hour discussing his tribe's many problems. He blamed these on the stifling bureaucracy the federal government had imposed on his people. Private companies – except for those attracted by the Nation's rich coal and oil deposits – were deterred from investing by the incredible red tape involved in obtaining land leases in a reservation where there was no private property, and by the fact that they faced both state and Navajo taxes. The tourist industry was hopelessly underdeveloped for that very reason, though the reservation had spectacular attractions in Monument Valley, ancient cliff dwellings and the great sheer-walled, green-floored Canyon de Chelly. Bootleggers were the leading entrepreneurs, Mr Hale admitted, but only because the maximum penalty a Navajo court could impose was a $500 fine or six months' jail and the 'Feds' were reluctant to get involved. He decried the Nation's own bloated bureaucracy, and presented himself as a reformer and moderniser striving to devolve power to the reservation's 110 'chapters' or local councils.

I have to admit I rather liked the man, but after breakfast I wandered over to the offices of the *Navajo Times*, the tribal newspaper, where my confidence in my own judgement was a little shaken.

Tom Arviso, the editor, rather sadly portrayed Mr Hale as some-one not far short of a Navajo Richard Nixon, though Peter MacDonald, a former president who was still behind bars, would seem a much stronger candidate for that title. The paper's lead story that day was how the Navajo attorney general's office was about to announce whether a special prosecutor was needed to investigate a raft of alleged offences by Mr Hale (it decided that one was). If Mr Hale was in fact guilty of transgressions he had certainly trans-gressed in style. Since winning the presidency in 1994 he had divorced his wife (who still insisted on calling herself the Navajo First Lady) and allegedly taken up with his former press secretary. He stood accused, amongst other things, of misusing the tribal credit card and airplane for jaunts to concerts in Las Vegas, the Superbowl in Phoenix and ski resorts in Colorado. He was already having $34,000 docked from his pay for questionable expenses, and his political future looked less than rosy.

My last stop in Window Rock was at the parliament building, or tribal council chamber, which is built in the shape of a hogan, the traditional eight-sided Navajo mud-and-log home. A mural around the inside walls tells how General James Carleton brutally rounded up the defiant Navajo people in the early 1860s and marched 8,000 of them 300 miles east to a thoroughly inhospitable area called Basque Redondo where he intended to subjugate them. The plan failed. More than a quarter of the Navajos died. In 1868 the gov-ernment relented and established the nucleus of the Navajos' present reservation in their former lands.

It was time for me to set off across that 'rez', blithely disregarding the guide book writer who warned of the roughness and remoteness of the roads and rather melodramatically advised: 'Make sure your vehicle is in tip-top physical shape. Check fanbelts, hoses, all fluid levels, tires and so on. If anything seems suspiciously close to being worn-out or broken, have it fixed. If it's a rental vehicle, trade it in for a new one.'

I rattled westwards out of Window Rock listening to someone called Red Bow singing 'My Friend the Buffalo' on KTNN, but almost immediately stopped to pick up a practitioner of the fine but almost obsolete art of hitchhiking. His name was Bo. He was an unemployed 'concrete mason' in his early thirties and was actually a Hopi Indian whose Navajo girlfrend lived in Window Rock. Initially we drove through pleasant but rather stunted pine woods, but after twenty or thirty miles these abruptly gave way to great brown plains stretching away to distant buttes and mesas beneath an immense blue sky.

Our road cut across these plains like a tiny thread of black cotton. Occasionally the endless sagebrush was interrupted by a dry river bed, a mud hogan or a shepherd's humble cabin (though rarely so humble it didn't boast a satellite television dish). In all this vast space there were no billboards, no businesses, no sign of entrepreneurial activity save the occasional 'trading post'. Settlements were few and far between and almost invariably named after some distinguishing physical feature of this barren land – Cow Springs, Steamboat Canyon, Indian Wells. They seldom consisted of more than a few trailer homes and some ugly prefabricated public housing.

In one, a dusty little place called Cornfields, two Navajos in a pick-up stopped to see if we were lost and told us they were off to visit their bootlegger. It was only mid-morning but they were already drunk, said Bo. He could tell by their flushed faces.

My companion was, it transpired, something of an expert on the subject. He had started drinking in 1980 when he was seventeen and still at school. He served an apprenticeship, married in 1984 and had two children, but his alcoholism grew steadily worse and his life collapsed. He served two prison sentences, one for drug possession and the other for aggravated assault on a police officer, and was arrested three times for drunken driving. In 1988 his wife divorced him. By the early 1990s, he told me, 'I was completely homeless and at the bottom of the pit. I was a bummer living on the streets of small cities in Arizona. I panhandled and stole and cheated. I became a beggar. I had lost my family, my occupation, my vehicle. I was barely able to walk. I was dying.' At that point he thought of his children and how they still looked up to him. Summoning what little willpower he had left, he entered a rehabilitation programme, and had now gone four years without touching a drop of alcohol.

As Bo was telling his story my eyes kept returning to the verges of the road. Here, in the middle of what was supposed to be a 'dry' reservation, the roadsides were littered with beer cans and whiskey bottles glinting in the brilliant sun. I don't mean just the odd one or two every other mile. It looked as if a recycling lorry had driven across the reservation with a large hole in its right side. No bald statistic so vividly illustrated the devastation the white man's 'bottle' has wrought on America's native Indians.

A couple of hours after leaving Window Rock we temporarily left 'Navajoland' and entered a nation within a nation within a nation. This was the Hopi Reservation, 4,000 square miles in the heart of the Navajo Reservation and a different world entirely. There were superficial similarities – the poverty, the alcoholism, the remoteness from modern America – but the Hopis and Navajos are actually very different peoples. They look different. They speak entirely different languages. The Hopis have lived in this desert region for a millennium or two, the Navajos for a mere 600 years. They are traditional enemies and are still embroiled in a bitter land dispute dating back to the 19th century. There are only about 10,000 Hopis, but they are a proud and independent people and guard their ancient culture even more jealously than the Navajos.

Visitors to 'Hopiland' are tolerated more than welcomed. They are not allowed to take photographs, make sketches or venture off the roads. They are asked to dress conservatively. While other tribes now stage religious ceremonies for the benefit of tourists, the Hopis recently banned outsiders from most of theirs because too many had acted disrespectfully.

At the tribal headquarters in Kykotsmovi village Kim Secakuku, a senior aide to her father, the tribal chairman, could not tell me the Hopis' per capita income. She said her people measured wealth not in material terms but in the richness of their culture and religion. Unemployment was very high, and nearly half those who worked had some sort of government job, but the tribal council discouraged outside investment unless it was 'culturally sensitive'. In fact the only non-Hopi business inside the reservation was the Peabody coal company owned by Britain's Hanson Trust. There was not one chain restaurant or motel, nor even a bank – just a handful of family-owned grocery stores.

The Hopis live in twelve semi-autonomous villages built on or by three great rocky mesas that point southwards like fingers down the reservation. I dropped Bo near the foot of the first, on the patch of dusty desert where his parents lived. They were not there, but Bo showed me around. There was a small field carved from the desert from which his father miraculously coaxed beans, corn, squash and melons despite an average annual rainfall of only 7.7 inches. There was the small wooden cabin with electricity, but no running water, in which they lived. Scattered around were pens holding a few sheep and chickens, a clay oven for baking bread, some sheepskins drying in the hot sun and a pile of coal. An assortment of ramshackle outhouses held chests full of blue and white corns, dried corn leaves for making Indian tamales and buckets of beans – proof that Hopi 'dry-farming' really worked. There were eagle feathers and a fox's pelt which Bo's father used for religious ceremonies. On the cabin's verandah was an old hand grinder for making meal from the corn. A few dogs dozed in the hot sun. The shimmering plain stretched away, unbroken, for perhaps twenty miles and in all that enormous space there was no sound. It was primitive and serene.

I climbed back into my car and followed a steep road up First Mesa to the village of Walpi, a jumble of ancient stone houses perched where the flat-topped mesa tapers to the finest of points at its southernmost end. The views across the sunlit plains below were quite stunning and the snow-capped peaks of the San Francisco Mountains were easily visible 80 miles away. The village had a fine plaza for its ceremonies, underground kivas for worship, bread ovens in the alleys and wooden privies balanced on the edge of the precipices. I should have loved Walpi, but I didn't. I had to take a guide, who was surly and uninformative and reprimanded me for taking notes. The place was crawling with hawkers of not very special Kachina dolls and Hopi pottery. It was overrun with mangy curs, and its waste disposal consisted, it appeared, of people simply throwing their rubbish, along with their excrement, over the mesa's edge.

On Second Mesa I ate a late but tasty lunch of fry bread covered in beans and cheese at the Hopi cultural centre, and on the tip of Third Mesa I found what, according to the Smithsonian Institution's guide to the historic south-west, is probably the oldest continuously-inhabited settlement in all America.

To my amazement there was not a single sign anywhere proclaiming this remarkable fact. Had I not idly pulled the Smithsonian guide from the shelves of Virginia's Mason District library several months earlier, I would have driven straight past the turning to Old Oraibi without a second thought. In fact the place was not even marked on my map. As it was I bumped down the dirt track leading off the highway and found a wonderful little village of perhaps 200 people dating back to at least 1150. Admittedly the French began building Notre Dame around that time, but by American standards the village was positively prehistoric.

Perched more than a thousand feet above a vast plain rent by a single river gorge and devoid of human life, Old Oraibi enjoyed the same incredible panoramas as Walpi but with none of Walpi's more offputting features. Here there were no other visitors, no hawkers, no guides telling you where you could and could not go. I parked in the silent, dusty plaza and wandered at will through the cluster of simple houses, many built on the foundations of previous homes and using the same rough-hewn yellow stones. It was one of those very rare places in America that had grown out of, and actually enhanced, its natural environment instead of being incongruously plonked down on it.

Here, too, there were underground kivas with homemade wooden ladders leading down to them, piles of gnarled tree trunks for firewood and, far below at the mesa's foot, tiny patches of ploughed earth where the villagers grew their beans and corn. Old Oraibi had no paved roads. It had no electricity and no mains water. The only obvious concessions to modernity were a few solar energy panels and television aerials on the flat-roofed homes and the occasional use of breeze blocks instead of stone. My initial reaction was to think that Old Oraibi had had a 500-year start on New York City and quite spectacularly blown it. On further reflection, I decided that the inhabitants of this beautiful, tranquil place would probably consider the Big Apple a modern-day Sodom or Gomorrah.

It was late afternoon by the time I re-entered the Navajo Reservation, and the sun was setting the red cliffs aglow. I passed a big yellow school bus coming the other way, and twice in the next few miles I spotted specks on the huge plains that were Navajo schoolchildren walking along dusty tracks to their distant homes.

I myself stopped for the night in Tuba City where I stayed in a student hostel that was infinitely nicer than the Sunset Motel, and dined off a tasty rice-and-mutton dish called hominy stew at the Tuba City Truck Stop Café. At the end of days like these I would occasionally switch on the television, see Dan Rather, Tom Brokaw and other familiar old East Coast anchormen broadcasting the evening news, and be faintly shocked to realise I was still in the same country.

19

Husband and Wives

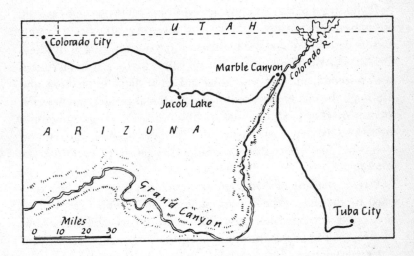

The next day was another scenic and geological treat. It was warm and cloudless, and I set off westwards from Tuba City through a lunar landscape of multi-coloured earthen hills devoid of vegetation – part of Arizona's 'painted desert'. I then turned north and for 40 miles followed a dramatic escarpment of crumbling red rocks called the Echo Cliffs until I reached the top of Marble Canyon. There a narrow bridge carried me high over the gorge of the Colorado river – a vivid green ribbon in a land of reds and browns – and out of the Navajo Reservation.

On the far side my lonely road trailed the equally dramatic Vermilion Cliffs westwards for another 40 miles and then climbed high up on to the Kiabab Plateau where, to my surprise, I found myself driving through snowy pine forests. By the time I descended on to the hot, scrubby plains the other side I had penetrated deep into Arizona's northern 'Strip', a remote and forbidding wedge of land that is more than 100 miles long and physically isolated by the Grand Canyon to the south and the mountains of southern Utah to the north. Until the late 1950s there was not even a proper paved road through the 'Strip'. It was, in short, a perfect place for people who wished to avoid the public gaze, which is one reason why Colorado City was founded where it was.

If you speed past Colorado City on Route 389 you might remark on its beautiful setting at the foot of towering red cliffs split by a narrow canyon. You would see from the roadsigns that it straddles the Arizona-Utah border. You would pass a petrol station, a restaurant, a secondhand car dealership and an artificial log factory, and you might be mildly surprised that after so many miles of desolation there is no motel. That would be about all you would remember unless you happened to venture off the highway, in which case you would quickly realise that Colorado City is a very curious place indeed.

Here in the land of shacks and trailer homes you would be astonished by the size of the houses, at least half of which seem to be having further extensions added. You would see children everywhere – riding bikes, running along the pavements, playing on extended swing sets in the gardens. You would be struck by how the women and girls all look as if they have stepped out of the 19th century with their long, braided hair, ankle-length skirts and dresses, and total lack of make-up or jewellery, and by how the boys all wear short hair, long trousers and buttoned-up, long-sleeved shirts. You would also become aware of people watching you with considerable suspicion. Colorado City has a strong aversion to prying outsiders. This is entirely understandable, for it is a town of polygamists.

I had stumbled on Colorado City completely by accident during a family camping holiday two years earlier. We had stopped one hot morning at the Pipe Spring national monument, a 19th-century Mormon ranch in a little oasis 20 miles to the east. Our guide was a pleasant, personable girl called Chris Cox and after our tour, as we picnicked in the shade of some ancient cottonwood trees, she came along with a barrow and asked if the children wanted to help her pick vegetables. We all spent a happy hour digging up potatoes and carrots from an irrigated patch of desert, and naturally got talking. She'd told us the 19th-century ranchers had practised polygamy so I asked if there were any polygamists still around.

'Yes,' Chris had replied, 'and I should know. My father has two wives and nineteen children.' She lived, she explained, in Colorado City which was seventy-five per cent polygamist and where families far larger than hers were commonplace.

We couldn't explore the town then for we had a date in Las Vegas, but I did now. It was pointless trying to engage people in the street so I went straight to the smart new town hall to meet the mayor – a genial, balding man in his mid-sixties named Dan Barlow. Colorado City reportedly had five 'first ladies', who allegedly had about sixty children between them, but I knew better than to ask the mayor directly about his familial arrangements, for it was clear that my presence would be tolerated only if I respected people's privacy.

He told me the town had been established back in the 1930s by a group of fundamentalists, including his father, who were being persecuted by the Mormon Church because they had never accepted its renunciation of polygamy – a central tenet of its faith – in return for Utah's statehood. Here, following the well-established American tradition of religious groups heading off into wilderness to practise their faith freely, they established their own church – the Fundamentalist Church of Jesus Christ of Latter-Day Saints – and resumed their practice of what they called 'the Principle'.

In those days the town was known as Short Creek. The authorities raided it in 1935, again in 1944 and, most famously, in 1953 when squads of police cars from both Utah and Arizona swept into the town at 4.00 a.m. to find the forewarned citizens gathered at the meeting house and singing 'God Bless America' beneath the Stars and Stripes. The men and several women were arrested, but the case against them largely collapsed. However the town's 263 children spent two years in foster homes before the courts ordered that they be returned to their parents. Since then Colorado City, which changed its name in the 1960s because Short Creek had gained such notoriety, has been left alone and quietly flourished.

Mr Barlow painted an extremely rosy picture of the town. Polygamy, or 'plural marriage' as he prefers to call it, had 'nothing to do with sexual or licentious feelings'. It was strictly a religious principle, but also one with great social advantages. Kids grew up in big, strong families. There were no 'latchkey children' because if one wife went to work a 'sister' wife stayed at home. Far from being a hotbed of libidinous behaviour, he said, Colorado City was actually a very conservative and patriotic place where alcohol and tobacco were banned, the Church actively discouraged television and the 'evils' it brought into the home, and any abuse of wives or children was dealt with very harshly. There was a great community spirit, a strong work ethic, practically no crime, and hardly any divorces.

'Why should anyone disapprove of us? We're doing things people all over America are crying out for – families, structures, homes and morals,' Mr Barlow argued. 'We have elements of small town America that have been lost throughout the United States – families, community spirit, people still working together, volunteerism and those type of things you just don't find in other communities. We still have some of the old-fashioned ways about us that are not wrong. They are good ways.'

Certainly it was a patriarchal society, he conceded, but it had to be. The woman's place in life 'was just as grand as a man's, but you need someone who's boss. If you get into a position where everyone's boss you're going to have a problem'. The outside world, being full of adulterers and fornicators, had 'no right to judge us', the mayor declared.

Mr Barlow drove me up to Colorado City's new 'Barlow University' – named after his father – in his luxury Buick to buy a history of the town. The bookstore, I noticed, was full of books such as *Is There Life After Housework?* and *Practical Parenting Tips*. The college offered a course called 'Fascinating Womanhood' that offered instruction on 'the highest goals in marriage' and 'helping women attain the greatest happiness and fulfilment possible in daily living and all their relationships'. He then whisked me round the town – the huge church, a smart high school, a small zoo, orchards of blossoming fruit trees and a pleasant park with a miniature railway and display of antique farm machinery.

Many of the men worked in the construction business, he said, and helped their neighbours extend their houses at weekends. The streets were broad, tree-lined and litter-free thanks to a recent 'community clean-up'. People grew their own fruit and vegetables. The children were freckled and rosy-cheeked and looked incredibly healthy. There were tennis and basketball courts, but no swimming pool as that would entail an unacceptable degree of nakedness.

By the time we returned to the town hall, with the town's almost biblical rocky backdrop glowing red in the evening light, I was beginning to think of Colorado City as some sort of Eden – albeit a puritanical one – carved from the desert by a group of brave and profoundly misunderstood men. It was hard to object to polygamy if it was entirely consensual, and Mr Barlow insisted it was. Church leaders offered advice, he acknowledged, but no girl was ever forced to marry against her will.

'There's no such thing as force in the gospel of Jesus Christ,' he said. 'The whole principle of the gospel is built on the principle of free agency.'

My favourable impression of Colorado City was only mildly disturbed by the implications of Mr Barlow's last little gesture that evening, which was to introduce me to the police chief so I'd not be troubled as I wandered round the town. The next day I did just that. I found, on Utah Avenue, the home of Rulon Jeffs, the church's eighty-six-year-old 'prophet', or spiritual leader, who was reputed to have at least ten wives though no one knew for sure. It was an opulent new edifice, surrounded by high railings, with a floodlit basketball court and a magnificent view across the town and the plains beyond. Unfortunately, the prophet spent most of his time at his other home near Salt Lake City and never gave interviews.

I visited the town's supermarket, which was also run by the Church and sold giant packs of cereal and cloth for making clothes, but no newspapers or magazines. I admired washing lines in back gardens dripping with dozens of pairs of children's socks. I visited the library, which was full of Mormon tracts and books on sewing and children's diets. I returned to the town hall where the clerk rather reluctantly let me see the 1990 census.

This showed Colorado City's population had virtually doubled every decade as its citizens had dutifully multiplied and now comfortably exceeded 5,000, two-thirds of whom were under the age of twenty. It was also a hundred per cent white, which was hardly surprising in a town where the Church could prevent any influx of outsiders because it owned almost all the land.

The clerk, incidentally, turned out to be Kevin Barlow, the mayor's nephew. I was encountering Barlows at every turn. One was the university administrator, another the school superintendent, a third had until recently been the town's marshall. A quick peek in the telephone directory revealed no less than sixty-four Barlow households, a number exceeded only by seventy-nine Jessops.

It was only when I sat down and talked to Chris Cox and her parents, Don and Katie, at a 20-foot family dining table in their eleven-bedroom home that I realised there might be a less wholesome side to Colorado City and its various *ménages à trois, quatre* or even more.

The Coxes were, admittedly, notorious dissidents. Mr Cox had come to the town from Salt Lake City in the 1960s so he could live openly with his two wives, but had grown steadily more disillusioned with the autocratic Church until, in 1984, he and two or three dozen other families had broken away and formed a rival congregation. The Church then moved to evict those families from the homes they had built on its property, triggering a lawsuit of positively Dickensian proportions that had still not been resolved a decade later.

The Coxes nonetheless painted a picture of the town that could not be lightly dismissed. My first impressions were all wrong, they said. Mr Barlow had 'left out a whole lot of chapters'. The town was a virtual dictatorship, not a paradise. A small religious élite ran the place through fear. Girls were taught from infancy to be entirely submissive, to marry whoever they were told to, and to spend their lives bearing and raising children. They were 'brainwashed' into believing that was the only way they would reach the 'celestial kingdom' and not go to hell.

'Dan Barlow said there were no forced marriages,' said Mrs Cox, 'but when a girl is raised in a system and taught every day, whether in school or at home or in church, that she's supposed to marry whoever the prophet tells her to marry I would call that a forced marriage.'

Polygamy, said Mr Cox, was 'neither right nor wrong, but enforced polygamy is wrong as hell'.

Still worse, said Chris, girls were treated as 'gifts to men to reward them for good behaviour in the community'. The prophet was very obliging in the 'revelations' he received from God. Sixty-year-old men were given beautiful teenagers. Senior or very loyal Church members were often granted many wives, but rank-and-file members just one or two. LeRoy Johnson, the previous prophet who had died at the age of ninety-eight in 1986, reportedly had sixteen wives who ranged in age from eighteen to one in her seventies.

The Coxes claimed to have received several calls over the years from girls desperate to escape impending marriages, and that those who ran away were chased and brought back. By contrast, said Mr Cox, young men were run out of town for the flimsiest of reasons in order to 'thin out' the male population. In short, the religiously persecuted had themselves become persecutors.

The Coxes also knew from personal experience that polygamous households were not always the happy, secure and supportive places Mr Barlow had suggested. In reality they were often torn by conflicts between jealous wives or rival siblings competing for the father's attention. Wives survived, said Chris, by making themselves 'comfortably numb'.

Chris was twenty and single and had, needless to say, no intention of entering a polygamous marriage herself. It was easy to tell she was a rebel because her hair was loose, she wore jeans, and had pierced ears. She took me to meet Cyril Bradshaw, an intelligent and highly articulate chemist of seventy-four, and you could tell he too was a dissident because he had a large satellite television dish outside his home.

Mr Bradshaw also insisted that the Church indoctrinated the young in order to maintain its power, but I was more struck by his own story. He'd had two wives and twenty-three children but now lived by himself. One wife had died. The other had left him after he joined the breakaway group in 1984 because, he said, the Church 'told her she could not be saved if she stayed with me. They told her she had to leave so she finally did . . . I feel they brainwashed her'. She'd taken seven of their eleven children with her, and some of those seven were still 'scared to death to come and visit me because their salvation depends on it'.

Happily Mr Bradshaw had retained his sense of humour. He told me he had seventy-five grandchildren. When I asked if he ever had family reunions he replied, in a horrified tone: 'I hope not.'

In a community as closed as Colorado City it was, of course, almost impossible to determine which portrait was nearer to the truth, but the town was clearly not the happy, harmonious place I'd first thought. Nor were its citizens as virtuous as Mr Barlow liked to think.

As I drove away I passed, a couple of miles beyond the town, a little cabin called the Canaan Store that sold beer. I turned round, went back, and asked the lady behind the counter whether she got many customers from Colorado City, where alcohol was supposedly taboo. 'Are you kidding!' she exclaimed. 'That's where most of our business comes from.' Even Church elders came in to buy alcohol, she said, though some asked for bags to hide it in. 'We had one lady in here who said she wanted some beer to wash her hair with!'

20

Lost in Space

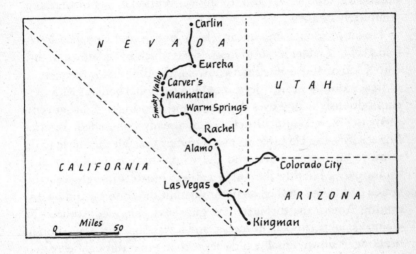

Not far beyond Colorado City I entered the little-known but fast-growing state of Paranoia. I knew I'd reached it because I saw a large homemade sign by the road that announced: 'Stop the New World Order. Get us out of the United Nations'. A hundred yards up a dirt track were a couple of caravans with a large Stars and Stripes fluttering above them. Like a fool, and out of some misguided sense of journalistic duty, I stopped. I bumped up the track and parked by another sign that read: 'No Government Officials. $1,000 Fine for Entering'. It was the edge of night. I approached the nearest caravan with some trepidation, not entirely certain that I wouldn't get my head blown off, but the door was opened by an elderly fellow whose face lit up when I told him I was from England.

'England!' he exclaimed. 'You know the Queen of England's behind all this? She's chairman of the board of the Club of 300.'

And so I met Ted Gubler. He was seventy and called himself a property developer, though to judge by his dilapidated caravan he was not a very successful one. He was a classic exponent of a bizarre conspiracy theory that has been very effectively disseminated throughout rural America by radio chat-show hosts, the Internet and a plethora of books, tapes and videos plugged by the far-right media. Mr Gubler was also, to my conventional way of thinking, completely bonkers.

He sat me down amid great piles of papers and launched into a remarkable if rather jumbled monologue which boiled down to this. The 'Club of 300', sometimes known as the Illuminati, was a group of tremendously wealthy Jewish-led international bankers who were surreptitiously taking over the world and creating a global government or 'New World Order'. They already controlled America financially – the US owed so much money that 'all they have to do is move up interest rates and the whole system would collapse tomorrow'. Militarily they were taking control through the UN, which had troops stashed away throughout the country, and by disarming Americans through new gun laws. They controlled the country's politicians and its media, and it was now 'just a question of breaking us down morally, and they're doing that through television and the movies,' he said. 'Just look at that Hollywood and television crap. They've put sex education in schools to help demoralise the schools. The best way to destroy a nation is to demoralise it.'

Once the bankers had control, Mr Gubler continued, they would exterminate about fifty per cent of the world's population, beginning with the rebellious Americans. They would keep the Chinese and Japanese as slaves because those people were 'used to being regimented'. There was still time to avert this catastrophe, but America had to wake up fast. The people were 'nitwits'. They didn't understand that personal freedom required constant vigilance. 'If we had a Congress with guts we could still whip them while we have an army and navy,' he said. 'I had high hopes that Ronald Reagan would get us out of the UN but he lost his guts after they shot him. It's too easy to give up. I hope I don't get that way. I intend to fight till I die for what I know is right.'

I extricated myself as rapidly as I could, but did I learn my lesson? I did not. I actually ventured deeper into Paranoia, which turned out to be a much larger and far more densely populated place than I'd ever imagined when I was sitting back in Washington.

I stopped for the night in the town of Hurricane, about 22 miles west of Colorado City, and telephoned a Mr Don Nickey in Kingman, Arizona. Someone who knew someone who knew someone had told me he was a prominent member of the Sons and Daughters of Liberty, one of a plethora of citizens' militias in this young, wide-open state where it is perfectly legal to carry a gun so long as you do so openly. He agreed to meet me. It was only then that I looked at my map. I knew Kingman was in the same county as Colorado City – indeed it was the Mohave County seat – but I'd forgotten momentarily that the Grand Canyon was in the way. Kingman was 120 miles south as the crow flies, but 250 by road and in completely the wrong direction.

I set off in a disgruntled mood the next morning but cheered myself up with a big and extremely inexpensive buffet lunch at the Circus Circus casino in Las Vegas. Remembering the old saying – 'If you aim to leave Las Vegas with a small fortune, go there with a large one' – I spent not a quarter in its slot machines. I nosed my way through crowds of tourists at the Hoover Dam, and reached my destination late in the afternoon with a sunburnt left arm and strong desire for air-conditioning in my car. Kingman enjoys – if that's the right word – a certain notoriety as the place where Tim McVeigh prepared for the Oklahoma City bombing. It is also a place where land is so plentiful, and so barren, that friends from crowded old England had, on impulse, bought forty acres for a mere $17,500 while passing through on holiday the previous summer.

Mr Nickey invited me to join him and his wife for dinner at a restaurant called JB's. He was, alas, an immense disappointment. My hopes of gallivanting around the night-time desert with a bunch of heavily-armed rebels were dashed the moment I set eyes on him. True, he wore a baseball cap emblazoned 'Militia of Arizona' and, on the front of his black shirt, an official-looking badge that read: 'Militia of Arizona – Mohave County Coordinator'. But he was a short, bespectacled man in his late fifties, a former electrical goods retailer who walked with a stick and could no longer work because of asthma. He was also just as barmy as Mr Gubler.

Mr Nickey shared Mr Gubler's conviction that the Club of 300 was out to take over the world, but added several embellishments of his own. The British royal family controlled the Chinese opium market, he informed me, but warned that if I printed that I would put my life in danger. He believed the government had bombed the federal building in Oklahoma City so it could blame and discredit the militias, and that McVeigh was merely its 'patsy'. Within a year, he told me, the government would manufacture some crisis so it could suspend the Constitution, declare martial law and disarm the people. Russian troops were massed in Mexico for that very purpose. 'When they come to take our arms away I guarantee you that the shooting will start. It will turn into guerrilla warfare.'

This funny little man solemnly explained that he was head of a 'brick' – a self-contained cell of five militiamen. There were at least thirty 'bricks' in Mohave County alone, and when the fighting began these 'bricks' would launch a campaign of 'leaderless resistance' similar to that of the Vietcong. 'We all have plenty of weapons, artillery, ammunition,' he said. 'We stockpile ammunition and food, sometimes in houses and sometimes cached somewhere.' The purpose was not to attack anybody, overthrow the government or 'strut around and be macho', but simply to protect one's family and liberty. There were more than 3 million militiamen in America, and another 17 million Americans who were supportive. The militias would ultimately prevail. 'It will be a long nasty fight,' he said, 'but we will win.'

Halfway through the meal a waitress joined us for a few minutes. Her name was Christie, and she too had bought into this whole bizarre conspiracy theory. She talked excitedly about a video she'd just seen called *The Imminent Military Takeover of the USA*. Mr Nickey's innocuous-looking wife, Donna, was another fervent believer. When I asked if she worked, she told me she had a job at a mental health clinic. 'She's trying to get me a room,' her husband joked. 'A lot of people probably think I need one.' Dead right, I said to myself.

I could understand why so many Americans distrusted their government. They had plenty of reason to after Vietnam, Watergate, the Iran-Contra affair, a catalogue of CIA and FBI excesses and the use of unwitting citizens as guinea-pigs in nuclear radiation and syphilis studies. I could understand why so many Americans found their law enforcement officials aggressive and their bureaucrats overbearing, for I did too. I could see how rural America felt excluded from the country's general affluence, and how the common man felt alienated from a political system dominated by big money. But to go from there to believing that the government was a profoundly evil institution controlled by some shadowy global cartel and bent on suppressing the people seemed to me preposterous, to put it mildly.

Paranoia is nothing new in America, of course. From its earliest days its citizens have periodically thought foreign conspiracies were about to subvert and destroy their young country. Their anger and fear has been directed at Catholics, Jews, Masons, Wall Street financiers, East Coast élitists and, of course, Communists. 'How can we account for our present situation unless we believe that men high in this government are concerted to deliver us to disaster?' asked Senator Joe McCarthy at the height of his communist witchhunt in 1951. 'This must be the product of a great conspiracy, a conspiracy on a scale so immense as to dwarf any previous such venture in the history of man.'

President Kennedy's assassination in 1963 induced a fresh surge of paranoia, and America is now gripped by yet another wave in which the government's every action is construed in the worst light possible. I'd learned from bitter experience, for example, the futility of arguing that the extremely modest gun control measures passed during my time in Washington were simply an attempt to make America's streets safer. To the likes of Mr Nickey such measures had one purpose only. Guns were an American's last line of defence against tyranny. If the government could disarm its people it could take away all their other constitutional rights. 'An armed man is a citizen,' he declared. 'An unarmed man is a subject.'

Mr Nickey wanted to spend the next day showing me piles of material corroborating his wild and wonderful theories. Instead I

rose early and fled back the way I'd come, past the equally fantasti-
cal but marginally saner world of Las Vegas, up to the great deserts
of Nevada. I once turned on the radio, but snapped it off when the
very first thing I heard was a chat-show caller ranting about 'a government that poisoned our troops in the Gulf War, that uses black
helicopters to spy on our people all the time'. Why, this man
demanded, were 'our people so willing to bear arms and go off to
fight foreign enemies when they won't bear arms and fight the
enemy within?'

Nevada is the seventh biggest state in the Union and probably the
emptiest save Alaska. Its 110,000 square miles contain just 1.2 million people, and the great majority of those live in or around Las
Vegas. I turned off the interstate about 20 miles beyond that painted
harlot of a city and travelled another 70 before I reached the tiny
town of Alamo and saw any form of human habitation. Then I
drove through a further 50 miles of desolation – along a road that
averages just fifty-three vehicles a day – till I reached a tiny cluster
of trailer homes in the middle of an enormous bowl of scrubby,
mountain-ringed desert.

This was the hamlet of Rachel, named after the only baby ever
born there, and its ninety-eight inhabitants have built an entire
industry on the fact that they live closer than anyone else to a place
that doesn't exist – officially at least. I am talking of Area 51 or
'Dreamland', the supposedly super-secret but actually world-famous
US Air Force base that appears on no maps but is hidden away
behind the nearest mountains.

'Dreamland' is where the Stealth Bomber and U2 spy plane were
developed and where the 5,000 mph Aurora war plane – the world's
fastest machine – is allegedly being tested. It is also the Holy of
Holies for America's legions of ufologists. It is, they insist, the place
to which the alien spacecraft and its occupants were taken after it
crashed near Roswell, New Mexico, in 1947, and where more UFOs
have been sighted than anywhere else in the world. Indeed, in 1989,
a physicist named Bob Lazar claimed there were no less than nine
crashed or captured flying saucers being kept in Area 51, and that he
had been employed there to try to replicate their propulsion systems.

Rachel is America's equivalent of Loch Ness. Like Roswell, 700 miles back east, its few residents have cashed in handsomely on America's seemingly limitless suggestibility when it comes to UFOs. I approached the tiny settlement along a road that the state of Nevada had obligingly renamed the Extraterrestrial Highway and whose roadsigns were adorned with pictures of flying saucers. I checked into Rachel's only motel, which was called the Little A'Le'Inn and had a sign outside that read 'Kneepsheep Nknock Ip Nknook' – 'univarian' for 'Welcome UFOs and Crews'. I spent the next hour exploring Rachel as a stiff wind whipped across the desert and blew dust into my eyes. I wandered round the 'Area 51 Research Centre' and the 'Totally Alien Information Museum' – both glorified gift shops housed in trailers – and Rachel's only store which advertised various guided tours alongside warnings that 'you are walking the boundaries of the most secured military base in the world. Crossing the border means imprisonment or death'.

You used to be able to hike up Freedom Ridge and look down on the distant hangars and 5-mile runway of the air base that isn't there, or watch an amazing private air show in the nocturnal skies above you, but sadly the military closed off the ridge in 1995 and it is now guarded by heavily armed 'cammo dudes' in jeeps. Today's tours are rather less exciting. They take you on a strenuous two-hour climb to the top of Mount Tikaboo, from which you can just about make out the base 25 miles away, or to the site of a crashed US Air Force jet, or to the 'world-famous black mail box' 20 miles back along the ET highway which is apparently 'the most popular spot in the world for UFO sightings'.

As darkness fell I returned to the motel where nine or ten people had gathered for dinner in a bar plastered with photographs of UFOs. There were two men from Las Vegas, two more from Los Angeles, a couple from France, a local astronomer and the motel owners, Joe and Pat Travis – a seemingly diverse collection of human beings thrown together in the middle of the desert for a single night. The evening had great potential, but before I knew it we were back on the subject of the New World Order with Joe, a wild-looking fellow with ruddy face and long grey beard, leading the charge, and everyone but me and the French couple in agreement.

'We're going to lose all our countries to one-world dictatorship,' Joe thundered. The American people would soon be living as slaves, mere peons of the élite. Everyone who had a gun and was willing to stand up and fight for his country was now a militiaman. If Texas seceded from the Union 'I'll load up my guns and go straight down there.'

Joe had several new pieces of information to impart. There hadn't been a free election in America since 1863. The last major piece of gun control legislation – the Brady Bill – was passed in the dead of night by just two senators and Vice-President Al Gore. Computer chips in roadsigns enabled the government to keep tabs on all its citizens. Here was a man suffering, if you'll forgive the pun, from extreme 'alienation'.

As the alcohol flowed and the night wore on, the conversation grew still more bizarre. Of course there were nine flying saucers at Area 51, Joe declared, and of course the government was concealing them. Not only that, said Pat, but there were six different sorts of aliens there – large and small-nosed grey ones, orange ones, blue ones, reptilian ones and humanoids. She launched into a string of stories about humanoids visiting this very bar, of strange lights penetrating its solid doors, and of human abductions. We were not to worry, however, as the aliens around here were 'full of love'.

The local astronomer, Chuck Clark, claimed personally to have witnessed a hovering object pulsating with orange light suddenly flash 8 miles across the desert, stop dead and vanish. To cap that he produced a video allegedly shot one night by a Californian couple sitting in their car near the famous black mail box. The car is suddenly filled with orange light and to gasps from the occupants, a great orange disk then wobbles off into the darkness from right overhead. Everyone was hugely impressed save the Frenchman, who was a professional photographer. 'Faked,' he whispered to me.

Really, really hard core conspiracy theorists believe the conspirators are planning a mock invasion of earth by man-made flying saucers in order to panic the world into accepting a single global government, but fortunately I was spared that.

Late in the evening, I said goodnight and returned to my room in an adjacent trailer. I found I was now sharing these rather cramped premises with a young couple from California and their two children. Like so many restless, questing Americans before them, they had recently sold their home in Sacramento for $17,000, packed all their belongings into a U-Haul van, and were now touring the south-west in search of somewhere new to live. They had come to Rachel because the father was a self-confessed UFO nut. 'People ask me if I believe in UFOs,' he told me. 'I'm way beyond that. It's like asking me if I believe I have a son.'

I fell asleep wondering whether wide open spaces made people crazy, or crazy people were attracted to wide open spaces. For some reason I woke at about 3.00 a.m., so I padded outside to admire a firmament of glittering galaxies. I searched the heavens in vain for UFOs, but I did see the magnificent Hale-Bopp comet, its tail easily visible in the brilliantly clear night sky of the Great American Desert.

Some 250 miles south-west of Rachel, in southern California, thirty-nine members of a cult called 'Heaven's Gate' were also watching the comet. A week later they committed mass suicide in the belief that a UFO trailing in Hale-Bopp's tail would transport them to eternal peace. We can't be sure that they weren't whisked away to some 'higher level' of course, but somehow I doubt it.

The next morning, I returned to Planet Earth and continued my journey northwards through a land so barren that Mark Twain once compared it to the hide of a singed cat.

My map showed a place called Warm Springs 62 miles north of Rachel, but its population proved to be precisely zero. It had long since been abandoned. All that was left was a payphone, a boarded-up bar and café, a few tumbledown homes, and a crumbling open-air swimming pool fed by the hot springs that gave the place its name. The pool was surrounded, unfortunately, by a high, wire-mesh fence and umpteen 'Keep Out' notices.

I kept on going, the road stretching straight out ahead of me till it tapered to a tiny point at the foot of the next line of mountains 10 or 20 miles away. Across those mountains was another basin, another range, and so it went on. This moonscape was so remote that you could stop and relieve yourself beside the car without the faintest concern about being seen. There were no turn-offs, no historical markers. I seized on any little diversions – the sandy beds of dried-up lakes, mini-whirlwinds drunkenly pirouetting across the desert, the tell-tale line of dust kicked up by some faraway jeep. Had my car had cruise control I could have stretched my legs along the front seats and read a book. Once or twice I passed small crosses marking spots where drivers had perhaps done just that and met a sorry end. Often, when travelling in America, I've found myself wondering how places must have looked to the first explorers, but here in this land of spartan beauty very little imagination was required.

After 130 miles the landscape changed suddenly and dramatically. I found myself driving up, not across, a valley, and this one was green and pleasant, not dry and barren. It was about 20 miles wide and a hundred long. It was bounded by the Toiyabe Mountains to the west and the Toquima Mountains to the east – forested ranges with 10,000-foot snowy peaks and any number of alluring little canyons from which clear creeks tumbled. This was Big Smoky Valley, and about a third of the way up it I reached a little town called Carvers. The entire place was for sale. For just under $2 million I could have bought a small shopping centre, laundromat, car wash, motel, petrol station, store, restaurant, bar, an old gold mine and a ranch home with ten acres. For different reasons the owners of these properties all wanted to sell, so an enterprising estate agent named Bill Kohlmoos had persuaded them to club together and offer the entire town as a package.

Bill was a tall, fit seventy-four-year-old with wiry white hair, glasses and *joie de vivre*. He invited me to dinner, so we drove 30 more miles up the valley in his outsized van to the next little community, Kingston. There we ate and drank in a splendid old lodge with a blazing wood fire, hidden away at the foot of the mountains. Selling property was, I learned, just a sideline. During Bill's long and colourful career he'd been a rancher, a bush pilot and a coppermine manager, but his real passion for the past half-century had been prospecting for uranium, barium and – above all – gold.

Bill had done most of his prospecting in Nevada, but he had once bought a yacht and spent five years prospecting along the coast of Alaska and Mexico and in the South Pacific. He was actually president of the Nevada Miners and Prospectors Association but, he confessed, there were now less than a dozen active gold prospectors left in the entire state. This was not because there was no gold left – Nevada still accounted for more than half of America's annual gold production – it was because eighty-seven per cent of the state's land was federally owned and excessive government red tape had killed the prospectors' market. Most small mining companies had been 'regulated out of business' and the big boys were now only interested in truly sensational new discoveries. To open a new mine they had to obtain more than fifty environmental, archaeological and other permits, a process that could take years and cost millions.

'You almost need a permit to blow your nose,' Bill complained. 'We don't see any young people coming into the business any more because there's no future in it. Old-timers are doing it out of habit. That's why I do it – because I love the mountains and the challenge and there's always a hope the rules will be relaxed a little bit.'

The next morning Bill and I hiked up into the mountains in gorgeous spring weather, disturbing a bald eagle on the way. Prospectors no longer panned for gold in rivers, he explained – at least not in Nevada. All that 'placer' or surface gold had long since been found and taken. What they looked for nowadays were tiny specks of gold in rocks that indicated high-grade gold-bearing ore. We finally reached a rocky slope that he'd stumbled across the previous autumn and considered promising. There were not only veins of quartz and mineralised rocky outcrops, but the remains of 19th-century mineworkings. The old-timers had wonderful noses for gold, he said, but they had left much of it behind because they lacked the technology to extract anything but the easy stuff.

Bill actually staked a claim that morning which we named after my son, Barney. He stuck a post in the ground, nailed an old film carton on to it, and into that carton stuffed a form proclaiming his rights to any minerals in a surrounding area 1,500 feet long and 600 feet wide. He then had ninety days to put up posts on every corner of the claim and register it in the county courthouse 150 miles away. The process had not changed since the 19th century, but the cost had. To register that claim he would have to pay about $150, plus another $100 annually to maintain it. 'It's a gamble just to take a look,' he said. 'When I started it was a dollar a claim.'

The next step would be to have rock samples tested by an assay office. If they contained flecks of gold Bill would hire someone to drill a 400-foot hole or two, and if that drilling revealed more gold he would then seek to persuade some big mining company to lease the land from him. The chances of the Barney Stake ever being mined were about one in 10,000, he admitted, but that was the thing about prospecting. You acquired the basic geological knowledge and worked hard, but the rest was 'horseshit luck'. It was 'like playing the slot machines in Reno. You pull the handle and hope you can win the big one'.

Bill had made most of his money from other minerals. He had discovered a couple of moderately profitable gold mines, and had watched a huge one slip through his fingers because his partner let their claims expire. The Barney claim might be the last he ever staked, he said. 'I still have plenty of energy and I'm young of mind and would continue, but the government has stopped me.' Somehow I doubted that. Bill seemed to me addicted, and that afternoon, further down the valley, he showed me another area which could, he confided, 'be a big one'.

It was at the foot of a mountain that faced a ranch a mile out across the valley floor. A few years back, he told me, the underground pipe carrying water to that ranch had cracked and the ranch's tap water had grown steadily sandier. One day the rancher's wife was cleaning the sandy sediment from the toilet bowl when she noticed flecks of gold. They dug up the broken pipe and found the leaking water had formed a subterranean hole that was full of placer gold. Bill reckoned the source of that gold must be in the mountain opposite and so had staked fifty claims. He had named them the 'Royal Flush'.

What really amazed me about these mountains was that they looked so pristine from a distance but were actually riddled with old mineworkings. Up every little creek and canyon were old shafts and rusted-up machinery, the remains of a miner's cabin or the wooden frame of an abandoned ore-loader. We hiked into what seemed wilderness and found ancient tobacco tins and whiskey bottles scattered among the rocks. Bill knew every nook. He took me deep into a mountainside along an abandoned 350-foot tunnel. High on a ridge he showed me a huge old forgotten mill for crushing ore, now open to the sky and with the foundations of half a dozen homes around it. These hills must have been absolutely crawling with fortune seekers in the late 1800s and early 1900s, but were now inhabited only by memories.

We ended up in Manhattan, an old gold-mining community in the mountains south of Carvers that was a far cry indeed from its New York namesake. At its peak in the early 1900s three thousand people had lived there. Today Manhattan's population is less than sixty with just a couple of small mining operations cleaning up after the old-timers. The surrounding hillsides are a honeycomb of old mineshafts – poignant reminders of Manhattan's glory days. Almost all the houses are now boarded up or derelict. Their yards are littered with rusting old cars from the Steinbeck era. Manhattan was just one step away from becoming a ghost town, but it still had a church, a post office and two ramshackle old bars. We had a beer in one of them, the Miners Saloon, and tried to fathom the timeless lure of gold. The funny thing was, said Bill, that 'if you took all the gold in the world and threw it in the ocean it wouldn't make any difference at all to the way we live'.

That night Bill took me to dinner with Dick Carver, a man of legendary status in the rebellious West who lived, it turned out, right behind my motel. Indeed the town of Carvers was founded by his family.

Mr Carver, a pudgy fifty-two-year-old rancher, is commissioner of Nye County, of whose 18,000 square miles ninety-three per cent are owned by the federal government. He'd just returned from an inspection of Yucca Mountain, a radioactive nuclear waste dump the government is planning to open in Nye County. Even the county's air space is largely controlled by the Pentagon because it contains the giant Nellis air force range and the Nevada nuclear test site. By 1994 Mr Carver had had enough of federal agencies dictating what Nye County's land could and could not be used for, of bureaucrats threatening the livelihoods of miners, ranchers, loggers and others who depended on that land for their survival. He decided on a dramatic gesture to grab the government's attention and bring the issue to a head.

The Forest Service was refusing the county's request that it re-open a weather-damaged dirt road through the Toiyabe national forest that linked Big Smoky to a neighbouring valley. On 4 July – Independence Day – that year, flourishing a copy of the Constitution and with an angry, gun-toting crowd of about two hundred at his back, Mr Carver sat on a flag-draped bulldozer and forced a way through while two armed Forest Service agents vainly ordered him to stop.

It was an act of civil disobedience that reverberated across the country and is compared, by Mr Carver's many supporters, to the dumping of tea in Boston Harbour or Rosa Parks' refusal to give up her bus seat to a white man in Montgomery, Alabama. Almost overnight Mr Carver became the top draw on the 'county supremacy' speech circuit. The government successfully sued Nye County to establish once and for all that it owned and had the right to manage the federal lands within its boundaries. But then it drew up a formal agreement to cooperate with the county in the administration of those lands, which is what Mr Carver had wanted from the outset.

'I was scared to death,' Mr Carver admitted as we drank wine in his living room beneath a framed *Time* magazine front cover that pictured him beneath the headline 'Don't Tread on Me'. He did not strike me as an extremist. He came across as a cheery, mild-mannered fellow and we had a very jolly St Patrick's Day dinner of corned beef and cabbage with his wife, Midge, her sister and his father-in-law. He simply felt that the federal government had become so arrogant and overbearing, so dismissive of local authorities and local people, that unless he took a stand there would soon be no more mining or ranching or logging left. 'It's tyranny when the people fear the government,' he said, 'and freedom when the government fears the people.'

Big Smoky Valley yielded one final surprise before I finally left it the next morning. At its northern end I turned right off the highway and rattled six miles down an unmarked dirt road in a cloud of dust, sending three antelope bouncing away through the sagebrush. There I found Spencer's Hot Springs, a place I would never have known of had some locals not told me about it. There was no one for miles around. I stripped naked, and for a blissful half-hour wallowed in a large tub of hot mineral water in the middle of an idyllic sage-scented valley enclosed by snow-capped mountains and a deep blue sky.

Refreshed and tingling, I rejoined the highway and was soon heading east on Route 50. Some years ago *Life* magazine dubbed this 'the loneliest road in America' after being told by the American Automobile Association that it was 'totally empty. There are no points of interest. We don't recommend it. We warn all motorists not to drive there unless they're confident of their survival skills.'

The state of Nevada seized on *Life* magazine's description to entice tourists, and so speedily debased it. In truth Route 50 wasn't nearly as lonely as the road from Alamo to Rachel, or Rachel to Carvers. Here the towns were a mere 50 or 60 miles apart and several cars passed every hour. Loneliness, I was discovering, also had nothing to do with numbers. The scenery was compelling. There was a camaraderie between travellers, signalled by a passing wave. I've felt far lonelier battling my way out of New York on a foul winter's night in a tangle of unfamiliar rush-hour freeways.

I stopped for a late lunch in Eureka, which proclaimed itself 'the loneliest town on the loneliest road in America' and was said to have acquired its name when miners struck silver there in the 1860s. I then left Route 50 and headed north towards the town of Carlin through what looked, from my map, to be 90 miles of complete emptiness.

The journey actually proved quite eventful. I crossed the old Pony Express trail, now covered with sagebrush. I passed a broken-down van; it would have been unthinkable not to stop, but the driver cheerily informed me that help was already on its way. Late in the afternoon I spotted a billowing cloud of dust ahead. As I drew nearer I saw it was caused by scores of calves charging around a large pen in a frantic effort to escape the lassos of several mounted cowboys.

This I had to watch, so I parked by the roadside and walked over to the corral. A middle-aged woman in jeans and a cowboy hat detached herself from the action and greeted me, with twinkling eyes, above the din of mooing calves. Of course I could watch, she said. Her name was Patsy Tomera. She and her husband Tom, who had a magnificent pointed moustache, were ranchers and owned 1,500 head of cattle. With the help of friends and neighbours, she explained, they were getting ready to turn the calves out on to the surrounding hills and had been at it since 5.30 that morning.

For the next hour I had a ringside seat at my own private rodeo. There were four cowboys on horseback and one cowgirl, the Tomeras' eighteen-year-old daughter Susan who was a member of her high-school rodeo team. With their lassoos they would expertly rope a calf around its legs and drag it to the centre of the corral. Patsy and others would then physically wrestle the bellowing beast to the ground. There it was branded with a red-hot iron that produced a loud sizzling, clouds of smoke and a stench of burning hair. Nicks were taken out of its ear and back leg for further identification, and after an injection of antibiotics from a frighteningly huge syringe the bloodied females were then released. Not the males. For them there was one more treat in store. A young man rummaged around in their nether regions, grabbed their testicles, and calmly castrated them with a large pair of clippers called a 'masculator'.

The Tomeras and their helpers had 170 calves to do that day and it was past dark before they finished. As the dust finally settled and the mooing subsided, and as the moon rose in a night sky already shimmering with constellations, they invited me to join them around the branding fire. There we cracked jokes and drank beers. We talked of the coyotes, mountain lions and mustangs – wild horses – in the surrounding hills. We cooked the calves' testicles – otherwise known as 'mountain oysters' or 'cowboy caviar' – on pieces of wire suspended above the embers, and, when their skins burst, ate them. It was all much as it must have been when Tom Tomera's grandfather first settled this magical land a hundred years ago.

My day was not yet over. There is much more to Nevada, of course, than just ranching and gold mines. It is a state where gambling is such a way of life that even laundromats and petrol stations provide slot machines. It is the state to which outsiders flock for instant marriages or divorces with no questions asked. It is also the only state in America with legalised brothels, and as I reached the edge of Carlin I spotted one – a long, low building with two red lights shining like beacons in the night.

I slowed, accelerated, then stamped on the brakes as I considered whether to delve deeper. My curiosity prevailed, and I parked on an expanse of rutted mud alongside two large trucks and a white stretched limousine with a vanity number plate that read 'SPARKY'. The place was called 'Sharon's'. I rang the bell. A youngish man with a droopy moustache opened the door, looked me up and down, and admitted me into a cosy little bar where three or four scantily-clad, heavily made-up prostitutes – one black, the rest white, and all well past their sell-by date – were sitting on high stools and ostentatiously preening themselves for my benefit.

Though I say it myself I remained admirably composed. There are times in America when a rather proper English accent sounds quite ridiculous, and this was most definitely one of them, but I explained to the assembled company that I was writing a book and this elicited shrieks of pleasure from the girls.

'You're writing about catshops!' exclaimed one of them, uncurling herself from her chair and sidling over. 'Let me help you, sweetheart!' Before I knew it she was leading me back to her room which seemed to consist entirely of bed, pillows and big soft cushions.

'My name's Star,' she said as she sat me down. 'My CB handle's "Bad Habit". I've worked in four houses but this is the one that treats its customers best, like it's home. We have a hot tub . . .'

We were interrupted, perhaps fortunately, at that moment by the moustachioed man who'd admitted me. He was the barman, and seemed less than thrilled with my presence. I'd have to sit in the front and wait for Charlie, he said. Star and I returned to the bar where someone lifted the lid of a lavatory seat hanging on the wall to reveal a picture of the aforesaid Charlie. He was a balding, middle-aged man who was evidently the brothel's owner.

Star pulled her stool close to mine. She began telling me how prostitution enabled her to support her three kids who lived with her parents in Los Angeles, but we were almost immediately interrupted again, this time by the laboured entrance of a considerably older woman with a brightly patterned jacket, watery eyes and gingery dyed hair. This was Charlie's mum, Pat Kendrick, who evidently ran the brothel on her son's behalf. She deposited herself on a stool the other side of me, ordered some black coffee and lit a cigarette. A badge on her jacket proclaimed: 'I'm a superior lover'.

'What d'you want to know?' she asked in a deep, slurred voice.

'All about your "establishment",' I replied.

'I call mine a brothel, honey,' she replied bluntly. 'You never been with a whore or prostitute before? How d'you do it? With a hand job?' Pat was what you might call tart of tongue.

Her son had had 'a fascination with brothels since he was fourteen', she told me. He went to college, qualified as an accountant and became Nevada's youngest brothel owner when he opened Sharon's nine years ago. He named it after his wife, a cardiac nurse. 'We told her daddy we'd put her name in lights, so we did,' said Pat. 'Since when she's run away, remarried and had a child.'

There was no local opposition to the brothel, she continued. 'The Mormons wanted it. The senior citizens wanted it.' There were mines and a large truck stop in Carlin. 'This was a town overrun with men, honey, and we didn't need rape.' Charlie was now part of the town's establishment. He had helped organise a chamber of commerce, established a scholarship, and fed the needy at Christmas with donations from the brothel's clients.

Pat herself had been a teacher of home economics and a hospital worker before becoming Charlie's 'hod carrier'. The children she'd taught now came to use the brothel. 'It's just like a kid said to me: "Don't you remember me? You taught me in second grade". I said "you didn't have a moustache then, did you?"'

I asked Pat how she was treated in Carlin. 'No one's spat on me recently,' she replied. 'The Baptist minister will excuse himself from a crowd of people and come over to talk to me.'

Star had been butting in, asking Pat if she was allowed to talk to me. Pat suddenly snapped at her. 'You're sitting there babbling anyway,' she snarled. 'Stop acting as if you're in some kind of prison.'

A few minutes later the doorbell rang and a huge trucker walked in. The fickle Star was by his side in an instant. 'Hi, Big Ben,' she purred. 'I'm still alive and kicking.' They disappeared in the direction of Star's room and another woman came and sat beside me. This was Jean. She had worked at the hospital with Pat and was now the brothel's cook and laundress. The two ladies cackled when they recalled how hard they used to work at 'running things, organising things, saving lives' before Charlie opened Sharon's.

Pat was becoming quite loquacious. She explained how the brothel would, if requested, use the limousine to collect lorry drivers from Carlin's truck stop. She told me that women truckers occasionally wanted to use the brothel – some of her girls would service them but others wouldn't. When I asked if sex was safe at Sharon's Pat got up, pulled me outside, and pointed to a sign by the front door that I hadn't spotted in the darkness. 'Public Health Notice,' it read. 'The law requires every brothel prostitute to be tested regularly. Customers must use a latex condom during all sexual activity. This does not guarantee freedom from sexually transmitted diseases.'

Pat was just explaining that the girls were tested monthly for AIDS, and weekly for other sexually-transmitted diseases, when she suddenly screamed and grabbed me. A large mouse was running across the floor just inside the open doorway.

When the commotion finally subsided and we regained our stools, Jean told me how she had given each of her three sons a night at a brothel for their 18th birthdays because, she explained, this was 'the safe way. Before that they got it underneath the bleachers'. Did they appreciate the present, I asked. 'What do you think, they ran round town telling all their friends?' she replied with a throaty laugh.

Pat seemed faintly contemptuous of her half-dozen prostitutes. 'I gave away more before breakfast than these girls ever sell,' she remarked at one point. 'They all have sick and sad stories,' she continued. Most had turned to prostitution because they had husbands or boyfriends in prison, or children to support, and this was 'fast and easy money for someone without any education'.

How much did they earn, I inquired? I'd have to ask the girls that, Pat replied. They were 'independent contractors'. They gave the brothel half their earnings, and $25 a day for food and lodging, but set their own prices. They and their customers had five minutes to negotiate, but then 'I spring through the door like the wicked witch of the West. You can't have someone in there killing time. Time is money, honey.'

The brothel did offer certain 'specials', however. 'Jon, give me a menu, will you honey?' Pat asked the barman. Jon produced a yellow sheet. Beneath a picture of a naked girl it read: 'Hors d'oeuvres: Garden Tub Bubble Bath, Hot Tub Party, X-rated Movies, Body Massage. Main course: Straight Party, Half and Half, Double Party, Vibrator Party. Desserts: Whipped Cream Party, Motion Lotion Party, Chocolate and Vanilla Party.' Money had to be paid in advance. Sharon's accepted Visa and Mastercard. The charges appeared on customers' credit card bills as 'Kendrick Enterprise Food Fruit and Gourmet'. Alternatively, Pat chuckled, 'We can give you a receipt that says "Front End Alignment".'

Pat told one of the girls to show me round. Her name was Marie Strawberry, and she wore merely a bikini and wide-open, see-through shirt. She smiled seductively, thrust out her ample bosom and led me off, but only after I'd stressed I was not a customer. The brothel was actually just a double-width trailer home and there was not much to see, so I soon found myself sitting on another outsize bed in Marie's cosy little room.

I didn't like to ask her age, but she had two grown sons and there was something distinctly maternal about her. She was from Washington state, she said, and had turned to prostitution because she had got into debt. She did it for a year, got married, and returned to it two years later when the marriage failed. She had maybe half a dozen customers a day. This was a nice brothel because they didn't force too much business on the girls and let them go out. It was also good money, and 'a good way for a girl to get from a bad place to a good place'. She herself would stay till she had earned enough to finish a nursing degree because 'as you get older you have to have something. I can't see myself doing this at the age of eighty and saying, "Hello, honey. Let me take my teeth out!"'

Marie charged anywhere from $50 for a fifteen-minute 'back massage and hand job' to $350 for a comprehensive six-hour package, with a whole range of different options in between. Most of her customers were lorry drivers – single, solitary men who lived in their trucks and were always on the go. Some wanted to act out their fantasies, she said, but 'I can't do "domination" so I just suggest another girl.' Others didn't want sex at all. 'Sometimes they will just ask you questions. A guy will come in and just ask you to hold him or to hug him. They're lonely. It's more about closeness than just plain sex.' After weeks on the road myself I understood exactly what she meant, and to judge by demand alone it seemed that Marie did much more to fulfill the human needs of truckers than Robert Richard, the truck-stop chaplain back in Mesquite, Texas.

Marie genuinely enjoyed her job because 'If I can make somebody feel good it makes me feel good.' Outside the brothel, however, she had to tell people she was a bartender. 'It's not because I'm ashamed of what I do. It's because society doesn't accept or understand it.'

The barman came in. 'Sweetheart, I have a trucker requesting you,' he told Marie. It was clearly time for me to go. I contemplated buying a Sharon's T-shirt for my wife – 'Things never get better' read the slogan beneath a picture of a naked girl – but decided she might not appreciate it. Star was still entertaining Big Ben so I said goodbye to Pat and Jean, who were still sitting at the bar, and slipped out into the night.

Later, in yet another charmless motel room, I studied my map for the next day's journey and was struck once again by the way you can travel from one state to another across a cartographer's random line and find utterly different social attitudes.

Directly north of Carlin, in permissive Nevada, was Gem County in conservative Idaho. Gem County's prosecutor, Douglas Varie, had recently achieved national notoriety by dusting off a 1921 Idaho law forbidding sex between unmarried couples. He was using this to prosecute unwed teenage mums as fornicators. He was enjoying a high degree of success as the evidence against the girls was unusually irrefutable.

21

Prophet without Honour

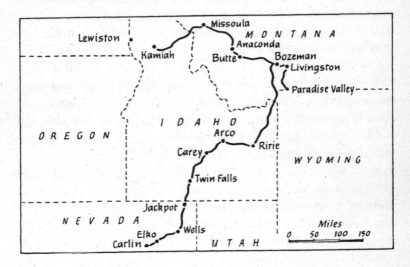

It was to Idaho and the Pacific North West that I was heading, but I had one chore to do before leaving Nevada. My back tyres had worn perilously thin, so I stopped in a largish town called Elko to have them replaced. This cost me $86, but I enjoyed some compensation. The mechanics were out to lunch, so to kill an hour I strolled into the centre of this rough old mining and ranching community. There I found not one, but three Basque restaurants in a row. This seemed about as likely as finding Navajos selling fry bread in the middle of Beijing. The restaurants were all closed till the evening, but I asked around and was directed to a woman called Anita, the mayor's wife, who ran the Elko General Merchandise Company, a wonderful old-fashioned store that sold boots, Levi's, stetsons and other western wear to the ranchers.

Anita's full name was Anita Anacabe Franzoia and she was Basque. One of her two assistants, Ruth Leniz, was married to a

Basque who ran yet another Basque restaurant. The second assistant, Maite Ugalde, was the daughter of a Basque. Elko bristled with Basques, Anita told me. There were hundreds, maybe thousands, of them. They spoke Basque. They gathered in the Basque restaurants in the evening to play a Basque card game called Mus. There was a Basque club where I could watch Basque children learning Basque dances that very evening. Elko's supermarkets sold imported Basque wines, and every July the town staged a two-day Basque festival. It even had a municipal pelota court next to the municipal tennis courts.

Basques had been coming to Nevada for well over a century, Anita said. The first ones were looking for gold, but mostly they came to pursue their traditional way of life as shepherds in the high Nevada deserts. Her own father had come over in 1901 as a bucka-roo, a man who broke horses. When his first wife died he returned to the 'old country' to find another. He had opened this store in 1937 to outfit the Basque shepherds, and Anita had been raised above it. As we were talking, her three-year-old daughter ran out of a back room. Anita spoke to her in Basque. Yes, she said, nearly a century after her father first arrived in the United States her family still spoke Basque at home.

Already on this trip I had heard Elizabethan English spoken in Chesapeake Bay, French in Louisiana and German in Texas, not to mention the Gullahs' African creole and widespread Spanish. America may be a melting pot, I thought, but there were still numerous ethnic lumps inside that pot which stubbornly refuse to dissolve.

I pressed on, that evening's Basque dancing class notwithstanding, and crossed into Idaho after one typical last Nevadan flourish. Right on the border, servicing visitors from the north-west and Canada, was a town that consisted of nothing but five casinos. It was called Jackpot.

North of the border the landscape changed abruptly. The sage-brush gave way to ploughed fields, dry gulleys to flowing rivers. The slogan on Nevada number plates was 'The Silver State', but in Idaho it was 'Famous Potatoes'. In Nevada the weather was warm and spring-like, but in Idaho it was still late winter with patches of snow on the ground.

My destination was an elementary school classroom in a tiny town called Ririe, some 250 miles north-east of Jackpot. By the time I reached it the following afternoon I had driven across a bleak, black, jagged lava field known as the Craters of the Moon, past a town called Arco that was the first in the world to be powered by atomic energy, and through a vast expanse of bare brown land dotted with mysterious installations. This was the Department of Energy's nuclear reactor testing site, and since 1949 more reactors have been built on this 900-square-mile plain than anywhere else in the world. The distances may be great, but if you avoid the inter-states there is no such thing as a boring journey in America.

I'd read about Ririe in the *Wall Street Journal*. The classroom belonged to a teacher named Tina Andersen and was hardly con-ventional. Behind the children's desks was a lifesized plywood model of a simulator used for training astronauts and a mock command centre. Plastered across the walls were autographed photographs of NASA astronauts. There was also a large poster proclaiming 'Reach for the Stars' – which was exactly what this tiny town was doing.

Ririe has just 596 people and sits amid endless grain and potato fields near the foothills of the Teton Mountains. It has no traffic lights, no motel and no supermarket, though it still has three bars. Like so many other farming communities it has been slowly dying, many of its buildings are boarded up, and two-thirds of the people that remain are past retirement age. But a few of its more dynamic inhabitants were searching for a way to save it, and in 1995 Mrs Andersen's obsession with space inspired one of the more audacious economic recovery plans ever to emerge from small-town America.

Mrs Andersen is a forty-two-year-old grandmother who so longed to be an astronaut that she joined NASA's 'Teacher in Space' programme and was periodically invited to NASA facilities. During a visit to Moffett Field in California, she discovered that NASA had a real simulator that it would literally give away to anyone will-ing or able to remove it. The only problem was that this $4 million contraption, used to train the early Mercury, Gemini and Apollo astronauts, was 60-feet high, weighed several tons and was incredibly complex.

Mrs Andersen hurried back to Ririe with the news. It caught the imagination of DeLayne Adams, a town councillor with an unusually forceful personality. The two women couldn't excite Ririe's staid town council, so they by-passed it and formed a twenty-seven-member Space Committee. They then flew back to Moffett Field to inspect what Mrs Adams termed 'this monstrosity' and agreed to take it. At the very least, they thought, the town could plonk the thing in a potato field near the E-Z Stop Café and attract tourists travelling along the nearby highway to Jackson Hole, Wyoming.

But why stop there, they asked themselves? Why not build a space museum? Why not open a space camp for kids? Why not have a visitors centre, a cinema, a food court? Why not make the simulator the centrepiece of a comprehensive 'Space Discovery Station' that would turn Ririe – a town with only the most tenuous links to America's space programme – into a tourist mecca?

Thus what began as one small step for Ririe quickly developed into the proverbial giant leap.

The Space Committee could not afford professional contractors to dismantle and move the simulator so it decided to do the job itself. The following spring, Mrs Andersen, Mrs Adams and six others – only one of whom had any relevant experience – drove the 600 miles to Moffett Field and spent the next ten days dismantling the simulator with wrenches and cutting torches. 'We're all farm people, and even though we were women we knew how to use wrenches,' said Mrs Adams, an accountant in her late forties. A local transport company lent them three flatbed lorries. 'We had hardly started when we had those three trucks loaded,' she said. Another Ririe company donated three more and they too were quickly filled. A seventh lorry had to be dispatched from Ririe a couple of months later to collect the final bits and pieces, and NASA threw in a second, smaller simulator for good measure.

The two simulators – and seven boxes of blueprints for reassembling them – are now stored all over Ririe while the Space

Committee attempts to raise $10 million in cash or kind to build the Discovery Station. By the time I visited, it had made some remarkable progress. NASA had offered a seemingly limitless supply of obsolete aircraft. 'We will probably limit it to twenty planes,' Mrs Adams told me in a rather blasé tone. The IMAX company had promised to build and operate a giant-screen cinema. The women had cajoled architects, fundraisers and lobbyists into giving their services free, secured the support of Idaho's politicians and rural development agencies, and were in line for several large grants. Working on the principle that every little helps, the committee was meanwhile selling T-shirts, had raised $400 with a stall at Ririe's harvest festival and was raffling a horse.

'DeLayne's a ball of fire on this,' said Brent Ferguson, owner of Ririe's T&T Auto Parts store. 'At first we thought "Yeah, right, it's never going to happen", but as we worked on it, it all came together.'

There was still an awful long way to go, of course. Shelley Landon, a potato farmer's wife and Space Committee member, gave me a tour of tarpaulin-covered computers, hulking pieces of machinery and great blue steel frames sitting in sheds and barns and yards all over Ririe. She took me to a ploughed potato field near the highway, and it was very hard to imagine it covered in asphalt, gleaming white domes, ranks of planes and one huge reassembled simulator. But in Mrs Adams' mind the Ririe 'Space Discovery Station' was already a reality. Based on existing traffic flows, she informed me with complete and utter confidence, the station would attract 450,000 visitors a year and generate $5 million.

I left Ririe thinking of a line in a speech delivered to the Democrats' 1996 convention by Christopher Reeve, the 'Superman' actor paralysed by a riding accident. 'So many of our dreams at first seem impossible,' he declared, 'and then they seem improbable. But then, when we summon the will, they soon become inevitable.' In Ririe, at least, that proverbial American can-do spirit was still very much alive.

One of the most bizarre stories I covered during my years in

Washington occurred in March, 1990, in Paradise Valley, Montana, about 150 miles north of Ririe. I had flown out to Bozeman, rented a car, and driven east to Livingston, then south down the valley, which was every bit as exquisite as its name suggested. Bison and elk grazed by the meandering Yellowstone River, and on each side the snow-covered Rockies towered skywards behind rolling green hills. It was the sort of perfect, idealised landscape that model railway enthusiasts create from glass, green baize and white paint, but there in that beautiful corner of Montana as many as 3,000 people were – grotesquely – preparing for a Soviet-inspired nuclear holocaust that they believed was imminent.

Halfway down the valley I had turned right and followed a dirt track two miles up into the foothills until I crossed a brow and encountered a hideous sight. A fleet of bulldozers, diggers and cater-pillar trucks were putting the finishing touches to a veritable warren of underground bunkers, perhaps forty in all. Where once there had been grass there were now great tracts of churned-up mud from which protruded radio masts, subterranean entrances, shiny new steel air ducts and the humps of giant 30,000-gallon propane fuel tanks. Trailer homes littered the hillsides, many flying the Stars and Stripes.

That was the community of Glastonbury and about 20 miles further down the valley, at a second secretive community called Corwin Springs on the edge of Yellowstone national park, another giant honeycomb of bunkers was nearing completion, though I was not allowed in to see it. That would hold 756 people in thirty 150-foot-long buried steel cylinders, and a seven-month supply of food and fuel, advanced communications equipment, computers, medical stocks and a little library had already been laid in. There was even a separate bunker for livestock – a latter-day's Noah's Ark.

By 1990, the Cold War was over, of course, but these people were religious fanatics, members of a New Age cult called the Church Universal and Triumphant, or CUT, that was the latest in a long line of apocalyptic movements in America. Their leader was a woman called Elizabeth Clare Prophet, also known as 'Mother' or 'Guru Ma', who claimed that through her spoke the saints in heaven or

'Ascended Masters'. Fervently anti-communist, she believed *glasnost* and *perestroika* were Soviet tricks to dupe the West into lowering its guard, and had issued warnings to the effect that March and April of that year would be a particularly perilous time in world affairs, with the danger peaking on 23 April.

Her followers knew exactly what that meant. Across America hundreds left their jobs, sold their homes, packed all their belongings into rented removal vans and set off with their families for CUT's 33,000-acre refuge in Paradise Valley, there to wait out the holocaust and the long, long night to follow. Many were armed. Some came from as far away as England. In the event, of course, Mrs Prophet's fears proved unfounded. The 'period of maximum peril' was marked only by the rupturing of three giant fuel tanks and the seepage of 32,000 gallons of propane into this precious and pristine environment.

I decided to return to Paradise Valley and see what had become of all those people. I called CUT and asked if I could visit. The answer was a flat and unequivocal no, but I set off anyway. Not far beyond Ririe I began climbing high into the Rockies on a highway bordered by thick pine forests and ever-higher walls of snow. I spent the night in the summer resort town of West Yellowstone, where I was the only guest in my motel and discovered to my dismay that I'd have to make a 100-mile detour as the road through the national park was not yet open. Admittedly there was no speed limit in Montana, but that was not much good to me.

I reached Livingston, the town at the northern end of Paradise Valley, early the next afternoon. I paid my customary visit to the local newspaper – in this case the *Livingston Enterprise* – and learned that Mrs Prophet was addressing a CUT dinner at Livingston's old railway depot that very night. At first I considered this an amazing stroke of luck, but by the time I collapsed on to my motel bed early the next morning I had somewhat revised that opinion.

The dinner began at 7.30 p.m. I gave it an hour to get going, then sneaked in the back and studied the assembled crowd. I was dismayed. What had become of my cult? These people were not freaks or weirdos. They didn't have wild eyes or messianic beards or crazy clothes. Some of the women were wearing purple – one of CUT's sacred colours – and a few besuited men were concealing running shoes beneath the tablecloths, but they were mostly old or middle-aged and looked so staid that I wondered whether I'd crashed a Rotary Club dinner by mistake.

My disappointment only deepened. The speeches began around 9.00 p.m. and droned on and on with not even the faintest allusion to titillating subjects like imminent nuclear holocausts. Senior officials spoke solemnly about how the Church needed to retrench, lay off staff, refocus on its core activities and be more customer-friendly. It sounded like a business seminar. There were occasional interludes when someone would play Rachmaninov or sing an old music hall song. The only vaguely interesting moment came when the audience stood as one and three times chanted: 'Hear O Universe! I am grateful.' By the time 'Mother' herself stood up to speak it was past midnight and even the truest believers were flagging.

Mrs Prophet was in the process of divorcing her fourth husband, the Church's executive vice-president. She had recently stepped down as the Church's president, but remained its 'spiritual leader'. She was a trim, well-groomed lady in her late fifties with a musical voice, and was reputed to be charismatic, but I must have caught her on a bad night.

She said she wanted to talk about Mark Prophet, the second of her four husbands who founded the Church in 1958 and died in 1973. In particular she wanted to talk about the incredible magnanimity he had displayed during his earlier incarnations as Lot, the disciple Mark, Lancelot, Saladin, Bonaventure, Louis XIV, Alexis, Longfellow and numerous other great men whose names she rattled off faster than I could take them down. It seemed he had never been anyone lowly or undistinguished. She then began working through the list, telling two or three interminable stories about each figure, but I'd had quite enough before she'd even reached halfway.

The Church wouldn't see me, but its critics were far more welcoming. The next morning I met Peter Arnone, a paraplegic who'd been a CUT member for twenty-two years before growing thoroughly disillusioned and resigning in 1992. His former wife remained in Glastonbury with their four children, but he had moved to a small flat in Livingston from which he published occasional newsletters attacking the Church. He had joined it as a confused young man in 1970, he told me, and there was a time when he would have laid down his life for Mrs Prophet, but now he considered her nothing but a fraud and her followers brainwashed.

Peter and I drove down the valley and I was amazed at what we saw. At Glastonbury, the scene of so much frenetic activity seven years earlier, the bunkers were now overgrown and neglected and relatively few scattered homes remained. At Corwin Springs the guardhouse was, to our surprise, unmanned so we drove unmolested around 'the ranch', as the headquarters of this previously impenetrable sect is known. Five miles up a dirt road behind the ranch, high in the mountains, we came to a barrier with a large sign reading: 'End of Public Road. Absolutely no public access beyond this point.' We had reached what was known as 'the Heart of the Inner Retreat'.

Again there was no guard, so I hopped over the barrier, sauntered half a mile further up the track and there it was – the master bunker prepared back in 1990 for Mrs Prophet, her family and the Church's staff. It was an awesome sight. From a great swathe of deforested hillside protruded seven or eight great concrete domes. Halfway along, a massive concrete entranceway, protected by giant steel doors and big enough to admit juggernaut lorries, had been cut into the hill. Just outside this entrance were at least two dozen steel cargo containers holding, I presume, supplies. The entire bunker was surrounded by high barbed-wire fencing. It was, in every sense of the word, a monumental folly.

Even Peter was shocked by the general lack of security and sense of abandonment. 'What we have seen today is a shadow of what this place used to be,' he said. The Church was dying. It had reached the peak of its power in 1990, but had been losing members and money ever since and there were probably less than 1,000 members left in the valley. 'We are seeing the whole thing disintegrate,' Peter declared as I drove him back to Livingston, and he sounded almost wistful. 'When I think of the hopes and dreams we shared in the past I feel bad the whole thing has turned out to be a fraud.'

My day ended delightfully and unexpectedly. During my visit in 1990 I had interviewed several newly-arrived Church members. Most had long since departed again, but not Michael and Jeannie Campbell. They were listed in the telephone book. I called and they invited me to dinner. So that evening I returned to Glastonbury and discovered that for them at least everything had worked out almost perfectly.

The last time I'd seen them, the Campbells had recently arrived from Seattle with their two young daughters and were living in a half-finished 'convertible' shelter that Michael was building himself. It was an amazing construction. The five back rooms were dug into a hillside and had foot-thick concrete walls and ceilings. The front living area had windows, but they were covered with sheets of steel and three feet of earth. There was mud everywhere, and it had seemed an unutterably miserable existence.

Now, seven years later, I drove high up into the hills, far higher than I remembered, and found the house transformed. The sheets of steel had been removed and the front rooms were flooded with light from plate-glass windows that offered breathtaking views across Paradise Valley to the great sunlit snowy mountains of Yellowstone. Here, at an altitude of 6,000 feet, the Campbells had renounced the intense materialism of our age and pursued the simple, more spiritual life they had dreamed of. Michael had built himself a large two-storey shed in which he did pottery and other crafts. Jeannie grew vegetables. Together they had been home schooling their daughters, Nicole and Rachel. A single woodstove heated the entire earth-covered house and – when it was working – a small windmill generated additional electricity. The family lived, Michael told me, on $700 a month which he earned by doing landscape gardening back in Seattle every summer.

It was a glorious evening and dinner was not ready, so Michael and I walked to the top of the hill behind the house and found ourselves looking down on five magnificent bull elk the other side. He took me around the hillside to a sheltered hollow at the head of a steep gully where he had placed a Buddha. This was where he came to meditate, he said. A little further down the gully was a gnarled pine tree from which he had hung a bell made from half a fire-extinguisher. He struck it once, and the reverberations went on and on, rippling outwards and filling the otherwise silent evening air.

Before dinner the family performed an 'om' – a sort of hum and a song – by way of a grace. We ate lasagna, salad, warm bread and the meat of an elk that Michael had shot, and drank a 'tea' that Jeannie had brewed from peppermint, nettle, camomile and liquorice root.

The Campbells told me they would have moved to Paradise Valley with or without Mrs Prophet's encouragement, though perhaps not so soon. They would have built an 'earth-bermed' house like this whether or not they believed a nuclear attack was imminent because it was intensely practical. They certainly paid heed to the 'dictations' Mrs Prophet relayed from the 'Ascended Masters', but they did not follow them – or her – blindly and were not meant to. That was the trouble back in 1990. Fanatics had interpreted her words too literally. Some gave up everything to come here. Others ran up enormous credit card bills believing they would never have to pay them. When nothing happened, they felt angry and deceived and left the valley. Others departed because they couldn't find work. What remained was still a spiritual community, but one far less frenzied and fanatical. Peace had returned to Paradise Valley.

After dinner Nicole played the piano and Rachel showed me her artwork. I found myself lulled by this charming family that I'd hardly met before that evening. They had not foisted their religion on me. They had not claimed to have all the answers. They were just idealistic people who believed, said Michael, that there was 'more to life than just having a job and growing old and dying'. All that really mattered, added Jeannie, was that 'you live a kind, caring, loving life, be responsible for your family, and you try'. It was a real effort to leave, and when I did finally rouse myself Jeannie gave me a slice of sweet-scented juniper wood to take with me. The two girls ran on outside, and my last sight was of them bouncing high on a trampoline against an amazing moonlit backdrop of plunging valley and soaring mountains.

*

I don't know about the girls, but I soon returned to earth. Within minutes I'd again been stopped for speeding.

'But Montana has no speed limit,' I protested to the officer.

'It does after dark,' he replied, and a few miles further on I learned why when two deer darted across the road just yards ahead of me.

To demonstrate literary solidarity I stopped that night at a Days Inn in Bozeman that advertised itself with a little poem:

> *Spring is sprung*
> *And melts the snow*
> *Come stay with us*
> *Our rates are low*

The next morning, at breakfast, I ran into an old acquaintance from my Washington days, and after so long in the boondocks it felt like meeting someone from a former life.

His name was Dan Glickman. He was now the US Agriculture Secretary, and he too had just experienced the rage of the rural west first-hand, though this time it was a conservationist doing the protesting. During the winter state officials had, with Washington's support, slaughtered more than a thousand bison that had strayed from the snowbound Yellowstone national park in search of food. This was in case they spread brucellosis to cattle herds. The previous evening Mr Glickman had attended a public meeting to discuss this highly emotional issue. His reward was to have an irate woman splatter him with a bucketful of putrefying bison guts.

Mr Glickman and his aides departed for Bozeman airport and the 2,000-mile flight back to Washington. I set off west along a 'Montanabahn', as Montana's interstates are now known. This carried me back up into the Rocky Mountains and just before the town of Butte I crossed the Continental Divide. Henceforth all rivers flowed west towards the Pacific, not south or east, and for the first time I began to sense that the end of my journey was approaching.

I stopped for petrol in Butte and ended up staying a couple of hours. The town is a mile above sea level and sits atop 'The Richest Hill on Earth'. In the course of a century an estimated $22 billion of copper and other minerals were plundered from the mountain beneath it, and there are said to be 10,000 miles of tunnels still down there, some a mile deep. Earlier this century the writer John Gunther described Butte as the 'toughest, bawdiest town in America' and 'the greatest mining camp ever known'. At its prime in the early 1900s the town boasted a population of 100,000, but today it has shrunk to just a third of that size and only one small mine still operates.

Butte is full, however, of poignant reminders of its heyday. There are the copper kings' mansions, the tall and elegant brick buildings that once housed fine hotels, the old Mother Lode Theatre, the many saloons. There are the towering black mineframes that dot the landscape like so many gallows, the narrow railway tracks that criss-cross the streets, and the vast, terraced Berkeley Pit, now gradually filling with water and huge enough to hold two or three Houston Astrodomes. There is St Patrick's cemetery, filled with the graves of Irish mineworkers who came out from Cork and Waterford and Donegal in the late 19th century. But what really caught my eye was a two-storey red-brick building standing alone on an expanse of razed land with a scantily-clad female mannequin on its front steps.

I stopped to investigate. A plaque on the wall informed me that this was the old Dumas Hotel and had been placed on the National Register of Historic Places. It was never a real hotel, however. It was built as a brothel in 1890 and continued as such until 1982, making it America's longest-running house of pleasure. More than a million satisfied customers was its claim. It might still have been open had it not been burgled in 1981. The thieves made off with a night's takings of about $4,500, got caught, and thus revealed that the madam, Ruby Garrett, had not been declaring all her income. Of Butte's infamous red light district, that fanned out from Venus Alley and was once the largest between San Francisco and New York, nothing else survives.

A sign said 'Come In' so I did. The front door was punctured with four ancient bullet-holes courtesy of a jealous wife who saw her husband's car parked outside and didn't realise it had simply broken down. Inside was a long, wide corridor lined with bedroom doors and windows, through which customers could inspect the wares within. Above the corridor was a balustraded balcony lined by two more rows of bedrooms, and above those was a skylight running the length of the building. I had stumbled – I later learned – on the last known example in America of a style of architecture known as Victorian Brothel, though it was somewhat obscured by the piles of junk in every room.

At first I thought the place was deserted, but finally a forlorn-looking middle-aged man emerged from a room at the far end of the corridor. He introduced himself as Rudy Giecek. He was a restorer of antique furniture, he said. He had delivered groceries to the Dumas Hotel as a boy, and had bought the place on impulse from Ruby Garrett in order to save it from destruction. It was now an 'antiques mall', he helpfully informed me, but confessed it was not doing very well.

Rudy showed me round. He took me down the main corridor, where he had converted each room into a little shop, up to the first-floor rooms where the classier prostitutes had worked, and around the madam's suite. It was all rather sterile, as reconstructions always are, but then he veered from his standard tour. 'Come and look at this,' he said conspiratorially. He took me to the very back of the building and down some rough wooden stairs to the windowless basement where the cheapest whores had worked.

I found myself in a veritable time capsule. Nothing had changed in half-a-century. Here the corridor was cold and damp and lit by dim red lights. The rooms off it were small and dingy and contained little more than single iron bedsteads. They had buzzers with which the prostitutes could order drinks or summon help. There were yellowed pin-ups on the walls, half-drunk bottles of grape brandy, jars of vaseline, a 1930s wireless, rotting floor-boards. On the faded wallpaper were scratch marks where men had lit their matches, and pencilled calculations of what the girls had earned. You could almost smell the sweat, scent and sex. At the corridor's furthermost end was a door through which Butte's more respectable citizens had been able to enter the brothel unseen via an underground passage.

I'd encountered nothing quite like it since 1979 when, in the course of writing a guide to London's greasy spoon cafés, a proprietor showed me the old, disused British Museum underground station which survived in pristine condition beneath his Bloomsbury diner.

Twenty-six miles beyond Butte I came to Anaconda, a town built by one of Butte's copper kings for the sole purpose of smelting ore so Butte could be spared even worse pollution. For a century, Anaconda was the archetypal company town, but unfortunately the company closed in 1980, leaving behind hundreds of unemployed workers, general industrial dereliction, and great tracts of land contaminated with arsenic and heavy metals. Like Ririe in Idaho, however, this gutsy little town of 9,000 people decided to fight back.

Its civic leaders came up with a seemingly preposterous idea for a town 500 miles from the nearest major city, lacking a single quality hotel and covered in snow for six months of every year. They decided to turn a large chunk of that blighted, toxic wasteland into a world-class golf course. This would, they hoped, attract tourists, retirees and businessmen and act as a catalyst for Anaconda's economic recovery. They persuaded Jack Nicklaus to design it for them. The government ordered the Atlantic Richfield oil company, owners of the now-defunct Anaconda Copper Mining Company, to finance the $15 million reclamation project. Thus it was that I found myself, early the next morning, touring one of the world's most unusual golf courses a month before its formal opening.

The Old Works Golf Course covers 220 acres reclaimed by laying a two-foot cap of limestone, clay and topsoil over the contaminated land and lining the bunkers, greens and ponds with plastic sheeting. It is dominated at one end by a giant slag heap and the old Washoe smelter's colossal 585-foot brick smokestack – the world's tallest. The surrounding hills have been denuded by a century of severe atmospheric pollution. The fairways are bordered by the remains of furnaces, piles of discarded rock and pieces of old machinery. The bunkers contain not sand, but a powdery black residue of the smelting process, and the holes have names like Calciner, Flue, Crusher, Refiner and Anode. The course is not exactly beautiful, but it certainly has character and where else could you play on a Nicklaus-designed course for just $30?

Having seen America's oldest golf course back in Middlesboro, Kentucky, I had now seen its newest one too. What I had also seen was a particularly vivid symbol – a golf course built on top of an old smelter works – of how Montana is becoming gentrified.

Montana is, admittedly, the state where the Unabomber Ted Kaczynski sent out mail bombs from his primitive forest hut for seventeen years before his arrest in 1996. It is the state where the same year twenty-one self-styled 'Freemen' – rebels who refuse to acknowledge the government's authority – holed up in a farmhouse and held off the FBI for eighty-one days before surrendering. But it is also a state where the super-rich and celebrities galore – Meg Ryan, Ted Turner, Peter Fonda, Brooke Shields, Michael Keaton, Whoopi Goldberg, Hank Williams Jnr., Andie McDowell – have bought themselves ranches, where art galleries and coffee houses are taking over Main Streets, and where tourism has leap-frogged past mining to become Montana's second biggest industry after agriculture. Even the infamous Militia of Montana has become almost mainstream, cashing in on its celebrity by setting up a lucrative mail order business that sells everything from chemical and biological warfare suits to survival guides with titles like *How to Disappear Completely and Never Be Found*. It was time to head on to the real 'wild west'.

From Anaconda I trundled westwards to Missoula, a small university town that has become a well-known writers' colony, then embarked on a spectacular 110-mile drive over the Bitterroot Mountains to the next small community. This was the route that Lewis and Clark took during their pioneering expedition across the continent to the Pacific in 1805, and it is scarcely more populated today.

I drove up and up into these densely-forested and rather

forbidding mountains. High above the snowline I came across Lolo hot springs where Lewis and Clark camped and bathed on both their outward and return journeys, and witnessed the Indian equivalent of a Scandinavian sauna. 'I observe after the Indians remaining in the hot bath as long as they could bear it run and plunge themselves into the creek, the water of which is now as cold as ice can make it,' Clark recorded with characteristically poor grammar in his journal.

The springs are now contained in a small pool with a broken roof. I meant to stop for just fifteen minutes, but there were three other men already there, we got talking and I ended up staying a couple of hours as snowflakes wafted in through the holes above and melted in the water. The occupations of my fellow loungers revealed a lot about modern-day Montana. One was a writer and poet from Missoula. Another was an artist who had returned to his native Montana after Los Angeles 'chewed me up and spat me out'. The third – bearded and long-haired – was a former property developer from Colorado who now lived in a tepee back near Anaconda and built furniture from wood he gathered in the forests.

It was getting late and dark by the time I left, and I still had a long way to go. I crossed into Idaho through the Lolo Pass and a veritable tunnel of snow. A little after that I passed a sign that warned: 'Winding Road Next 77 Miles'. I was several thousand feet up in the mountains, the snow was becoming heavier, and mine was the only car on the road. It was then that a large log edifice surrounded by great snowdrifts appeared like a warm and welcoming apparition in the night – the Lochsa Lodge.

The Lodge had been built as a hunting and fishing cabin back in the 1920s, long before the road came through. It was now owned by the Denton family who kept it open all year round though they had few winter visitors. For $25 they gave me a little log cabin of my own, and with my key came newspaper and kindling to light the wood-stove. I had a beer at the bar and ate dinner in a dining room lined with bear skins, elk heads and assorted stuffed critters. I wandered back to my cosy little cabin, enjoying the silence of the mountains and the forest, and fell deeply asleep. At 4.00 a.m. I woke up shivering because the fire had gone out. I rebuilt it, poked my head outside, and disturbed a large deer that bounded off into the darkness.

The next morning, I followed the swelling Lochsa River down through seventy more miles of wilderness, stopping at occasional historical markers that showed I was covering as much ground each hour as Lewis and Clark managed in a day. Where the Lochsa finally joined the Clearwater River I turned north and soon reached Kamiah, a pretty little timber town in the bottom of the great, green Clearwater Valley.

It was from Kamiah that I began a mini-odyssey up through the Idaho Panhandle, a gorgeous wedge of lakes, rivers, forests and wild, rolling mountains that extends about 200 miles northwards to the Canadian border and contains as strange and eclectic a population as you could hope to find anywhere in America.

22

Their Own Private Idahos

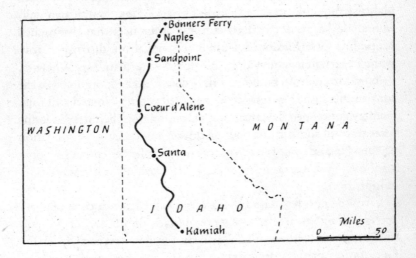

I found Steve in a field where he was laying the foundations for a barn he was building for a farmer. He was a cheery, middle-aged fellow with concrete splashed across his face and moustache. His wife begged me not to use his surname because he's a tax resister – one of at least 752 in Idaho according to the Internal Revenue Service – and has paid no federal income tax for eighteen years.

'Our government was founded on the faith that Christian man could govern himself. We don't rely on government to provide for us,' he told me. 'The government provides for nothing. All it does is take and redistribute wealth. It becomes a thief, not a provider, except for those on welfare. When those people on welfare can vote away your property it's legalised theft.'

The IRS claims Steve owes $500,000 and is threatening to seize the house in which he lives with his wife and eight children, all of whom are taught at home so they don't have to attend 'godless' public schools. But Steve will not capitulate. He no longer has a bank account or credit cards, or anything through which the IRS can gain access to his funds, and builds his barns for cash or barter only.

George Bernard Shaw once described Britain and America as two countries divided by a common language, but he'd never visited Idaho's panhandle and met men like Steve. Here, more than anywhere else I'd been, the deep cultural differences that distinguish Americans from Europeans – their individualism, distrust of government, religious conviction, idealism – are manifest. Where in Britain, for example, could you find counties abandoning building controls because they restrict personal freedom? Where in Europe would you find people retreating to mountaintops because the scriptures warn of some future Armageddon?

The 'Handle', as it is known, was not literally the end of my journey, but in a metaphorical sense it certainly represented its culmination.

Over the next few days I met a remarkable kaleidoscope of characters, though scarcely any were natives of Idaho. They were outsiders lured by the panhandle's beauty and remoteness, by its distance from America's degenerate cities, by the cheapness of its land and by its live-and-let-live attitude. 'Up here,' said a storekeeper in the tiny village of Naples, 'you can be or do just about anything so long as you don't harm your neighbours.'

These outsiders have poured in over the past thirty years to chase their dreams, pursue their personal utopias, build their own private Idahos. They are all in their own ways trying to recreate an America of some mythical golden age. They are decent folk fleeing the violence of metropolitan America – an astonishing number have come from California which was once a mecca itself but is now a place from which thousands of whites are bolting. They are hippies and back-to-the-landers inspired by Henry David Thoreau and that peculiarly American longing for the wilderness. They are self-styled survivalists and religious-right fanatics seeking somewhere remote enough to escape a tyrannical government and an apocalypse they believe is imminent. They are white separatists, attracted by the fact that Idaho's 1.1 million population includes barely 3,000 blacks, who see the 'Handle' as the core of an all-white Aryan homeland.

The panhandle is becoming positively crowded with these escapees. They live up rutted dirt tracks that wind high into the hills, in tepees and rough log cabins, on compounds guarded by dogs and ringed with 'Keep Out' and 'No Trespassing' signs. Time and again I was told that northern Idaho was really no different to any other part of America, but I beg to differ. In Helen Chenoweth it has elected – and re-elected – arguably the most extreme member of the US Congress, one who defends the militia movement and considers the white Anglo-Saxon male an endangered species. The Idaho legislature has had to legislate against institutions like common law courts set up by rebellious citizens to challenge the authority of public officials. At a rally against racism in the seemingly serene town of Coeur d'Alene I was amazed to find police ringing the hotel to protect it from right-wing extremists – and with good reason. The master of ceremonies was a former priest named Bill Wassmuth whose home was pipe-bombed in 1986.

At the same rally, incidentally, I met a large, bearded Vietnam veteran named Jim Hall who lived out in the woods near the Canadian border and gave me a strip of home-cured coyote meat to chew.

Hippies were the first group of outsiders to arrive in substantial numbers – people like Larry and Sheryl Nims who now run Granite Memorials, a stone-carving business on Kamiah's main street. They were once students in Oregon, but in 1970 packed everything they owned into a 1958 Packard and horse trailer and set off to return to nature with just $58 in their pockets. Two miles outside Kamiah, by a creek at the mouth of a secluded canyon, they found forty acres going for $12,000 which they bought with a borrowed $1,000 deposit and monthly payments of $100. For eighteen months they lived in a tepee while they built a six-sided three-storey log home, and there they still live out their youthful ideals. They grow corn, beans, tomatoes, squash, cantaloupes. They raise goats and chickens. They use horses to farm and cut hay, fell trees by hand instead of chainsaw, draw their water from a spring and use kerosene lamps for lighting. 'Until a couple of years ago,' said Larry, 'this really was utopia' – but then 'they' came.

'They' are the residents of 'Almost Heaven' and other so-called 'covenant communities' being established high in the mountains above Kamiah by Colonel Bo Gritz, a swaggering former Green Beret commando and populist presidential candidate with apocalyptic views and strong links to the far-right militia and survivalist movements. 'They' are the hippies' end-of-the-century conservative counterparts – religious right-wingers and self-styled 'patriots' fleeing a civilisation they consider doomed. 'Now's your opportunity to leave the hustle and bustle, murder, rape and pillage of the cities,' says Gritz's promotional literature. 'Here's a mountaintop paradise where you can survive the coming Armageddon' is the implied subtext. The only condition for joining is that you must swear to uphold the Constitution and the Bill of Rights, and to defend your neighbours against outside threats. More than fifty families from across the United States have so far heeded Gritz's call.

To reach 'Almost Heaven' I followed a steep gravel road 12 miles up into the mountains till I came to a grassy, windswept plateau crossed by dirt roads and dotted with new or half-built homes. A large sign warned: 'Do Not Enter Private Driveways Without Permission'. The first house I came to was flying the Stars and Stripes upside down because, I later learned, the owner considered the Constitution so defiled that America was now in 'distress'.

Gritz's home was a large, pale grey affair on the plateau's far edge which looks down on birds of prey circling over the magnificent Clearwater Valley 2,000 feet below. From a tall white flagpole flew the Stars and Stripes. Below it flew the black-and-white flag commemorating American servicemen missing in Vietnam, Gritz having achieved notoriety in the 1980s by leading covert missions into the jungles of Indochina to search for his former colleagues. Gritz was away, teaching a survival course in Florida. So was his business partner, Jerry Gillespie, who lived in the second biggest house with the second-best view, so I sat in Mr Gillespie's elegant entrance hall with its portraits of Lincoln, Washington and Jesus and did my best to draw out his wife, Mary. She was not unfriendly, but clearly shared the community's strong antipathy towards the mainstream media.

Mrs Gillespie was a buxom, middle-aged lady with five children aged twelve to twenty-one and would have been quite at home in any American suburb. Her husband was a former insurance salesman and Arizona state senator, and they had moved up here from the city of Mesa, Arizona, two years earlier. They had come to escape the gangs and drive-by shootings and live an independent life, she said – but also because they believed the apocalypse, in the form of an economic collapse, was imminent. The government, she suggested, might even engineer such a collapse as an excuse to impose martial law and achieve total control over the American people. It could then force Americans to accept the 'mark of the beast'.

During the chaos before Christ's second coming, warns the Book of Revelations, Satan would force 'all, both small and great, rich and poor, free and bond, to accept the mark in their right hand, or in their foreheads: and that no man may buy or sell, save he that had the mark, or the name of the beast'. That mark, said Mrs Gillespie, could be an implanted microchip through which the government could monitor everything you did. Those who accepted it would be damned. In the cities it would be impossible to reject it and survive, but up here you could.

Most families had solar power or generators. There was water, wild fruit and berries, and you could grow your own food. She herself had laid in a year's supply of wheat, rice, cereal and vegetables, and was building a greenhouse. 'The government may try to make you believe everything's wonderful and fine and dandy,' said Mrs Gillespie, 'but it's like a volcano. There's always something stirring and some day it has to erupt.'

Mrs Gillespie doubted that anyone else in 'Almost Heaven' would talk to me. I wandered back to my car, smiling at the satellite television dish, the trampoline, the basketball hoop and other suburban accoutrements scattered so incongruously around the Gillespies' isolated home, but as I was about to drive off she called me back. I was in luck, she said. A neighbour, Greg Heun, had just called and was coming over. He might talk, but only because he was such a nice guy.

A few minutes later I watched a battered old Chevy pick-up approaching across the plateau and out stepped a man in his late thirties wearing a red baseball cap, old torn work clothes and two days' worth of stubble. A bumper sticker on the back of the pick-up showed caricatures of Bill and Hillary Clinton beside the words 'Dual Airbags'. His house had no running water, Greg explained. I could talk to him if I wanted while he filled the dozen white plastic barrels in the bed of his pick-up from a nearby standpipe. And so I stood in the mud as an icy wind swept across the top of the world and engaged in yet another distinctly surreal conversation.

Greg had resigned as a power company's security officer in Phoenix, Arizona, sold his home, and moved up here with his wife and baby in 1995. At first he suggested that he'd come simply to escape the urban violence, but acknowledged when pressed that there was a deeper reason. He too had studied the scriptures. He too believed America was heading for a cataclysmic crash, an economic Armageddon engineered by world bankers bent on global domination. There would be 'turmoil, starvation, famine, anarchy, a general breakdown of law and order'. The lowlands would be reduced to warring, marauding gangs. But for the residents of 'Almost Heaven', Greg told me, it would be 'like Bo said. You will be sitting up on a mountain and you will be watching it from here'.

The barrels filled, Greg took me back to his home a mile across the plateau. This was a half-finished wooden structure of eccentric design that he was building himself one section at a time. A couple of hundred yards away was a still stranger construction, a half-buried home with walls made of earth and old car tyres that had been temporarily abandoned by its owners when it became saturated. By now I was shivering, but Greg didn't invite me in. Around here, an American's home was his castle. We instead continued our conversation outside while he siphoned water from one of the barrels into a horse trough. He had three horses. 'I tell people up here "If the economy ever does crash, what's going to be the principal means of transportation?" Horses!' he said. They could pull a wagon. They would enable him to plant crops. He had actually found and was planning to buy a horse-drawn plough.

Greg was moving further and further 'off the grid' in his pursuit of a mythic frontier lifestyle, eschewing public services in pursuit of self-sufficiency. He hauled in his own water. He had a generator for electricity, kerosene for lamps and used coal and wood for heating. He had a vegetable garden, berry patches and had planted an orchard of thirty young fruit trees. His second child, Gabriel, had been born in the Gillespies' kitchen shortly after their arrival in 'Almost Heaven', and his third in his own house. All three would be taught at home instead of a secular public school. Greg had thrown away his credit cards, and during the past two summers had been teaching himself exactly what you could and could not eat from the forest.

I was by now so cold that I was beginning to think of 'Almost Heaven' as almost hell. Through chattering teeth I asked one last question. How would you respond, I asked, to those who say that the economy has rarely been stronger, America is at peace, and prophets of doom like yourself are crazy.

'They said just the same thing before the 1929 stock-market crash,' Greg replied with unshakeable conviction.

The village of Santa, two hours north of Kamiah, was bound to east and west by hundreds of square miles of wilderness and national forest. Stuck on a board outside its tiny post office were advertisements for an odd-job man willing to barter for his services, a 'prophecy conference' entitled 'Will Christ Return by the Year 2000?', and counselling for anyone stuck in an 'unhealthy relationship'. These betrayed a mild liberalism not normally associated with redneck lumberjacks, and hidden away in the hills behind the village was Pokey Creek where perhaps half a dozen old hippy families still lived. Most had now built themselves ramshackle homes with newish trucks and satellite television dishes outside, but not Hari and Judie Heath. They still lived in a tepee with their children and clung tenaciously to their old ideals.

I reached Santa long after dark, and drove helplessly around a

maze of snowy tracks until eventually Hari came out and found me.
With his beard and great long dreadlocks tumbling out from
beneath a tam o'shanter, he looked like some fierce Scottish high-
lander from the cast of *Macbeth*, but the very first thing he
suggested was that I stay the night if I didn't mind roughing it.
Anything but another cheap motel, I replied, though there was not
a motel in miles in any case. He led me back to his tepee, a magnificent affair that glowed in the darkness of a small forest clearing.
Inside were Hari's wife Judie, a big, strong earth mother type, his
father Wally, and three refreshingly uninhibited children –
Tenadore, Shawna and Ian –the latter aged five but with dreadlocks
longer than Hari's.

I'd searched out the Heaths because Hari was such an apparent
contradiction. He was a hippy who had joined the so-called 'Patriot'
movement of the Right, though I eventually came to realise that
there was little real difference between the Left's cherished civil lib-
erties and the freedom from government demanded by the Right.

Thoroughly apolitical for most of his forty years, Hari had been
radicalised by two experiences – the collapse of his small timber sal-
vage business thanks to an arbitrary US Forest Service ruling, and a
protracted battle with the judicial system to gain custody of two
children by a former wife. 'They fucked me out of a job and took
my kids' as Hari succinctly put it. He began delving. He became
convinced America no longer had a government of the people, by
the people, and for the people. It was ruled by an 'unlawful regime',
a malign and oppressive federal government that had seized powers
far beyond the very limited, specific functions granted it by the
Constitution. He had begun publishing his own newsletter called
'Brushfire', joined a self-styled citizens' committee and helped set up
a 'common law court' to try and reassert the power of the people. If
that meant joining forces with 'close-circuit Christian types' of the
far right – hippydom's harshest critics – so be it.

'The truth is the truth whether you have long hair or short,' he
declared. 'There's a war on. We have a common enemy. We can
fight over our differences later.'

Hari was no crackpot. He spoke softly, earnestly and intelligently, but by now I was tiring of all this agin'-the-government stuff. What did fascinate me, however, was Hari's home and lifestyle.

He and his pregnant first wife had arrived in Pokey Creek in a hippy's archetypal old school bus in 1984 after years of living on the road. They divorced, Hari later married Judie, and together they had built the tepee with poles cut from the surrounding forest that they covered with canvas and a synthetic sheeting.

It was like some fantastic film set. They had essentially chopped a conventional round tepee in two and inserted a long, straight section in the middle in the style of a Nez Perce Indian longhouse. It had a sunken floor with wooden walls perhaps four-foot high so the interior was far bigger than you'd ever guess from the outside – about 1,000 square feet in all. There was a large woodstove in the middle for heating and cooking, a set of rough-hewn bunks at the one end for the children, and a loft at the other where Hari and Judie slept. There were rugs and chairs and chests of drawers, dim lighting courtesy of a generator, and it was all surprisingly warm and cosy.

We talked till nearly midnight. I then crawled into my sleeping bag on one of the children's bunks and was asleep in an instant. I was woken at six by Judie chopping wood into kindling and soon the fire was crackling. I watched from my bunk as she vigorously ground corn into flour for pancakes that we ate an hour later with a sauce of serviceberries culled from the forest. The sun was now up and light streamed through the tepee's translucent walls. Judie put out a bowl of warm water from the stove for me to wash with, and I emptied my bowels in a rough wooden lean-to on the far side of the snowy clearing which was filled with evidence of the Heaths' resourcefulness. There were skis and snowshoes hanging in a shed, a snowplough Hari had fashioned from old oil drums, and a horse which he used for hunting elk, deer and grouse.

The Heaths were 'off the grid' and self-sufficient to an extent that Greg Heun could only dream of. Indeed Hari was distinctly scornful of the 'Almost Heaven' crowd. 'You cut those folks off from going to town or going shopping,' he said, 'and they're all going to be fucked as quick as anyone else.'

The Heaths fetch drinking water from a neighbour on a sled, but collect rainwater for washing. They have a telephone, but no mains electricity, no television, no radio, no credit cards. Their children were, with one exception, born at home and all are taught at home. They are not immunised. Hari still earns a little money from logging, but his real craft is making exquisite bows and arrows which sell for several hundred dollars each. In the summer he teaches bow-making at 'primitive skills' gatherings where kindred spirits go to learn how to make knives from stones, bowls from gourds and tools from bones. He doesn't earn enough to pay income tax, but wouldn't pay it if he did because he considers the Internal Revenue Service constitutionally illegal, and the tepee attracts no property tax because it is not considered a permanent structure.

For her part Judie 'wild forages' in the woods for food, collects nettles for tea, and makes her own medicines from plants and herbs. She tans hides from which she makes moccasins, and is learning to make them into clothes as well. She also weaves willow baskets that she trades at the sixties-style 'barter fairs' still held in these parts each spring and summer. She loves living in a tepee, she says, because 'you are still connected with the environment. I can tell what time of night it is by the moonlight on the tepee. You can hear things on the outside, coyote and the footsteps of wild turkey'. It was also 'a real dynamic lesson in the sharing of space, and when I feel the kids are all over me there's the great expanse of outdoors'.

The Heaths are no 'trust-fund hippies'. They would have little to fall back on if things went wrong, but for them life remains an adventure. 'An awful lot of hippies became yuppies and shoed right on into materialism,' Hari lamented. 'To me it's a challenge to maintain my own personal ideals . . . I did try cutting my hair and dressing nice and living in a city for a few years but it just wasn't me.'

Further up the panhandle I reached a fenced compound off a gravel road in pleasant countryside outside the little town of Hayden Lake. Long ago this was a 20-acre dairy farm. At first glance, in the bright afternoon sunshine, it still retains a bucolic air with six or seven buildings scattered around beneath majestic pine trees. But then you spot the sign nailed to a tree by the entrance. 'Whites Only,' it declares. Another, on the side of the empty guard hut, reads: 'Welcome Kinsmen'.

The compound is in fact the headquarters of Richard Butler's Church of Jesus Christ Christian and its political arm, Aryan Nations. Butler, a former Lockheed aircraft engineer, is the grand patriarch of America's white supremacists, though he is now in his late seventies and no longer the force he was. His church is the most militant ministry in the Christian Identity movement, which preaches that people of North European descent are the true Israelites, that Jews are descendants of Satan, and that blacks are mere animals.

Since Butler moved his church to northern Idaho in the 1970s – southern California having become a 'cesspool of non-whites' – this compound has been a notorious meeting ground for Klansmen, militiamen, skinheads and neo-Nazis. It has hosted celebrations of Hitler's birthday and an annual Aryan World Congress at which Butler has demanded the creation of an exclusively white homeland in the Pacific north-west. In the 1980s a violent offshoot of his church called The Order, or the Silent Brotherhood, bombed, killed, robbed and counterfeited to advance the cause of white supremacy, and in 1988 Butler himself was tried on sedition charges but acquitted.

I found the self-styled 'pastor' sitting at a metal desk in the cramped and cluttered office he shares with his secretary, a girl named Christian who had moved up from Phoenix because Idaho was 'ninety-seven per cent white and you can't beat that'. The walls are lined with anti-Semitic booklets, pictures of young followers giving Nazi salutes, a German World War Two helmet and various portraits of Adolf Hitler.

The Führer was 'the only man to lead a worldwide battle for the salvation of the white race', Butler told me.

Where did that leave Churchill, I asked?

'Churchill fought for the death of the white race, the elimination of the British empire, the elimination of white Christian morals,' he replied. The Holocaust never happened, he added for good measure. 'There were no gas chambers. All you have is Jewish lies.'

I spent an hour talking to Butler while his two large German shepherds – Hans and Fritz – growled menacingly at my feet. In appearance he seems a grandfatherly figure, with silvery-grey hair and a face cracked like an elephant's hide, but from his mouth spewed pure vitriol. Jews were 'evil', he declared. They were like a deadly virus systematically destroying the world's white nations and their Christian values. They would not succeed, but it would take a 'great bloodbath' to defeat them.

Butler was not even talking of Jews in the abstract. He appeared to hate each and every one of them. If any of his four grandchildren married a Jew, he said, 'they would not be my grandchildren any more'. Blacks were evidently little better. Had I been black he would not have let me visit him because 'I don't have them on my property'. If he had his way he would send all Jews to Israel and all blacks back to Africa, and any whites married to Jews or blacks – those guilty of the 'mongrelisation of our race' – would have to go with them. An all-white, racially-pure America would be, of course, 'the most progressive nation on the face of the earth. We would not only walk on the moon but walk on Mars. There's nothing we couldn't do'.

I ventured to suggest that the Christian virtues of tolerance and compassion were somewhat lacking from his diatribe. Tolerance, Butler responded, was 'the most evil word in the dictionary. Tolerance means putting up with evil. You can put up with a certain amount of evil. You can take a certain amount of rat poison and live, but take too much and it kills you.'

As for compassion, he felt compassion 'for every living thing', he insisted, 'but I don't want them (non-whites) destroying the culture we are ordained to live and bringing immorality in place of our morality'. But whites frequently did immoral things, I interjected. 'Wherever you have integration of cultures you have the degradation of both cultures,' Butler replied. He did reluctantly acknowledge that there were white homosexuals but 'sodomites' were, he insisted, 'the genetic defects of our race' and should be eliminated.

Butler could be accused of many things, but not of mincing words. He supported violence 'one hundred per cent', he said, if that was the only way of saving his kindred. Far from disowning those members of The Order convicted in the 1980s, he argued that they had sought to hasten the white counter-revolution and 'would have been heroes' had they succeeded. He talked to patently unsympathetic reporters like myself, he said, because 'I have a commission to deliver the word. I have an obligation to tell people the truth so they can't say they were never told when judgement day comes'.

What, I asked as my parting shot, would he like his epitaph to read? Butler thought for a few moments. 'I tried,' he said at length. Tried what, I asked? 'I tried to call the race to its destiny.'

Before I left, a young man named Mike, Butler's 'head of security', showed me the compound's chapel. It was a bit run down, as was the entire compound, but it seemed like any other Christian chapel until you spotted the swastika flag in the lobby, the clock with the swastika motif on the piano, and the allegorical picture of Christian killing a serpent with a Cross of David on its back. The stained-glass window behind the pulpit was punctured, I noticed, by two bullet-holes. Adjoining the chapel was a new kitchen, the old one having been destroyed in 1981 by a bomb designed to blow up the chapel. Unfortunately it failed.

Beyond Hayden Lake a single two-lane road unwinds northwards towards Canada, and this took me to Sandpoint, a picturesque resort town of 5,200 people on the northern shore of Lake Pend Oreille.

Sandpoint has a Buddhist mayor, a lively arts programme and a main street lined by chic little shops, but is also saddled with a reputation for being America's foremost white supremacist stronghold. It is where Mark Fuhrman, the racist Los Angeles cop, retreated after being exposed and disgraced during O. J. Simpson's trial, and where more than 1,000 people had recently turned out for Fuhrman's booksigning session in a local bookstore. It is where Louis Beam, an infamous former Ku Klux Klan Grand Dragon, has taken up residence. It is the home of three white separatists being tried, at the time of my visit, for a series of bombings and robberies in neighbouring Washington State. Sandpoint boasts just one black resident – a postman named Robert Mitchell who was summoned to play basketball with Wynton Marsalis when the black jazz star performed in the town a few years back.

It was a Sunday, so I went to church in an octagonal wooden building on the very edge of town, out beyond Sandpoint's industrial fringe, out beyond where the paved road ends, and out – many would say – beyond the pale.

There were two dozen of us in the congregation: parents, children, a few older worshippers. We sang hymns, said prayers, and listened to a sermon. In its outward form the service resembled that of any other church. In its actual content, however, it was utterly different, for this was the headquarters of America's Promise, another Christian Identity church convinced that whites are God's chosen people and have been targeted for destruction by a Jewish 'religious empire' bent on global domination.

Members of the congregation stood up and denounced efforts by the US Forest Service to import Mexican labour to northern Idaho. The hymns appeared to have been chosen for lines like 'Oh precious is the flow/ That makes me white as snow'. And the sermon of Pastor David Barley, which seemed to have been composed largely for my benefit and in which I actually featured, was unlike any I'd ever heard before in a house of worship.

Barley was a large, balding, jowly man and a father of six children. He had inherited the church from his father-in-law and moved it here from Arizona in 1991 because, he said, America's cities were 'going to hell in a handbasket' and northern Idaho was like America as it used to be. Though he decried Butler's overt Nazism, he too favoured a white homeland and virulently opposed inter-racial marriages. But if Butler's message was one of raw hatred, Barley's was one of paranoid, self-righteous rage and – to my suburban way of thinking – equally fanatical.

Like Jesus in his day, Christian Identity followers were being demonised for daring to preach the true word of God, Barley protested from his pulpit. They were being painted as 'monsters', as

'bad, wicked and terrible people', for opposing socialism, multicul-
turalism and internationalism and being politically incorrect. The
persecutors, he insisted, were the 'anti-Christs' of international
Zionism who controlled the government and media and were determined not to let true Christians stand in the way of their new world
order.

Before I knew it, I found myself being subtly linked with those
'satanic' forces. 'We have a writer with us here today, Martin
Fletcher, and he's from Washington DC,' Barley informed the congregation. 'I have been to Washington DC. Now he may be
perfectly at home there, but me? I feel like I'm in a jungle. I feel like
I'm in a den of vipers. There's something about looking at the
Capitol building. There's something about looking at the White
House. There's something about looking at those massive concrete
structures around there that makes me feel a little uncomfortable as
well.

'You know I don't see how you can be a Christian and even be in
some of those buildings and in those environments and know what
they do and what they represent . . . How can you go to churches
and claim that you are a Christian and say "we love you Jesus" and
read his word and see what the truth of his word says and pick up
your stuff and go in the next morning to those bureaucratic agencies
knowing what they're doing, what they're representing, and feel
comfortable? I don't see how you can do it.'

The truth, he thundered, was that 'those who are ruling over us
are traitors, whores, criminals and parasites' and that 'most of those
in government are bought and paid for'. As Christians 'we are called
to take a stand'. The world may label us fanatics, he concluded, but
'you better believe that I'm a fanatic for what I believe in, and I
thank God that you people are fanatics for what you believe in too'.

After the service we gathered, as any other congregation might, in
the church's vestibule. Someone produced a cartoon from the
Spokesman-Review newspaper of Spokane, in neighbouring
Washington State, that showed a crowd of children with one or
two wearing KKK hoods. 'Who are the kids from Idaho?' the cap-
tion asked. This caused general outrage, but then one of the men

quietly confided to me that he really didn't mind all the bad publicity. It scared off blacks, he said.

As I departed, Barley presented me with a tape of his sermon, but I have to say that I felt neither inspired nor uplifted by my morning's worship, and it was a relief to meet Steve and Elizabeth Willey that afternoon and discover that Sandpoint had a gentler side.

The Willeys are Quakers and took me to a Quaker meeting in the basement of a community hall. They sat in a circle and spent an hour discussing what it was about Quakerism that attracted them. In almost every case the answer was the same, and after so many encounters with religious zealots in the past few months it was refreshing to hear. It was the lack of dogma, they said, the absence of anyone claiming to have a monopoly on truth. I nearly signed up there and then.

The Willeys invited me home for the night. They too were former hippies who'd arrived from California in a purple school bus in 1973 and bought land in the mountains for next to nothing. They'd erected a windmill for power, begun peddling windmills to their fellow immigrants, and today sell more than $1 million worth of solar equipment a year to people with homes deep in the backwoods.

Their own home turned out to be a mountaintop palace built around the original windmill tower. Located miles up a rutted track, it is an amazing hi-tech, environmentally unimpeachable, Heath Robinsonian affair three or four storeys high, crowned by solar panels and looking like the fabulous creation of some eccentric professor. And, as if the view across a forested valley to the snow-clad Cabinet Mountains was not sufficiently inspiring, the Willeys have built themselves a helicopter to admire it more closely.

Between Sandpoint and Canada there remained just the small town of Bonners Ferry, the even tinier community of Naples and a vast expanse of apparent wilderness in which more people live than you'd ever guess.

In Bonners Ferry I found a municipal tap to which scores of backwoodsmen made periodic visits in order to collect 150 gallons of water for 25 cents. The town's shops were amply stocked with such staples as guns, chainsaws, snowmobiles and snowshoes. During the winter the area had received more than 13 feet of snow, and in the *Bonners Ferry Herald* I read not only that trains had killed thirty-five moose that had been using the railway tracks as paths, but that a man's corpse had just been found in a remote mountain cabin where it had lain since the previous autumn.

In the window of the old wooden general store in Naples were advertisements for everything from the clearing of mudslides, bulldozing and the digging of drainage trenches to workhorses and Rottweiler puppies. Linda Berwick, the store's owner, told me her customers ranged from reclusive artists and scientists to a man who had arrived on horseback one day and offered his rifle in return for a year's supply of food.

Until 1992 Mrs Berwick's customers had also included a self-styled Christian survivalist and white separatist whose deadly showdown with federal agents that August is now cited by every conspiracy theorist in America – along with the Waco tragedy – as irrefutable proof of the government's determination to suppress the people and quash dissent. His name was Randy Weaver, and the headwaters of the great tide of paranoia that has swept across the western United States can be traced back to the tiny clearing on Ruby Ridge, high above Naples, where this wiry, intense man from Bible-belt Iowa moved in the early 1980s to escape the coming apocalypse.

Weaver and his wife, Vicki, had studied the scriptures. They had read of the chaos that would precede Christ's second coming, of the 'wars and rumours of wars' and of the 'famines, and pestilences, and earthquakes in divers places'. They had read the injunction in Matthew 24 – 'When ye therefore shall see the abomination of desolation, spoken of by Daniel the prophet, stand in the holy place, then let them which be in Judea flee into the mountains' – and interpreted it quite literally. They packed up their belongings and moved to Idaho.

In that remote clearing, 4,000 feet up in the Selkirk Mountains where grizzly bears and caribou still roam, the Weavers built a flimsy 25-foot by 32-foot plywood cabin for themselves and their three biblically named children – Sara, Samuel and Rachel. They stock-piled food and guns and ammunition, home-schooled their children and lived according to their interpretation of the Bible. They called God and Jesus by their old Hebrew names of Yahweh and Yashua. They erected a sign at the entrance to their property on which they painted in blood-red lettering: 'Every Knee Shall Bow to Yahshua (sic) Messiah'. They celebrated the Sabbath for the twenty-four hours that began at 6.00 p.m. on Fridays, and built a shed where Vicki and the girls went when menstruating because they considered themselves unclean. They were convinced they were amongst the true Israelites who would be saved to build a new Kingdom of God from the ashes of the old.

Unfortunately the 'great tribulation' foretold in the Bible arrived, for the Weavers, in a form very different from anything they'd expected.

By late 1989 Weaver was nearly out of money. Down at Richard Butler's Aryan Nations compound, where he occasionally attended Christian Identity rallies, he met a biker named Gus Magisono who told him he needed sawn-off shotguns to advance the cause of white supremacy. Weaver offered to get him some and duly provided two. Unknown to Weaver, Magisono was part of a federal 'sting' opera-tion. The Feds tried to persuade Weaver to become their informer inside the white supremacist movement, and charged him with gun-running when he refused. Weaver believed he'd been framed by the 'Zionist-Occupied Government', failed to appear for his trial on 20 February, 1991, and became a fugitive from justice.

He remained holed up in his cabin for eighteen months, during which Vicki gave birth to a fourth child, Elisheba. The Feds covertly monitored the family's every move but stayed their hand until, on 21 August, 1992, the Weavers' labrador, Striker, began barking and ran off into the forest. Weaver, fourteen-year-old Samuel, and a young family friend named Kevin Harris gave chase and ran straight into three camouflaged US marshals. In the ensuing gunfight Samuel, one of the marshals and the dog were killed.

At that point the Feds moved in a small army of law enforcement officers supported by helicopters, armoured personnel carriers and humvees, while a large crowd of angry protestors gathered at the foot of the mountain. FBI snipers surrounded the cabin and the next day, when Weaver and Harris emerged, one of them opened fire. A bullet wounded Weaver in the arm. Another killed Vicki, who was standing in the cabin doorway with Elisheba in her arms, and went on to wound Harris. Weaver, his three terrified daughters and Harris held out for another week alongside Vicki's bloody corpse before Bo Gritz arrived on the mountain and persuaded them to surrender.

The following year, Weaver was acquitted of all charges save failing to turn up for his trial, for which he was fined $10,000 and served sixteen months in prison, but four top FBI agents have been suspended pending a criminal investigation, another has pleaded guilty to destroying an internal FBI report on the shoot-out, and the Justice Department has paid the Weaver family $3.1 million in compensation.

It was a warm spring day so I decided to visit Ruby Ridge. I stopped for directions in the Naples general store where Mrs Berwick gave me her opinion on the whole débâcle. It was the biggest fiasco she'd ever seen, she said. Every move the Feds made was worse than the one before, but the ultimate responsibility lay with Weaver. She knew him well because he used to come down to the store to spew out his dogma and at least twice she'd had to ask him to leave – once when he denied the Holocaust and again when he welcomed the Chernobyl explosion because, he claimed, the grass was greener after the nuclear attack on Hiroshima and everything was better.

'There are so many people who believe they have a direct line to God,' Mrs Berwick lamented. Weaver was one of them, and he got so caught up in his own little world, in his own propaganda, that he put his own children in harm's way – something for which she found it almost impossible to forgive him.

I drove north out of Naples on the old highway, disturbing a huge osprey that flapped along in front of the car for thirty yards before wheeling away above the fir trees. Just before the Deep Creek Inn I turned left up a dirt road into the wooded mountains until I came across a fellow sawing logs into planks on a sliver of open space between the road and the swollen Ruby Creek.

He was a man of positively biblical appearance – gaunt and bearded with deep, dark, gentle eyes. I stopped and we chatted in the sun. His name was Chris and he too had fled from the decadence of California so he and his wife could raise their three children 'out in the woods where they can be free to learn from the Creator through his creations'. They had bought forty acres high up in the mountains just a mile and a half from the Weavers' old cabin. There they grew vegetables, kept chickens and a milk cow, hunted for meat, fetched water from the creek and home-schooled their children because 'we want to acknowledge the Creator in everything we do all day long and don't want him out of any part of our lives'.

His family liked creature comforts and were more accepting than he of 'the way things are going in the world', he confessed. Left to his own devices he would 'just go out into the wilderness quite a ways and survive if that was possible or die trying'. Alone in the wild 'it just seems like it's easier for the Creator to speak to you, and if you quieten yourself down enough to listen you might hear something worthwhile'.

Chris had known Randy Weaver well and their children had played together. He shared Weaver's belief that the government was an instrument of Satan and preparing to introduce a one-world system in which everyone would have to accept the Mark of the Beast – a chip or a tattoo that would damn them eternally. 'I don't plan on getting stamped,' he said. 'I will starve to death rather than get stamped.' Come Judgement Day the Creator would 'throw away the chaff and keep the grain', and the grain was 'the ones who believe in the Messiah and live according to his will to the best of their abilities'.

Where Chris had differed from Weaver was in his response. Chris believed this satanic government was part of God's plan for Christ's second coming. Instead of resisting, you had to put your faith in God, accept things as they were, and 'turn away from evil'. Randy, by contrast, 'was an extremist. He used to say our job was to stop them from doing this evil, by force if necessary. He was a very moral, upright individual in his beliefs, and was standing up for what he believed was right.'

Chris was still tortured by what had happened. 'I saw the whole dang thing coming and I couldn't do a thing about it,' he lamented. 'I tried to dissuade him from judging before the time – I didn't have the reasoning power in me to go and talk to Randy about a possible peaceful solution.' In the event the government had used Weaver to set an example to all resisters. 'It boils down to one word – oppression,' Chris concluded.

Half a mile further on, the track had been washed away by the winter's snow, so I abandoned the car and continued on foot. I climbed up through the mud to a large meadow where there were two or three small cabins. On the far side I picked up an old logging trail that zig-zagged up and up through dense forest and melting snowdrifts for another two miles. Finally I spotted a path leading off to the right around a rocky knob. There was a profusion of 'No Trespassing' and 'Keep Out' notices, but I knew for certain that I'd reached the right place when I found, half buried in the snow, a broken board bearing the words 'Yahshua Messiah' in blood-red lettering.

After five long years I hadn't expected to find anything left save the clearing itself. Weaver and his daughters had returned to Iowa following the siege and I imagined the cabin would have been torn down long ago. There was not a soul in miles so I ignored the 'Keep Out' signs and followed the path around the knob till I came upon a scene that stopped me in my tracks.

In the middle of the clearing was the remains of the Weavers' cabin, its walls collapsed outwards under the weight of the winter's snow. Beyond the land simply fell away and there, thousands of feet below, were the wild and glorious forests of the glacial Kootenai River valley bounded by the soaring white peaks of Montana's Purcell Mountains.

If the panorama seemed designed to fill even the flintiest soul with awe, the remains of the cabin were poignant beyond words. It was as if the whole place had simply been abandoned to nature the day Weaver surrendered back in 1992. There were Scrabble letters and Monopoly money scattered around in the snow. The porch was still standing, and so was the doorway in which Vicki died, but the collapse of the walls had exposed to the elements the lino floor, the sink, the cooker, various cupboards, shelves lined with boots and kitchen equipment and sodden books: *Modern School Geometry*, *Practical Mathematics* and *Jane Lends a Hand*. Above the door, on the inner wall, there was still a sticker proclaiming 'Yashua is the Messiah'.

Around the edges of the clearing were the family's pit toilet, a small wooden hut with a barrel on top for showering, Striker's kennel and a couple of sheds piled high with cardboard boxes containing the Weavers' belongings. In the first shed I spotted two children's bikes, pillows, blankets, a frilly blue baby's dress, a boy's khaki shorts, acrylic paints, a pressure cooker, dozens of fruit jars, a radical right-wing newspaper called *The Spotlight* and magazines entitled *Soldier of Fortune, Gun World* and *American Survival Guide – The Magazine of Self-Reliance*. The second was filled with Vicki Weaver's stockpiled provisions – white plastic buckets containing flour, dried corn, couscous, and oatmeal, and silver packets of a 'delicious whey-based drink' called Yenka Nutri-Whey.

In a clearing once rent by screams and gunfire there was now no sound save the breeze in the surrounding fir trees and the rustling of a few chipmunks. I sat on a rock in the sun, savouring the pine-scented air and a view that would have brought tears to a glass eye. As tufts of white cloud drifted down from Canada, I pondered the irony of it all. The Weavers came here for the express purpose of survival, but two of them died. They came to escape a worldwide Armageddon, but engendered their own.

After three years' work, millions of dollars and the loss of three lives, the government managed to convict Weaver on a single minor charge, made him a folk hero to the radical right, and provided a rallying cry to militia and other extremist groups across the country that grew more, not less, potent as time passed. It was on Ruby Ridge that the Weavers' fanaticism reached such a tragic conclusion, and in the process inspired so much of the dangerous paranoia I'd encountered over the past few weeks.

I found no sign that anyone else had visited the clearing since the previous autumn, but for two or three years after the siege it attracted hundreds of visitors. Amongst them, apparently, was Tim McVeigh, the angry young man who subsequently killed 168 people when he blew up the federal building in Oklahoma City.

23

End of the Road

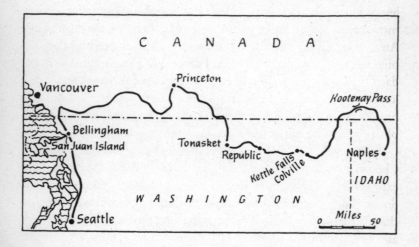

I came down from Ruby Ridge and suddenly I'd had enough –
enough of fast food and cheap motels, enough of talking to strangers
however unorthodox or friendly they might be, enough of the vast
and glorious scenery of the West and the dark, conspiratorial nether-
world it concealed. Rudyard Kipling wrote in 'From Sea to Sea':

> There is a great deal in the remark of the discontented traveller:
> 'When you have seen a pine forest, a bluff, a river and a lake
> you have seen all the scenery of western America. Sometimes
> the pine is three hundred feet high, and sometimes the rock is,
> and sometimes the lake is a hundred miles long. But it's all the
> same don't you know. I'm getting sick of it.'

I knew how he felt.

It was already late afternoon, but I got in my car and drove. I couldn't go directly west because the Selkirk Mountains blocked my way, so I went north till America ran out and crossed into British Columbia and took a Canadian highway west over the 5,800-foot Kootenay Pass where the snow was piled as high as houses, and it felt like deepest winter. I followed this tiny ribbon of road as it cut across a land of massive mountains and plunging valleys that God had constructed on an altogether grander scale than most other places in the world. I passed signs saying 'Avalanche Area – Don't Stop' and signs warning of bighorn sheep and then the bighorn sheep themselves. When I came down the other side it was dark. I turned south and re-entered the United States through a lonely customs post in the middle of a forest where there was just one officer on duty, and he spent fifteen minutes talking on the telephone before coming out to wave me through.

I had reached Washington, the last state before the Pacific Ocean. I began to sense the exhilaration that Lewis and Clark must have experienced as the Clearwater River carried their dugouts into the Snake River, and the Snake turned into the mighty Columbia, and the Columbia swept them towards the sea, the current flowing with and not against them for the first time in their amazing six-month journey from St Louis, Missouri.

I stopped for petrol in Metaline Falls where the cashier told me Kevin Costner was shooting a film about a postman who tries to persuade nuclear holocaust survivors not to lose faith in the government – we laughed simultaneously at the idea that people had not already lost it. I kept going, fast now, no longer concerned about whether the car would make it, my hands clenched on the wheel and my eyes fixed firmly on the central yellow lines as the empty road snaked through endless black forest. I felt like I was playing one of those video arcade games. I flashed past a large flood-lit dam on the Pend Oreille River, sped through tiny communities with names like Ione and Tiger, caught a couple of startled deer in my headlights in the depths of the Colville national forest. In Colville itself I gawked at the mountains of felled timber in the lit-up yards beside the highway, and at the claw suspended from a giant crane above them that could grab several trunks like so many matchsticks.

I finally stopped for the night at Kettle Falls, but early the next morning I was off again. I crossed the Columbia River where it was backed up like a lake fully a hundred miles above that monument to the usefulness of government – the Grand Coulee Dam. I trailed labouring timber lorries up and over the 5,575-foot Sherman Pass. I stopped for food in an old mining town called Republic where the Klondike Hunting and Fishing store was advertising airtight steel containers for burying guns against the day the government tries to disarm the American people.

Beyond Republic was another mountain pass, the Wauconda, and beyond that the town of Tonasket where my hopes of driving over one final range of mountains, the formidable Cascades, in time to watch a fiery sun slip into a silvery sea were dashed. It was now mid-April, but the road over the Cascades was still blocked by snow.

For once the Canadians had outdone their southern neighbours. Their equivalent road was open, so I headed north up the temperate Okanogan River valley with its endless apple orchards on a 280-mile detour. Having crossed back into British Columbia I turned west on the same Canadian highway as before and headed high up into the mountains and deep winter once again. It was a fabulous road that followed churning rivers through narrow passes between rearing walls of rock to whose sheer sides clung – miraculously – dense forests of fir. There was thick snow on the ground and trails of fog wreathed around the mountainsides, and as darkness began to fall so did lashing rain. It was all wonderfully atmospheric, but rendered faintly surreal by the Canadian radio programme I was listening to. This featured a couple from Ottery St Mary in Devon whose vibrating beds frequently went berserk in the middle of the night, and a Scottish ornithologist who kept finding right shoes washed up on a beach while a Dutchman in Holland kept finding left ones.

About 40 miles before Vancouver I turned south, re-entered the United States, and sped down to the coastal town of Bellingham with Robert Frost's description of the west coast running through my head:

> *The shattered wave made a misty din*
> *Great waves looked over others coming in*
> *And thought of doing something to the shore*
> *That water never did to land before . . .*
> *The shore was lucky in being backed by cliff*
> *The cliff in being backed by continent.*

My arrival was in fact a very far cry from the way I'd envisioned reaching the Pacific. It was pitch black, the rain was drumming on the roof, and while I could sense and smell the sea somewhere out beyond the lights I couldn't see a damn thing.

I spent the night in Bellingham, but my journey was not quite over yet. I knew exactly where it should finish. Happily the wind and rain abated overnight, and the next morning I drove another 25 miles down the coast then out on to a peninsula, past the town of Anacortes, to where the road abruptly ended at a dock. There I locked the car and sprinted to catch a departing ferry just as I had dashed for the ferry to Chesapeake Bay's Smith Island five months earlier.

I paid my $5 fare, and off we glided across the smooth blue water through an archipelago of humpbacked wooded islands with the snowy, cloud-capped Olympic Mountains and Canada's Vancouver Island as distant backdrops. It was a glorious day, gulls wheeled in our wake, and the passengers shrieked with excitement as a minke whale briefly broke the surface of the dimpled waters right in front of us.

Seventy minutes later we reached Friday Harbour on San Juan Island, the north-westernmost point of the lower United States. By happy coincidence San Juan Island was also the last place in North America – and quite possibly the world – where British and American troops squared off against each other, albeit over an errant hog.

The so-called Pig War was the product of a long-running dispute between Britain and America over the ownership of Oregon Country, a vast expanse of wilderness covering the present-day states of Washington, Oregon and Idaho and the Canadian province of

British Columbia. That dispute was supposedly settled by the Oregon Treaty of 1846, which awarded America all land south of the 49th Parallel up to 'the middle of the channel which separates the continent from Vancouver's Island'. Unfortunately the treaty failed to spell out who owned San Juan Island which lay right in the middle of that channel.

Both countries claimed the island, and in 1853 the Hudson Bay Company dispatched an employee, John Griffin, to establish a sheep ranch there and cement the British claim. Griffin landed with nearly 1,400 sheep and a few pigs. The Americans protested, then sent about eighteen settlers of their own including one Lyman Cutler from Kentucky. Tensions built until, on 15 June, 1859, Cutler woke to find one of Griffin's Berkshire boars rooting in his potato patch and shot it dead.

Cutler quickly apologised and offered Griffin $10 in compensation. Griffin demanded $100, and the incident spiralled rapidly out of control. British officials threatened to arrest Cutler. The American settlers ran up their flag and sought military protection. Brigadier General William Harney, Oregon's headstrong military commander, sent about sixty infantrymen, whereupon James Douglas, British Columbia's equally hot-headed governor, dispatched three warships with orders to remove the American troops. The military build-up continued, and by late August 461 Americans, protected by fourteen cannons and an earth redoubt, were facing five British warships with 167 guns and 2,140 troops.

For two or three weeks the island was a tinderbox. A single shot could have triggered a bloodbath, but then Rear Admiral Robert Baynes, the British naval commander in the Pacific, reached the scene. 'Tut, tut! No, no! Damn fools!' he allegedly exclaimed, and informed Douglas that he had no intention of involving 'two great nations in a war over a squabble about a pig'.

On 5 September news of the crisis had reached Washington. President James Buchanan was equally appalled and immediately dispatched General Winfield Scott, the commanding general of the US army, to defuse the confrontation. He brokered an agreement whereby both countries would keep token forces on the island until a permanent settlement was reached, and thus ended a military confrontation in which a single pig was the only casualty.

The American Civil War erupted two years later, and the island remained under joint military occupation for twelve years before Kaiser Wilhelm of Germany agreed to arbitrate and finally awarded it to the United States.

I found San Juan Island utterly enchanting – a maze of narrow lanes and woods and vivid green fields with stunning views across the deep blue waters of the straits. The trees were in blossom and the fields were carpeted with wild flowers. A park ranger named Mike Vouri showed me around the American Camp which straddles the island's grassy southern tip and where you can still see the remains of the earth redoubt and Griffin's chimney. Mike then drove me up to the English Camp, a dozen miles away on a lovely inlet called Garrison Bay near the island's northern end.

High on the hillside behind the camp is a tiny graveyard where six British marines and one civilian lie buried in this far corner of a foreign land. Down by the water several white weatherboarded buildings – the old barracks, the commissary, the blockhouse and the surgeon's quarters – stand beneath ancient maples on a sward of lush green grass. At one end is a little ornamental garden surrounded by a white picket fence which the camp's second commander built for his wife in 1867.

This was where I wanted to finish a journey that had begun with the raising of the Stars and Stripes on the roof of the US Capitol the previous summer. Fortunately Mike had a well-developed sense of humour. Together we walked over to the camp's 80-foot flagpole, unfurled an 18-foot Union Jack and hoisted it high into the sky by way of celebration.

Occasionally, said Mike, he inadvertently flew it upside down and got indignant calls from people with British accents in Victoria a dozen miles across the water.

To be honest I felt not elated, but a little melancholy. It was the end of my journey. It was also the end of my family's wonderful eight-year adventure in America – a country the novelist John Updike once called 'a vast conspiracy to make you happy' – and we were now being posted to the very different and far grimmer world of Belfast in Northern Ireland. I knew I had to look forward, not back, but at that moment I found it hard to do so.

The following day I drove down to Seattle and back into the world of suits and traffic jams and flashy homes and people endlessly jostling for position. At 2.00 p.m. I began hawking my car around secondhand car dealers. It had just completed 12,000 miles without a hiccup, but the Bazille Auto Centre, purveyors of 'the best used cars in the North West', displayed not a flicker of interest. They directed me to a wrecker's yard which was equally uninterested because, I was told, 'there's no market for scrap right now'. A to B Autos offered $200, but that felt like selling a child for a bottle of whiskey, so at 2.40 p.m. I pulled into a dingy little garage on the Pacific Highway and asked a Sikh called Joga Singh whether he bought cars as well as mended them.

Joga got into the car, started it and disappeared down the highway with my laptop and five months' worth of notes. To my great relief he returned five minutes later and offered $250. I beat him up to $300, plus a lift to the airport, and we shook hands on the deal. By 3.15 p.m. thirty-five minutes after pulling into Joga's garage, I was aboard Northwest Flight 162 and taking off for that 'den of vipers' called Washington DC, for that estranged and distant capital of this amazing nation, for my wife, my children and for home.

Bibliography

Applebome, Peter, *Dixie Rising: How the South is Shaping American Values, Politics and Culture.* Times Books, New York. 1996.

Bradley, Martha Sonntag, *Kidnapped from that Land: The Government Raids on the Short Creek Polygamists.* University of Utah Press, Salt Lake City. 1993.

Davies, Nick, *White Lies: Rape, Murder and Justice Texas-style.* Pantheon Books, New York. 1991.

Dees, Morris, *Gathering Storm: America's Militia Threat.* HarperCollins, New York. 1996.

Dize, Frances W., *Smith Island, Chesapeake Bay.* Tidewater Publishers, Centreville, Maryland. 1990.

Horton, Tom, *An Island Out of Time.* W. W. Norton & Co., New York. 1996.

Kennedy, N. Brent, *The Melungeons: The Resurrection of a Proud People.* Mercer University Press, Macon, Georgia. 1997.

Kimbrough, David, L., *Taking Up Serpents.* The University of North Carolina Press, Chapel Hill. 1995.

Lipset, Seymour Martin, *American Exceptionalism: A Double-Edged Sword.* W. W. Norton & Co., New York. 1996.

O'Clery, Conor, *America: A Place Called Hope?* The O'Brien Press, Dublin. 1993.

Walter, Jess, *Every Knee Shall Bow: The Truth and Tragedy of Ruby Ridge and the Randy Weaver Family.* Regan Books, New York. 1995.

Yapp, Peter, *The Travellers' Dictionary of Quotation.* Routledge and Kegan Paul, London. 1983.

Abacus now offers an exciting range of quality titles by both established and new authors. All of the books in this series are available from:

Little, Brown and Company (UK),
P.O. Box 11,
Falmouth,
Cornwall TR10 9EN.

Fax No: 01326 317444.
Telephone No: 01326 372400
E-mail: books@barni.avel.co.uk

Payments can be made as follows: cheque, postal order (payable to Little, Brown and Company) or by credit cards, Visa/Access. Do not send cash or currency. UK customers and B.F.P.O. please allow £1.00 for postage and packing for the first book, plus 50p for the second book, plus 30p for each additional book up to a maximum charge of £3.00 (7 books plus).

Overseas customers including Ireland, please allow £2.00 for the first book plus £1.00 for the second book, plus 50p for each additional book.

NAME (Block Letters) ....

....

ADDRESS ....

....

....

☐ I enclose my remittance for ....

☐ I wish to pay by Access/Visa Card

Number [ ][ ][ ][ ][ ][ ][ ][ ][ ][ ][ ][ ][ ][ ][ ][ ]

Card Expiry Date [ ][ ][ ][ ]